A Gift of the Spirit

A volume in the series

PSYCHOANALYSIS AND SOCIAL THEORY
edited by James M. Glass and C. Fred Alford

For a list of titles in the series, see www.cornellpress.cornell.edu

A Gift of the Spirit

Reading *The Souls of Black Folk*

Eugene Victor Wolfenstein

CORNELL UNIVERSITY PRESS
ITHACA AND LONDON

First published 2007 by Cornell University Press
First printing, Cornell Paperbacks, 2007

Printed in the United States of America

Library of Congress Cataloging-in-Publication Data

Wolfenstein, E. Victor.
  A gift of the spirit : Reading The souls of Black folk /
Eugene Victor Wolfenstein.
       p. cm— (Psychoanalysis and social theory)
    Includes bibliographical references and index.
    ISBN 978–0–8014–4522–4 (cloth : alk. paper)—
ISBN 978–0–8014–7353–1 (pbk. : alk. paper)
    1. Du Bois, W. E. B. (William Edward Burghardt),
1868–1963. Souls of Black folk.   2. Du Bois,
W. E. B. (William Edward Burghardt), 1868–1963—
Psychology.   I. Title.   II. Series.
    E185.6. W84   2007
    305.896'073—dc22   2006101253

Cornell University Press strives to use environmentally responsible suppliers and materials to the fullest extent possible in the publishing of its books. Such materials include vegetable-based, low-VOC inks and acid-free papers that are recycled, totally chlorine-free, or partly composed of nonwood fibers. For further information, visit our website at www.cornellpress.cornell.edu.

Cloth printing   10 9 8 7 6 5 4 3 2 1
Paperback printing   10 9 8 7 6 5 4 3 2 1

For Gabriel and Moses,
with love and respect

Contents

Preface

Ralph W. Ellison describes the way a disembodied "ironic, down-home voice" intruded itself upon a story he had been writing and led him into the "self-willed and self-generating piece of fiction" that became *Invisible Man* ([1952] 1989, intro.). My reading of *The Souls of Black Folk* (hereafter *Souls*) originates in a less dramatic experience of this type. I had been working on a collection of essays, psychoanalytic in perspective and loosely united as "narratives of descent." Two essays on *Souls* were to initiate the journey, which was to continue through *Invisible Man* and *Juneteenth* (also by Ellison) and then to *Tar Baby*, *Beloved*, and *Jazz* by Toni Morrison. The line of descent was to be both generational (Du Bois through Ellison to Morrison) and phenomenological (from surface to depth, in each text and in the advance from one to the next). *Souls* came first, not only because it is first chronologically but also because it establishes themes (e.g., the Veil and its equivalents, two-ness of various kinds, voluntary and involuntary sacrifice) that are carried through and elaborated in the other texts.

Initially those essays on *Souls* had a relatively narrow focus. One of them explored Du Bois's ambivalence about the enactment of anger, an ambivalence that cuts across and complicates the two-ness of African-American identity. The other was to take up the (perhaps inversely) related theme of death-as-liberation, obtrusive in the later chapters of the text, which could be viewed as consorting with the roughly Platonic aspect of Du Bois's conception of racial leadership. Both themes, although more obviously the second, can be traced back to the incident with which Du Bois begins *Souls;* that is, the moment in his New England childhood when a white classmate refused his offer of a visiting-card and he experienced for the first time

both the falling of the Veil and the desire to fly above it. So, more by instinct than by choice, I began the essay on Du Bois's "Platonism" with an
interpretation of that incident. Thereafter, at first without my permission or
even awareness, the project became "self-willed and self-generating." Placing myself as best I could in that schoolroom, I could see the topography
of *Souls* taking form around it—a horizontal plane of racial contestation
centered in the problematics of recognition intersected by a vertical plane
that could be signified by the idea of renunciation (voluntary and involuntary sacrifice). The vertical plane extended upward through high culture
and the self-sacrificing role of the Talented Tenth of black folk, to whom Du
Bois assigned the role of racial leadership, to the home over yonder that is
so movingly evoked in the Negro hymns and spirituals he named the Sorrow Songs. It extended downward into an abyss of pain, ultimately into the
waters of the Middle Passage and the long years of slavery that gave birth
to the Sorrow Songs. Still, I wanted to believe that this psychological and
topographical view of the text could be contained within the frame I had
initially set for it. This was wishful thinking, more precisely a resistance to
turning away from the project I had chosen in favor of another one that (so
it seemed) had chosen me. For I had already experienced something akin
to the interpellation Ellison describes. *Souls* kept drawing me in, in part
because Du Bois's authorial voice was so plainly audible, in part because
a unifying authorial vision became increasing apparent. This combination
of voice and vision, once heard and seen, left me feeling my only choice
was to give back what had been given and, by so doing, offer my own
recognition of Du Bois's singular achievement. The next steps down my
self-defined narrative line would have to wait.

I did not, however, set aside an interest in narrative when turning from
the one project to the other, and this for two reasons. First, *Souls* unfolds as
a story about black folk, with its characters, scenes, themes, and plotlines,
told in good part as a first-person narration. This is not to deny that it
contains and is indeed structured by a well-articulated theory of African-
American identity and interracial relations. But Du Bois's aesthetic intent
is unmistakable; and it is fair (if too simple) to say that the social theoretical content of *Souls* is presented in narrative form—joining in this way
the social scientific and imaginative dimensions of its author's personality.
Second, it seemed to me that I could best recognize Du Bois's twofold,
aesthetic and theoretical, achievement by mirroring it; that is, by telling a
story about his story.

As must necessarily be the case, I bring my own predispositions and
perspectives into this engagement with *Souls*. As to predispositions, I am
personally inclined toward storytelling and, on the theoretical side, toward
seeing dialectical Gestalten where others might see less organic phenomena.
This latter inclination consorts with a somewhat Cartesian—also Hegelian
and Marxian—desire to identify the simple elements out of which complex

unities are constructed. I might even acknowledge that these predispositions bespeak a certain interpretive will to power, a form-imposing impulse
that, if unchecked, would be incompatible with recognition freely given.
Knowing this about myself, I have accepted the necessity for methodological self-discipline—for a kind of interpretive restraint I have elsewhere
characterized as the disciplined suspension of the will to power (Wolfenstein 2000a, chap. 3). I cannot say I am a master of this demanding art, but
I am a student of it.

As to perspectives, the most basic is psychoanalytic, in part as a matter
of relying on psychoanalytic concepts, even more as a matter of sensibility.
This orientation leads me to ask, how does the manifest structure or narrative form of a text both defend against and express underlying aesthetic/
affective configurations and pulsations? (I do not answer, however, by in-
dulging in the familiar psychoanalytic tendency of reducing the manifest to
the latent.) And it helps to account for the weight I place on the visiting-card
incident, on the one hand, and the later and more personal chapters of *Souls*,
on the other. Next, there is the influence of Hegel. Although Du Bois himself
was unquestionably conversant with Hegelianism, it did not play a decisive
role in his intellectual development. By contrast, Hegelian problematics are
integral to my theoretical perspective and played a formative role in my approach to clinical practice. In the present instance, I have used the concepts
of recognition and mis-recognition to facilitate a synoptic interpretation of
the problem of the color-line; and traces of Hegelian phenomenology can
be seen in the psychoanalytic method I employ to explore the "deeper
recesses" of the world within the Veil (*Souls*, p. 5). Finally, I have an in-
volvement with Plato extending back to the earliest days of my intellectual
career. This is, one might say, an experience I share with Du Bois, who early
on read both the *Republic* and the *Phaedo*. Hence it is difficult to resist the
temptation of seeing Platonic leanings in his conceptions of culture, leadership, and spiritual life.

Along with the matter of predisposition and perspective, there is also
a question of cultural—racial—location. In a conference she organized on
"Du Bois and the Scientific Study of Race," Ange-Marie Hancock rearticu-
lated the notion of the "conscious pariah" made famous by Hannah Ar-
endt (Hancock 2005a; see also Hancock 2005b, pp. 80–82). Such individuals, aware of their outcast status, simultaneously base themselves in it and
struggle against the exclusions that define it. They, of necessity and by
choice, live on the margins, where identities intersect but the intersections
are normatively denied. Affirming that very position, they might serve as a
model of democratic empowerment and citizenship. Du Bois, who rejected
what he termed the path of revolt and revenge but would not rest from
confronting *his* America with its injustices and exclusions, is paradigmatic
of this political and ethical position. Just so, he calls forth a movement from
center to margin on the other side of the color-line.

In the spirit of engagements at the margins, I would add this note. Ethel and Benjamin Schub, the parents of my wife Judy, were friends of Dr. Du Bois and his wife, Shirley Graham Du Bois, during his final, decidedly left-leaning years in this country. Judy herself had the privilege of doing the research for her high school senior thesis on Ghana in Du Bois's library. I like to imagine myself there, with *The Souls of Black Folk* open before me. My eyes come to rest on a passage close to the end, in which Du Bois calls the reader's attention to three gifts of black folk to American life, most of all to the "gift of the Spirit" (*Souls*, p. 162). I think to myself, *The Souls of Black Folk* partakes of that Spirit and is just such a gift. How can we fail to be grateful for it?

The late Claudia Tate was notably generous in her response to my first attempts to write about Ellison and Du Bois. My friend Jean Wyatt provided me with an extraordinarily astute, thorough, and sympathetic reading of the manuscript. I am in her debt. Robert Gooding-Williams' subtle appreciation of *Souls*, displayed both in his own work and conveyed personally, has helped me to refine my own. Thanks also to Ange-Marie Hancock for her dedication to maintaining the space where it is possible to talk about things that matter; to Michael K. Brown, Brian Walker, and Frederick Lee for taking the time to read and offer comments on the manuscript; to C. Fred Alford and James Glass, for many years of intellectual comradeship; and to Raymond Rocco and Mark Sawyer, for continuing the struggle.

I am pleased to be continuing my relationship with Cornell University Press. Roger Haydon has once again provided me with astute and good-humored editorial guidance. Candace Akins and Cathi Reinfelder combined professional acuity with respect in their approach to editing the text. Susan Barnett performed the often unremarked task of keeping the reading public in mind, David Prout prepared the index, and Scott Levine found a way of transforming a book cover into a singular visiting-card.

To Judy I owe more than I can say.

EUGENE VICTOR WOLFENSTEIN

Los Angeles, California

A Gift of the Spirit

1

Setting the Stage

No more auction block for me,
No more, no more;
No more auction block for me,
Many thousands gone.

AFRICAN-AMERICAN FOLK SONG

In this book I advance two principal claims. First, *The Souls of Black Folk* has both the formal and substantive unity of a great novel or one of the classical works of political theory. Second, its narrative structure is built up around an aesthetic and affective core, common to both text and author, that can be signified by the concepts of recognition (more precisely, misrecognition) and renunciation. By way of introduction, I offer a preliminary elaboration of these claims and a few remarks on my own approach to the discipline of reading psychoanalytically.

The Souls of Black Folk

Souls is one of the masterworks in the African-American/American literary canon. Its cultural and political significance was evident from the time of its original publication in 1903, and in more recent years it has begun to receive the scholarly recognition it deserves.[1] But despite several important gestures in the direction of elucidating the narrative subtlety and complexity of the text (Byerman 1978, chap. 2; Lewis 1993, chap. 11; Rampersad 1976, 1990, chap. 4; Stepto 1979, 1991, chap. 3; Sundquist 1993, chap. 5; Zamir 1995, pt. 2), the greater part of the scholarly literature has been focused on various of its parts rather than the whole, specific themes rather than the narrative they comprise, its principal concepts (such as the Veil, two-ness, and double-consciousness) rather than their deployment within the text.[2] These are plainly valid modes of discursive appropriation, indeed the stock and trade of canonical interpretation; and one might say that Du Bois himself authorizes them. In *Dusk of Dawn* he notes that when the publisher, McClurg and Company, asked him to put together some of his essays for a book, he "demurred because books of essays almost always fall flat" (Du Bois [1940] 1975, p. 80; hereafter *Dusk*). In the event, he accepted the offer, and *Souls* includes nine previously published pieces.[3] Hence it is not surprising that, in the "Forethought," he does little more than indicate the content of each chapter. Yet *Souls* is not just a compilation of these articles. As David Levering Lewis says, the preexisting essays were "cut, polished, and mounted with a jeweler's precision for the McClurg collection" (1993, p. 278), and five new essays were added. Each chapter is introduced by a verse of poetry and a bar or two of an African-American hymn or spiritual. At a minimum, this provides *Souls* with a consistent aesthetic frame or mounting. The Forethought also includes a lightly drawn line separating the text into two parts. In the first part, Chapter V is new, and one of the earlier articles is divided to form Chapters VII and VIII. We will see later that this suggests a concern about how the chapters interface with each other. The second part, composed almost entirely of the new material, is at least loosely unified by the idea of permitting the reader to "view faintly" the "deeper recesses" of the Veil (*Souls*, p. 5). Thus there are clear indications of a unifying authorial intent. Nonetheless, *Souls* has the lingering appearance of a collection, a number of set pieces that have been brought together after the fact. It is understandable that this appearance, rich and variegated as it is, would be the primary object of interpretive attention.

I started out with exactly the view of *Souls* just described, and I stayed close to Du Bois's stated intentions when thinking about and teaching it. Over time, however, the veil of appearance began to dissolve and *Souls* took form in my mind as an intricate and coherent narrative, indeed as an organic whole and even at times as a living presence. It contains, as has long been recognized, a well-wrought theory of race relations and racial leadership. But beyond that, it reads *as if* it had been carefully plotted on a topographical map with vertical and horizontal dimensions, on the one hand, and designed to advance in phenomenological fashion from sociohistorical surface to psychological-spiritual depth, on the other. There are even strong hints of dialectical form, although not of the formal and closed sort one associates with Hegel or even Marx. Second, if we reverse perspective and look at the narrative structure from the bottom up, we can identify an underlying source of psychological unification that complements and intensifies the formal and empirical/theoretical unity of the manifest content. At least as I read it, *Souls* grows out of an aesthetic/affective configuration consisting of *a situation of insult and injury both personal and racial; anger as the native and direct response to the humiliating wound; and, when the anger is suppressed, a melancholy retreat from the site of the injury.* At the level of lived experience, this is the problem of the color-line. It is solved in twofold fashion: through proud and disciplined resistance to the impositions and injustices of white supremacy, and through the developed capacity to rise above the field of battle and survey it from on high. These are the modalities of mastery and self-mastery that parallel the affective responses to the originating situation of insult and injury. Taken in conjunction, they set up the horizontal and vertical dimensions of the text. Third, because this topographical structure of lived experience, affect, and action is common to narrator and narrative, something akin to a palindromic relationship is established between them. Just as in a palindrome one can read the same sentence both forward and backward, so in this instance one can read equally from author to text and text to author. The topography of *Souls* is Du Bois's personality writ large while, conversely, he appears within the text as an exemplification of the souls of black folk.[4]

If *Souls* has the formal and substantive unity I have attributed to it, then it can be placed in a lineage that includes such kindred spirits as Plato's *Republic*, Hegel's *The Phenomenology of Spirit*, Goethe's *Faust*, and the *Gesamtkunstwerk* (total artwork) of Richard Wagner.[5] Du Bois did not claim for *Souls* what I am claiming for it, however, and so one rightly might wonder if I am displacing his intentions with my own. Even if I am not guilty of mistaking him for one of his cultural ancestors, it still might be possible that the reading I am suggesting is a function of my will to knowledge, as Michel Foucault might put it, expressed through an *a priori* need for unification, on the one hand, and the use of a psychoanalytic optic, on the other. After all, in a post-Kantian and post-Nietzschean age, one can hardly claim hermeneutic innocence—as if the subjectivity of the interpreter did not form the object of interpretation, or the instrument of knowledge could be subtracted from the knowledge its use produces. Yet it is not necessarily the case that textual interpretation and reconstruction do nothing more than imprint the interpreter on the interpreted object. Rather—to cut a long methodological story short—the hermeneutic question is one of recognition: Is the interpreter's will to knowledge limited by the imperative of recognizing the autonomy of the object of interpretation? Or, if we frame the question of truth and meaning in narrative terms, is the original story recognizable in the one we tell about it?

In an initial stab at satisfying such criteria of recognition, here's a way of depicting the manifest form of *Souls*. The Forethought and Chapter I ("Of Our Spiritual Strivings") frame the narrative prospectively. They introduce the powerful signifiers of soul and spirit, terms that will become filled with meaning as we are guided through "the spiritual world in which ten thousand thousand Americans live and strive" (*Souls*, p. 5).[6] More specifically, they include the notions of the Veil, double-consciousness, and two-ness; a preliminary sketch of the historical situation of black folk; and a first look at the person and perspective of the author. The narrative grows out of this beginning, like the proverbial oak from the acorn. At the other end, Chapter XIV ("The Sorrow Songs") and the After-thought frame the narrative retrospectively. Du Bois's discussion of the songs (the hymns and spirituals mentioned earlier) takes us through the text again, seeing it this time from a different angle. The brief After-thought is a plea to readers to allow the book to take root in them: "Let there spring, Gentle One, from out its leaves vigor of thought and thoughtful deed to reap the harvest wonderful" (p. 164). Or, varying the metaphor, the first and last chapters are the portals through which we enter and exit Du Bois's world.

Within this frame, the text breaks into two parts. Chapters II through X depict the collective lives of black folk, principally in the South.[7] Du Bois appears as protagonist as well as interpreter in these chapters, but his dominant concern is with the empirical depiction and historical/sociological analysis of black life in white supremacist America. The narrative plays out on a horizontal plane, marked by a vertical distinction between high and folk culture. By contrast, in Chapters XI through XIII, the relationship between the horizontal and vertical dimensions of the text, as well as between Du Bois's individual experience and the collective experience of black folk, is reversed. At the same time, the vertical dimension takes on a more subjective hue, so that the vast expanse of the social world becomes a background for the exploration of spiritual and psychological heights and depths. The tales in this second part are more personal and autobiographical, and each of them is shadowed by death. Chapter XI, "Of the Passing of the First-Born," concerns the death of Du Bois's young son Burghardt, a loss that left a lasting mark on him. Chapter XII, "Of Alexander Crummell," is a eulogy for the great black cleric, whom Du Bois treats with filial respect and with whom he is deeply identified. Chapter XIII, "Of the Coming of John," is a tragic tale of racial enlightenment. Its protagonist, John Jones, is manifestly a black Everyman, who advances from childish innocence to worldly and world-weary wisdom. He is a lonely figure, carrying the burden of enlightening black folk without the whole-hearted support or understanding of black folk themselves. In this regard he resembles Crummell, in Du Bois's portrayal of him, and Du Bois himself, in actuality.[8] He is not, however, simply their double. He enacts the anger they abjure and death is his punishment, or perhaps reward, for this transgression. One might say that he is ambiguously related to them or, more precisely, that he is Du Bois's shadow self, the expression of a profound tension in his authorial and actual persona. Thus the body of the text might be divided into "the souls of black folk" and "the soul of W. E. B. Du Bois," so long as we recognize that individual and racial identity are interpenetrative and mutually constitutive.

A further step can be taken by following Robert Stepto, who reads the text as a "symbolic geography" (1991, p. 61) of African-American experience. Its antipodes are the North and the South, as they are in so many

African-American narratives. The *Narrative of the Life of Frederick Douglass* (Douglass [1845] 1997) is the archetype. Born to slavery in the South, he ascends to freedom in the North. By contrast, *Souls* depicts a "cultural immersion ritual" (p. 66), as Du Bois descends from the Berkshires in western Massachusetts through Tennessee to Atlanta, Georgia, and from Atlanta into the Black Belt of Dougherty County. Although literal slavery is now a thing of the past, it has not passed beyond memory, in part because its painful aftermath was the reality of Du Bois's present and foreseeable future. Thus the most powerful symbols of this geography remain slavery and freedom.

In the first ten chapters of *Souls*, freedom and slavery are unambiguously this-worldly matters. Du Bois views even religious experience from a mundane perspective; and he is expressly critical of the ways in which the Christian promise of eternal life functioned, in the antebellum South, as an ideology of adjustment and acquiescence (*Souls*, p. 125). In the chapters on Burghardt, Crummell, and John Jones, by contrast, death is treated as liberation, an escape from the vale of tears or, in Du Bois's language, a flight above the world of the Veil.[9] And because these chapters are personal, riven with pain and touched by an unmistakable melancholy, they drop us below the relatively less personal and more dispassionate symbolic geography that earlier organized the narrative. Hence the claim that *Souls* follows the classical phenomenological method of descending from surface to depth—so that, when viewed from below, it can be seen as an organic whole growing out of the aesthetic/affective configuration in which author and text are united.

Let me assume, if only for purposes of argument, that *Souls* is recognizable in these characterizations of it—that if you were to take these preliminary sketches and compare them to the text, you would find a near resemblance between them. Still, you might object that it is not fair to beg the question of authorial intent. How are these rather elaborate claims about *Souls* to be reconciled with the laconic statements with which Du Bois introduces it? The honest answer is, incompletely. Yet the gap between them is not quite so great as it at first appears. In a brief meditation on *Souls* written in 1904, Du Bois first comments on the diverse elements of which it is made: "bits of history and biography, some description of scenes and persons, something of controversy and criticism, some statistics and a bit of story-telling" (1904, p. 255). All this, he says self-critically, "leads to rather abrupt transitions of style, tone and viewpoint and, too, without doubt, to a distinct sense of incompleteness and sketchiness." We need not agree with this judgment; but the fact that he proffers it suggests that coherence and completeness were standards he aspired to meet. This reminds us that the text as we have it is the product of careful consideration and reworking, extending from the order in which the chapters are presented to the compelling thematization provided by their poetical and musical settings. Du Bois, in other words, plainly attempted to turn his collection of essays into an organic whole—an actual book. My view is that he succeeded more fully than he himself believed.

Yet from another perspective, Du Bois had no doubts that *Souls* was of a piece. "On the other hand," he continues:

> there is a unity in the book, not simply the general unity of the larger topic, but a unity of purpose in the distinctively subjective note that runs in each essay. Through all the book runs a personal and intimate tone of self-revelation. In each essay I sought to speak from within—to depict a world as we see it who dwell therein. (Ibid.)

In this passage Du Bois effects a characteristic glissade from "I" to "we," so that the self being revealed has a doubled meaning. But the "personal and intimate tone of self-revelation" is not effaced, with the result that we might even say of *Souls* what Nietzsche says of his autobiography: *Ecce Homo!*—behold the man! And this way of looking at it has the further implication that, when we are engaged with the text, we are simultaneously engaged in a process of recognition: "The reader will, I am sure, feel in reading my words peculiar warrant for setting his judgment against mine, but at the same time some revelation of how the world looks to me cannot easily escape him" (ibid.). This is not to say that the meaning of the text lies on its surface, even for its author. "It is difficult," Du Bois tells us, "strangely difficult, to translate the fine feelings of men into words. The Thing itself sits before you; but when you have dressed it out in periods it seems fearfully uncouth and inchoate. Nevertheless, as the feeling is deep the greater the impelling force to express it. And here the feeling was deep" (ibid.). We might understand him to be asking us to recognize the Thing—the feeling, the heart of the matter—even if it is difficult to find it in his words. And he tells us where to look: "In its larger aspects the style is tropical—African. This needs no apology. The blood of my fathers spoke through me and cast off the English restraint of my training and surroundings" (ibid.).

W. E. B. Du Bois

Nietzsche famously remarked that a great philosophy is "the personal confession of its author and a kind of involuntary and unconscious memoir" (Nietzsche [1886] 1966, p. 13). As we have just seen, Du Bois most assuredly would agree that *Souls* is part personal confession, but he would deny that the memoir is involuntary and unconscious. It is explicitly, in Walt Whitman's words, a "song of myself." Or, in Stepto's felicitous characterization, Du Bois is the "hero-narrator" of the tale he tells ([1979] 1991, p. 62). Because our efforts at textual reconstruction presuppose the part he plays, we must bring him into the story before we go any further.

William Edward Burghardt Du Bois was born February 23, 1868, in Great Barrington, Massachusetts, and died on August 27, 1963, in Accra, Ghana. He received his first B.A. from Fisk University in Nashville, Tennessee, in 1888, and a second B.A. *cum laude* in philosophy from Harvard University in 1890. After taking an M.A. in history at Harvard in 1891, he studied for two years at Friedrich Wilhelm University in Berlin. He returned to Harvard and was awarded the Ph.D. in history in 1895. His thesis, *The Suppression of the African Slave-Trade to the United States of America, 1638–1870*, was published in 1896 as the first volume of the Harvard Historical Monograph Series. His first, brief, teaching stint was at Wilburforce University, where he met and married Nina Gomer. Their marriage flourished in its earliest years, despite his consuming racial and intellectual passions, but never quite recovered from the traumatic impact of Burghardt's death. It was still intact, however, when Du Bois was hired to do a sociological study of Philadelphia's Seventh Ward by the University of Pennsylvania in 1896. The results were published as *The Philadelphia Negro* in 1899. In 1897 he was appointed professor of history and economics at Atlanta University in Atlanta, Georgia, where he edited a series of sociological studies of African-American life. He attended and was appointed secretary of the first Pan-African Congress in London in 1900, by which time he had also published a number of widely read articles in such journals as the *Atlantic Monthly*, the *Dial*, and the *Independent*. Not yet thirty-five, he was already one of the leading public intellectuals in African-American/American life.

Du Bois was a formidable scholar. He was also a novelist, a poet, and a brilliant polemicist. He was one of the founding members of the NAACP, and he founded its official journal, *The Crisis*, and edited it from 1910–1933/34. His political position changed over the years. Beginning as an aristocratic critic of socialism, he ended up as a communist. But from early on, he rejected the path of accommodation laid out by Booker T. Washington, and he was reluctant to adopt the view that the world could be changed for the better by the use of force. Thus in *Souls* he rejects both "an attempt to adjust all thought and action to the will of the greater group" and action motivated by a "feeling of revolt and revenge," arguing instead for "a determined effort at self-realization and self-development despite environing opinion" (*Souls*, p. 37). Despite environing opinion, and against it: "By every civilized and peaceful method we must strive for the rights which the world accords to men, clinging unwaveringly to those great words which the sons of the Fathers would fain forget: 'We hold these truths to be self-evident: That all men are created equal; that they are endowed by their Creator with certain inalienable rights; that among these are life, liberty, and the pursuit of happiness'" (p. 45).

This role of racial advocacy and leadership came naturally enough. Du Bois was a proud black man in "'nigger'–hating America" (Du Bois 1968, p. 183; hereafter *Autobiography*). His temperament did not suit him for deference and acquiescence. Yet his racial identity was achieved as well as ascribed. He, northern born and bred, chose to go south to Fisk; it was there, he reports, that he became a Negro:

> So I came to a region where the world was split into white and black halves, and where the darker half was held back by racial prejudice and legal bonds, as well as by deep ignorance and dire poverty. But facing this was not a lost group, but at Fisk a microcosm of a world and a civilization in potentiality. Into this world I leapt with enthusiasm. A new loyalty and allegiance replaced my Americanism: hence-forward I was a Negro. (p. 108)

It would be difficult to overemphasize the importance of this experience for Du Bois's subsequent development. Had he not gone south, perhaps he would have seen black folk primarily as a "lost group." But at Fisk and during two summers spent as a schoolteacher in rural Tennessee, he experienced first-hand both black community and white supremacy. He began a process of rooting himself in the history and culture of the African-American people, and he self-consciously affirmed the racial identity that was his birthright and his burden. He did not, however, surrender his northern and European aspirations (including the aim of eventually attending Harvard) when he immersed himself in black southern realities. If he became a Negro at Fisk, he also became a man with a double identity or consciousness.

Du Bois was keenly aware of this cultural duality and its accompanying stresses. One might even say that he embodies Nietzsche's desideratum of having "the ability *to control* one's Pro and Con and to dispose of them, so that one knows how to employ a *variety* of perspectives and affective interpretations in the service of knowledge" ([1887] 1967, p. 119). The Pro and Con, the dialectical oppositions in his authorial personality, are announced in the first chapter of *Souls*: "an American, a Negro; two souls, two thoughts, two unreconciled strivings; two warring ideals in one dark body, whose dogged strength alone keeps it from being torn asunder" (*Souls*, p. 11).[10] Inherent to that "dogged strength" is the aim of self-overcoming, and not for Du Bois alone: "The history of the American Negro is the history of this strife,—this longing to attain self-conscious manhood, to merge his double self into a better and truer self." In this truer self, he adds, "neither of the older selves [is] to be lost" (ibid.). Here, in this portentous fusion of his personal identity with that of his people, we see one of the portals through which the author enters the text.

The two-ness of Du Bois's cultural identity reflects and is a function of the Veil—the barrier of stereotypical beliefs and oppressive practices that splits or diremnts the historical and social space of African-American life. On the sociological level, the Veil signifies the color-line, the placements of power that maintain the relationship of white over black. On the psychological level, the Veil transforms the hyphen in African-American identity into the painful two-ness of self-alienation. Yet—if ambiguously—through suffering comes wisdom:

> After the Egyptian and Indian, the Greek and Roman, the Teuton and Mongolian, the Negro is a sort of seventh son, born within a veil, and gifted with second-sight in this American world,—a world which yields him no true self-consciousness, but only lets him see himself through the revelation of the other world. It is a peculiar sensation, this double-consciousness, this sense of always looking at one's self through the eyes of others, of measuring one's soul by the tape of a world that looks on in amused contempt and pity. (pp. 10–11)

Initially, the Negro is placed in the position of the seventh son and the veil is a caul. In African-American and other cultures, such a nativity implies special, even magical or shamanic, powers.[11] Here the gift is "second-sight," the ability to see beyond and beneath the surface of things, perhaps also to see them from more than one perspective. But at the textual juncture where "this American world" becomes "a world that yields him no true self-consciousness," second-sight becomes double vision. Black people see themselves through the eyes of white people, hence as deformed and inferior. This is the classic situation of mis-recognition, with its expectable yield of split and falsified consciousness.[12]

The epistemic ambiguity of the Negro's second-sight and double vision is fundamental to Du Bois's interpretive perspective. On the one hand, throughout *Souls* he presents himself as someone who knows life on both sides of the color-line. He guides the reader into the world of the American Negro and reveals its secrets, and he demonstrates at every step along the way his deep knowledge of European culture. He precludes the possibility of denying him his twofold cultural heritage. And because he puts himself forward as racial exemplar, this dual legacy is claimed for black folk generally. On the other hand, European culture, especially in its American implantation, is the mirror in which African identity is distorted and its value minimized. How, then, to internalize it as a cultural ideal without bringing the wooden horse of self-doubt into the citadel of the soul?

This ambiguity can be substantially reduced if not quite dissolved by thorough-going assimilationism or thorough-going separatism. The strength and dignity of Du Bois's position is his refusal of those options. He surrenders neither side of his cultural identity, but rather engages in the struggle to lift the Veil that renders them contradictory—to solve through social and political action the problem of the color-line.

On Renunciation and Recognition

The idea of renunciation is fundamental to Du Bois's conception of white supremacy and the struggle against it. The imposition of white supremacy can be interpreted as a situation of mis-recognition and the struggle against it as a battle for recognition. We will take up these notions in turn, at first through recourse to Johann Wolfgang von Goethe's *Faust*.

In the beginning of the tragedy, the philosopher Faust is tormented by the finitude of human knowledge. He wishes to "learn the things that hold the world together at its core," but the goal eludes him (Goethe 1965, p. 19). Burdened by Care, by a gnawing dissatisfaction with life, he contemplates suicide, willing to take the "risk of passing into nothingness" in order to find in death the knowledge that he cannot find in life (p. 30). He brings a phial of poison to his lips:

> The flood tide of my spirit ebbs away,
> To open seas I am shown forth by signs,
> Before my feet the mirror-water shines,
> And I am lured to new shores by new day. (Ibid.)

Easter bells sound before he drinks the poison, and he is recalled to life. Yet his yearning to cross the waters to new shores remains. He says to his student Wagner:

> Two souls abide, alas, within my breast,
> And each one seeks for riddance from the other.
> The one clings with a dogged love and lust
> With clutching parts unto this present world,
> The other surges fiercely from the dust
> Unto sublime ancestral fields. (p. 42)

A bit later, when Mephistopheles is attempting to snare him with promises of earthly delights, he says more bitterly and plainly:

> What can the world give me? Renounce,
> Renounce shalt thou, thou shalt renounce!
> This is the everlasting song
> Dinned in our ears throughout the course
> Of all our lives, which all life long
> Each morning sings until it's hoarse. (p. 56)

Renunciation, not gratification, is the song of experience. At least so it seems to Faust in the midst of his melancholy. But with his desire for true knowledge frustrated and his suicidal impulse not strong enough to lift him out of this world, he makes the fateful compact with Mephistopheles that suspends the imperative of renunciation and sets him on the course of striving and the gratification of desire.

Although Du Bois did not compact with the devil (which for him would have meant yielding to the temptation of revolt and revenge), the hero-narrator of *Souls* has an evident kinship with Faust as we first encounter him. The famous formulation of two-ness, cited above, racializes the Faustian dilemma: "an American, a Negro; two souls, two thoughts, two unreconciled strivings; two warring ideals in one dark body, whose dogged strength alone keeps it from being torn asunder." Thus where Goethe's protagonist was torn between corporeal delights and spiritual sublimity, ultimately between life and death, Du Bois is torn between Africa and America. But the identification with Faust's dilemma goes further. In Chapter V ("Of the Wings of Atalanta"), Du Bois lauds the founders of Negro colleges in the South, to whom the "voice of Time" says, "*Entbehren sollst du, sollst entbehren* [Renounce shalt thou, thou shalt renounce]" (*Souls*, p. 59). These dedicated souls "spread with their own hands the Gospel of Sacrifice." They were willing to forego much of life's sweetness in the present so that their children and children's children would not need to forego it in the future. Later, when mourning Burghardt, Du Bois identifies himself with these spiritual ancestors:

> Surely there shall yet dawn some mighty morning to lift the Veil and set the prisoned free. . . . But now there wails, on that dark shore within the Veil, the same deep voice, *Thou shalt forego!* And all I have foregone at that command, and with small complaint,—save that fair young form that lies so coldly wed with death in the nest that I have builded.
>
> If one must have gone, why not I? Why may I not rest me from this restlessness and sleep from this wide waking? (p. 134)

Bending the meaning of the concept in *Faust*, Du Bois accepts the command of renunciation that his responsibility to the future of his race imposes on him. But beyond the pragmatic meaning of renunciation and compounding it, there is his inevitable sadness in the loss of his son and heir, bringing home in the most painful way the lost possibilities of those who live within the Veil. At that moment his experience approximates to Faust's at the beginning of the tragedy and, he, too, is pinioned between life and death.

We will return to the theme of renunciation recurrently as we proceed, but we can already see that its meaning in *Souls* is overdetermined; that is, that several lines of thought and feeling are condensed in it. Along the horizontal or mundane dimension, it intersects with the problematic and project of racial advancement. Renunciation is a necessary condition for the realization of emancipatory aims. Along the vertical or spiritual dimension, it is joined by an affective link of melancholy to the notion of death-as-liberation, and more generally to the desire of rising above the field of battle. The two dimensions meet in the Veil itself, which vertically splits the horizontal plane.

The meaning of the Veil is also overdetermined, but several of its significations can be brought together through an adaptation of the Hegelian notions of recognition and mis-recognition, as famously articulated in the fourth chapter of the *The Phenomenology of Spirit* ([1807] 1977).[13] Hegel sets up a situation in which each of two selves desires to be recognized as an autonomous being by the other. A battle ensues, in which one of the combatants is willing to sacrifice his life rather than yield and the other is willing to yield rather than sacrifice his life. In the resulting relationship, the former emerges as lord, the latter as bondsman. This is Hegel's conceptualization of the origins of slavery.[14] There is no room in it for the circumstance that characterizes the origins of the slavery of African-Americans; that is, conquest based on superior power. But the upshot is the same—a relationship of domination in which the self who is denied recognition must recognize the self who will not recognize it. The concept of the Veil makes present this recognitive asymmetry, and in just such a way as to capture the painfully negated desire of black folk. *Souls* is intended (in part) as a contribution to solving *this* problem of the color-line. The "Gentle [white] Reader" (*Souls*, p. 5) is being given the chance to see within the Veil; that is, to see black folk as they truly are. Put differently, and in the vocabulary of the fin de siècle, the issue is one of human sympathy. As Du Bois states it in the chapter on Crummell, "the nineteenth was the first century of human sympathy,—the age when half wonderingly we began to descry in others that transfigured spark of divinity we call Myself" (p. 136; see also Mizruchi 1998, p. 316). Human sympathy approximates to the affective dimension of mutual recognition, and one of the functions of *Souls* is to engage the sympathy of those white folk who are capable of it. At the same time, black folk are being offered a mirror of their own experience, with the attendant possibility of taking a step toward their own true self-consciousness. And, from a slightly different angle, we might see the encounter as a publicly staged battle for recognition between Du Bois, the hero-narrator of *Souls*, and his white interlocutors. Black folk reading the text see themselves doubly represented: They witness Du Bois speaking *of* them and *for* them to their oppressors. He is their champion, akin in this regard to Joe Louis when he fought and defeated Max Schmeling in 1938 or Malcolm X when he debated a variety of white folk during the 1960s. In these ways, the project of self-recognition and mutual recognition is advanced, but—and this is the central point—the very existence of the project presupposes both the desire for recognition of black folk and its negation. And that negative moment, the Veil in its signification as the negation of desire, is the point of intersection between the horizontal and vertical planes of *Souls*.

In sum, the symbolic geography or topography of *Souls* is shaped by the problematic unity of the negated desire for recognition and the imperative of renunciation. Read psychologically, recognition and renunciation point to the situation of insult and injury with which *Souls* begins, and to which we will presently turn.

On Psychoanalytic Interpretation

In a late paper, Freud distinguished between interpretations and constructions in psychoanalysis: "'Interpretation' applies to something that one does to some single element of the material, such as an association or a parapraxis. But it is a 'construction' when one lays before the subject of the analysis a piece of his early history that he has forgotten . . . " (1937, p. 261). Extending the latter notion, we can say that, in constructions, the analyst uses the available data of a patient's life-history imaginatively. S/he fills in the gaps of memory and, in the process, lends a narrative coherence to the patient's experience. Of course, the two modes of analysis are not opposed. Constructions are in part built up from interpretations, which provide the foundation for the imaginative or inductive leap the more integrative perspective involves; and once the larger view has emerged, interpretations find their place within it.

The approach I am taking to *Souls* might be conceived in similar terms. In common with, and often borrowing from, other readers, I offer a variety of specific interpretations of the text. These are combined with larger themes—the topography of the Veiled world, with its horizontal and vertical dimensions; the problematics of recognition and renunciation; the sojourning of Du Bois as hero-narrator, resembling at times a stranger in a strange land. And both the specific interpretations and these larger themes are viewed as (at least in part) expressing an underlying aesthetic/affective configuration or dynamic. But beyond this, my aim is to offer a construction or reconstruction of the text as a whole, to re-present it in such a way that its narrative and conceptual coherence is made visible. I am not, however, placing myself in the position of the analyst as the one-who-knows in relation to the text or its author as the unknowing patient. That distribution of roles violates the requirements of respect and recognition on which clinical psychoanalysis de facto depends, and it would be totally inappropriate here.

As noted in the Preface, I employ two, or perhaps two and one-half, optics in this work of construction or reconstruction. A Platonic topography mirrors the topography of *Souls* in certain respects, and at times I make interpretive use of it. Hegelian problematics have an even closer fit with the problem of the color-line, as Du Bois conceives it. And my native perspective is psychoanalytic. But psychoanalysis means different things to different people and can be employed in a variety of ways. Here it functions primarily as a technique of textual interpretation and secondarily as a psychological theory. In the former regard, the original model was first presented in Freud's *The Interpretation of Dreams* (1900), and it retains its relevance in the current instance. As in dream interpretation, we differentiate between manifest and latent content. The manifest content consists of the lifeworld of black folk, as Du Bois re-presents and re-creates it. It contains various signifiers of Du Bois himself, including symptomatic expressions of his internal conflicts;

and these point toward one set of latent meanings. There is also a network of metonymic and metaphorical relations, akin to the condensations and symbolizations of what Freud calls the dream-work. The Veil is the point of greatest density in this network, but other notions constituting the surface of the text (e.g., renunciation and sacrifice, the temptation of revolt and revenge) point downward as well. Then there are recurring scenarios, most importantly the mise-en-scène of mis-recognition, that link the manifest and latent levels of the text and bring us into contact with the aesthetic/affective dynamic that I view as animating *Souls* as a whole. But—and this proviso is of the utmost importance—in contrast to the epistemic assumption that guides classical psychoanalytic dream interpretation, here the manifest text is not reduced to the latent one. The lifeworld that Du Bois re-presents and re-creates is not mere day residue, the raw material of the dream-work gaining its meaning only from below. It is rather irreducible. Its elements may point elsewhere, but they themselves are also the point. Put differently, the configuration of insult, anger, and melancholy is not to be taken as essence, with the lifeworld of black folks as appearance. The epistemic relationship is not one of an underlying Truth and its manifestations. Rather, the unity of the reconstructed text is constituted by the interpenetration of its various elements and by the perspectives through which we view it. Psychoanalytic perspectivism, not psychoanalytic reduction, is the vehicle for the elucidation of textual meaning. So we, no less than Du Bois, must hope for "the ability *to control* one's Pro and Con and to dispose of them, so that one knows how to employ a *variety* of perspectives and affective interpretations in the service of knowledge" (Nietzsche [1887] 1967, p. 119).

Adopting a nonreductive or perspectival approach to textual interpretation involves the willingness to listen to the voice or voices through which the text articulates its meaning, and to listen with something akin to what Buddhists term beginner's mind.[15] Along these lines, Paul Ricoeur, in his now-classic *Freud and Philosophy* (1970), distinguishes between interpretation as the recollection of meaning and interpretation as the exercise of suspicion (pp. 28–36). Quite rightly, he places the methods of Marx, Nietzsche, and Freud in the latter category. The truth-claims of a given consciousness are viewed skeptically. Employment of the relevant method reveals the falsity of these claims and the underlying reality that has been concealed. Surface is reduced to depth and, having been revealed as merely defensive, is then permitted to drift away into oblivion. Or, if this is too extreme, the outer layers of the subject are seen as character-structure serving (perhaps necessary and appropriate) defensive functions. Long ago, however, the clinical practice of psychoanalysis convinced me that every defense is also an expression of what it defends against, indeed that the expressive dimensions of subjectivity—often limited in their richness by biographical circumstance—are the ultimate objects of analysis. Their elucidation requires a method approximating to Ricoeur's recollection of meaning, in which the object is believed to speak, to reveal itself to or "address" the interpreter who listens in the right way (p. 29). Put differently, although all interpretation involves interpellation or hailing of the Other, it is equally important to accept being interpellated by the Other. The interpretive *action* of entering into the inner world of person or text must be complemented by a kind of *inaction* that permits its entry into the interpreter's inner world. The hermeneutic equivalent of mutual recognition depends on this double process.

What, then, is the role of psychoanalytic theory in this hermeneutic endeavor? Stated simply, it provides a sounding board, an (optimally open) set of meanings that remain in the background until they are called forth by the interpretive transaction. For the most part, in reading *Souls* I've not attempted to bring them forward, choosing instead to stay close to the language and aesthetic/affective tone of the text. The conspicuous exceptions are the notions of racialized oedipal and pre-oedipal relations. Their employment seems warranted on two grounds. First, beginning with slavery, a perverse familial paradigm has been built into the everyday practices of white supremacy. White men are positioned as fathers, black men as sons, and women (black and white) as objects of masculine desire and prizes in the contestation of men. The white men in this peculiar triangulation claim to have God on their side; that is, that they are enacting the Law of the Father even when the action in question is the sexual violation of black women and the lynching of black people, male and female. Black men and black women contest the validity of this claim. But the paradigm itself is masculinist, and the voices of the women are seldom heard. Insofar as women are granted agency, it is in the performance of maternal functions; that is, in pre-oedipal relations of nurture. But even here they are viewed, indeed conceived, from a masculine perspective—as a mother-world, a surround or environment providing blissful gratification at one time, the threat of abysmal pain at another. It is from this matrix that the stereotypical figure of the black mammy emerges in the white imaginary, and the archetype of the strong—enduring and indomitable—mother in the lives and dreams of black people.

Unsurprisingly, when women, black women in particular, approach the problem of the color-line, this masculinist paradigm loses its position of dominance and a much richer field of psychological exploration replaces it.[16] But—and this is my second justification for bringing it forward here—I believe the paradigm is of a piece with the underlying psychology of *Souls.* Hence it emerges at certain critical junctures in my reading of the text, as one of the stories within the story and as a narrative construction that aids in the reconstruction of the text. It does not, however, displace the fundamental problematic of recognition and renunciation, which touches more nearly on the painful issues of identity and selfhood with which Du Bois frames his exploration of the souls of black folk.

Here it might be emphasized that recognition and renunciation, although drawn from a register of philosophical meaning, are themselves psychoanalytic concepts, or at least conceptual fellow travelers. The basic setup of recognition, the interaction of two selves with questions of identity in the balance, is paradigmatic of the human condition. The archetypal first instance is the fateful union of mother and child, which feminist psychoanalysts have done so much to elucidate. For, as already noted, in once-conventional (patriarchal, phallocentric, masculinist) psychoanalytic narratives, the subjectivity of the woman who is a mother is as invisible as Ellison's invisible man. Yet infantile fantasies of the mother-world can be properly assessed as fantasies only by bringing in the mother's experience as the baseline of comparison. More generally, problems of gender identity were hidden behind a veil of normative masculinity, in which the problems themselves were distorted beyond recognition.[17] Further, and in-house psychoanalytic issues aside, no tale told of black folk can be considered adequate if the subjectivity of women is occluded by that of men. In this regard, *Souls* is imbalanced, in ways that are characteristic of the times generally and of the strivings of black men for recognition by white men in particular. We catch glimpses of the spiritual strivings of black women, but these are, relatively speaking, of a fugitive sort.

Renunciation would not ordinarily be viewed as a psychoanalytic notion, although it could be said that, in Freud's classical articulation of drive theory, the shift from the immediate gratification of the Pleasure Principle to the delayed gratification of the Reality Principle is the paradigmatic instance. Du Bois's major use of the idea, the Gospel of Sacrifice that guided the work of racial progress, might be taken as a further, historically more specific, step along this road of sublimation. But the more melancholy imperative of renunciation that accompanied the death of his son is of a different sort. So here, too, there is a doubling of consciousness.

Both forms of renunciation can be given a psychological grounding by reference to a theory of basic drives quite different from Freud's. We assume a primary drive toward pleasure and a parallel drive away from pain. We may term the first the life-drive, because pleasurable experiences are life-sustaining in the primary instance. The second, with somewhat greater license, may be termed the death-drive: If the quantum of pain in living crosses a certain, individually variable, threshold, the imperative of avoiding painful stimulation dictates the cessation of life itself. This is the drive behind the fantasy of death-as-liberation. Characteristically, however, the experience of living brings us neither pure pleasure nor pure pain, but rather the two varyingly commingled. This sets up the field of operation of a third drive, the one most consequential for human development. Borrowing from Nietzsche but radically altering his use of the term, we may identify this as the domain of the will to power, defined generally as the drive to overcome resistance and more specifically as the drive to overcome pain to gain pleasure, including the pleasure of overcoming pain (Wolfenstein 2000a, chap. 2). This is also the locus of aggression, which at its simplest is the energy and affect of overcoming resistance. And when the resistance, the experience of pain, imposes itself upon us with sufficient intensity—when it intrudes or is forced on us—aggression turns into rage (the primary, unmediated response) and anger (when there is more mentalization).

Although the psychological story is far more complicated than I am making it out to be, we may say that renunciation as a modality of racial advancement involves a sublimation of the will to power in the mode of life-affirmation. It builds upon a creative restraint of impulses, even rageful and angry ones. Renunciation as form of retreat reflects the influence of the death-drive and may result in death itself. Short of this eventuality, it serves to establish a psychical territory apart from the site of painful interaction. Yet even in the extreme instance, it may bespeak not a paralysis of the will but rather a proud unwillingness to bear the "slings and arrows of outrageous fortune" (Shakespeare, *Hamlet*, act 3, scene 1). There are even circumstances, special and awful ones, in which the renunciation of life is its affirmation: "there is some shit I will not eat," the conscientious objector Olaf "ceaselessly repeats" as he is being mercilessly beaten by the soldiers assigned to break him (Cummings 1972, p. 339).

Itinerary

Our exploration of *Souls* begins, in Chapter 2, with Du Bois's self-presentation in the first chapter of "Of Our Spiritual Strivings." This will give us an initial image of the unity of text and author. It is the kernel from which both *Souls* and the present interpretation of *Souls* unfold. Chapter 3 portrays the author as a young man; in Chapter 4, this portrait is rounded off with a brief review of his educational experiences and the tensions in his emergent worldview. Taken together, these two chapters add a biographical dimension to the character of Du Bois as hero-narrator but do not subtract from it—that is, the character of hero-narrator is not reduced to biography. Then, having established Du Bois's identity as the principal actor in the drama we are staging, we will follow him along the horizontal and vertical paths of his spiritual odyssey. In Chapter 5 we look over his shoulder as he proceeds, in dialectical fashion, to reveal the collective souls of black folk. In Chapter 6, we accompany him as he takes what can been seen as a phenomenological plunge and reveals the depth of his own soul.

2

Through a Glass Darkly

There was a time when meadow, grove and stream,
The earth, and every common sight,
To me did seem
Aparell'd in celestial light,
The glory and the freshness of a dream.
It is not now as it hath been of yore;—
Turn wheresoe'er I may,
By night or day,
The things which I have seen I now see no more.

WILLIAM WORDSWORTH,
"Ode: Intimations of Immortality from
Recollections of Early Childhood"

Each substantive chapter of *Souls* is headed by a stanza or two of poetry,
set above a bar of one of the spirituals or hymns that Du Bois names the sorrow songs.[1] These twofold inscriptions might be read as signifiers of two-
ness, of the duality in Du Bois's personality and worldview, or equally of
the merging of his "double self into a better and truer self" in which "neither
of the older selves [is] to be lost."[2] Arthur Symons's mournful apostrophe
to ocean, "The Crying of Waters," which heads Chapter I, "Of Our Spiritual
Strivings," captures the pain at the heart of this duality. The poet's voice
(the "voice of my heart in my side") ambiguously merges into the "voice
of the sea": "O water, crying for rest, is it I, is it I?" (*Souls*, p. 9). The sorrow
will not cease until "the last moon droop and the last tide fail,/ And the fire
of the end begin to burn in the west." Until then, "the heart shall be weary
and wonder and cry like the sea/ All life long crying without avail/ As the

water all night long is crying to me" (ibid.). In the poet's words we feel the presence of the troubled waters of the Middle Passage, the terrible defile through which Africans were transported to the Americas and slavery.[3] Indeed, the poem is virtually a sorrow song, with its joining of weariness and melancholy with the foreshadowing of the end of days—joined as well, and almost seamlessly, to "Nobody Knows the Trouble I've Seen," the actual sorrow song that follows. And joined a third time to Du Bois himself ("is it I? is it I?"), who—speaking in his own voice—begins: "Between me and the other world there is ever an unasked question: . . . How does it feel to be a problem?" (*Souls*, p. 9). In this way a stamp of melancholy is placed on *Souls* and, by virtue of proximity and the continuity of the first person singular, on its author as well. This personalization of the race problem echoes the first words of the Forethought ("the problem of the twentieth century is the problem of the color-line"), a formulation that also is used to frame Chapter II ("Of the Dawn of Freedom"), prospectively and retrospectively. Thus from the start, Du Bois presents himself as an exemplar of his race—which is also to say, of the problem of being black in a land of white supremacy. No less than *Dusk of Dawn* ([1940] 1975; hereafter *Dusk*), *Souls* might have been subtitled "An essay toward an Autobiography of a Race Concept."[4]

Having set the stage for himself, Du Bois turns to a recollection of childhood, the moment in (perhaps) his tenth year when he recognized as a matter of personal identity the problem of being black in a white world.[5]

> I remember well when the shadow swept across me. . . . In a wee wooden schoolhouse, something put it into the boys' and girls' heads to buy gorgeous visiting-cards—ten cents a package—and exchange. The exchange was merry, till one girl, a tall newcomer, refused my card,—refused it peremptorily, with a glance. Then it dawned on me with a certain suddenness that I was different from the others; or like, mayhap, in heart and life and longing but shut out from their world by a vast veil. I had thereafter no desire to tear down that veil, to creep through; I held all beyond it in common contempt, and lived above it in a region of blue sky and great wandering shadows. The sky was bluest when I could beat my mates at examination-time, or beat them at a foot-race, or even beat their stringy heads. (*Souls*, p. 10)

Shanette Harris shrewdly argues that "this incident of social rejection produced great discomfort because the severity was of a magnitude to dismantle a denial system that previously offered protection from the harsh reality of racial overtones in New England" (2003, p. 226).[6] David L. Lewis has a more cautious assessment of its meaning: "A permanent, anchoring sense of Du Bois's racial identity *could* have come from a single traumatic rebuff. . . . The incident must have occurred, and his account is psychologically plausible; yet sympathetic skepticism is advisable whenever Du Bois advances a concept . . . by way of autobiography" (1993, p. 33). Thus advised, we'll consider the biographical evidence in the next chapter. But a useful way of combining the unique occurrence and a background of racial tension would be to see the incident as a screen memory—an actual event that gains emotional intensity because more diffuse but associated affective experiences are condensed in it. Taken this way, its emblematic value is enhanced rather than diminished.

Let's imagine, then, that Du Bois, in offering his classmate the visiting-card, was expecting a sympathetic response, that he was consciously unguarded against and therefore unprepared for a rejection of this kind. The girl's gesture of contempt came as a shock, but took hold and resonated because an awareness of racial prejudice already hung cloudlike in the New England skies. And just because he was at that moment open-hearted, he would have felt humiliated by the insult, injured in his amour propre and his pride. If so, there would necessarily be a feeling of anger, even rage—the kind that shows up in a reddening of the face or in a blow to the face of the offender.[7] But in his account, these feelings are warded off, in twofold fashion. First, a veil drops between him and the others—dropped by them, to be sure, but also protectively held in place by him. He breaks off contact with them and, in the process, disavows the painful feelings of the contact that precipitated the break. He claims that he "had thereafter no desire to tear down that veil." More likely, he suppressed the desire to tear it down, except insofar as it shielded him against further insult. Either way, anger was controlled by removing or at least reducing the occasion for it. Second, mirroring inversely the humiliating gesture of the white girl, he "held all beyond [the veil] in common contempt, and lived above it in a region of blue sky. . . . " Thus we have an upward retreat to the realm of intellectual superiority. Not that Du Bois completely abjured physical contestation, with its opportunity for a displaced and sublimated expression of anger. But his character was formed as a defense against the lacerating and explosive affects that racialized contempt engendered. The defense was not perfect. Even in his blue skies there were "great wandering shadows," no different in kind from the shadow that swept across him on that fateful day.

Such an interpretation emphasizes the dynamic role played by repressed anger in the formation of Du Bois's character. Additionally, we see here how the problem of the color-line became a problematic nexus of personal identity—two-ness in a twofold sense. On the horizontal or mundane plane, the girl's insulting gesture broke the bonds of commonality and sympathy between the boy and his white-skinned contemporaries. We might say it transformed the hyphen in African-American identity into a broken link and so began the process through which he came to recognize in his own experience the history of his race. It also generated or at least accentuated a vertical split between the mundane and the spiritual/intellectual planes— between a body dwelling within the Veil and a soul soaring proudly above it. The contempt *of* white folks was then matched by contempt *for* white folks. Yet this is not the whole story. There are shadows in the sky, Du Bois has already joined his voice to the mournful voice of the sea, his troubles to the unseen troubles of his people. And time, he tells us, drummed home the lesson learned in that wee schoolhouse: "Alas, with the years all this fine contempt began to fade; for the worlds I longed for, and all their daz-zling opportunities, were theirs, not mine" (*Souls*, p. 10). He did not cease to strive after them, unlike less fortunate black boys who sank into "silent hatred of the pale world about them and mocking distrust of everything white." Still:

> The shades of the prison-house closed round us all; walls strait and stubborn to the whitest, but relentlessly narrow, tall, and unscalable to sons of night who must plod on darkly in renunciation, or beat unavailing palms against the stone, or steadily, half hopelessly, watch the streak of blue above. (Ibid.)

The wings of his proud independence could carry him only so far before he, too, must return sadly to earth, within the Veil.

Thus our first acquaintance with the souls of black folk is the moment when Du Bois's own soul became divided within itself.[8] Gone were the days when he could say of Great Barrington that it was a "boy's paradise" (*Dusk*, p. 13). Now innocence was lost, and from this time forward he would be bedeviled by double-consciousness. Perhaps, in recalling this experience, he had Ralph Waldo Emerson's depiction of the transcendentalist's double consciousness in the back of his mind:

> The worst feature of this double consciousness is, that the two lives, of the understanding and of the soul, which we lead, really show very little rela-tion to each other, never meet and measure each other: one prevails now, all buzz and din; and the other prevails then, all infinitude and paradise; and, with the progress of life, the two discover no greater disposition to reconcile themselves. Yet, what is my faith? What am I? What but a thought of serenity and independence, an abode in the deep blue sky? (Emerson 1950, p. 100)

The soul of the transcendentalist, akin to that of the young black man, seeks to rise above the buzz and din of mundane affairs and make its home in the deep blue sky of serene and independent thought. But whether or not Du Bois was intentionally echoing Emerson in telling his own story, he was certainly invoking William Wordsworth's ode, "Intimations of Immortal-ity from Recollections of Early Childhood" (1807; hereafter "Intimations"). "Shades of the prison-house," says the poet, "begin to close upon the grow-ing Boy," a darkening of vision that in time will blind him to the celestial light. We are not born blind: "trailing clouds of glory do we come from God, who is our home: Heaven lies about us in our infancy." (in George 1904, p. 354).[9] But we are forgetful and so we stumble on with only a this-worldly light to guide us. In this way Wordsworth makes use of Plato's notion that the immortal soul becomes amnesiac at birth and loses access to its preexistent knowledge of the divine. As he remarks in his preface to the poem:

> a pre-existent state has entered into the popular creeds of many nations; and, among all persons acquainted with classic literature, is known as an ingredient in Platonic philosophy. Archimedes said that he could move the world if he had a point whereon to rest his machine. Who has not felt the same aspirations as regards the world of his own mind? Having to wield some of its elements when I was impelled to write this poem on the "Immortality of the Soul," I took hold of the notion of pre-existence as having sufficient foundation in humanity for authorising me to make for my purpose the best use of it I could as a poet. (p. 353)

In like fashion Du Bois takes hold of Platonic, Romantic, and transcendental concepts and metaphors to express the divisions consequent upon the falling of the Veil. Yet the pain thus signified overflows the signifiers themselves, and it is not to be wondered that he would require the solace of a return to his airy spiritual home to tolerate living and striving in the prison-house of white racist America.

Postscript

The aesthetic/affective meanings of the visiting-card incident can be translated into the language of recognition and renunciation. The humiliating response of the white girl to Du Bois's offering is a paradigmatic instance of mis-recognition. His repression or suppression of his anger, followed by its sublimation into the will to contest white supremacy, initiates a battle for recognition. Renunciation in the sense of voluntary self-sacrifice is required to wage the battle. Hence he does not follow in the path of those "sons of night who must plod on darkly in renunciation"—who accept their exclusion from the kingdom of light. But there are affective resonances of their despair in the melancholy accompanying his retreat from the scene of the injury. No doubt he is able, as they are not, to take flight into a sky-realm detached from the earth below, his own kingdom of the mind where freedom of self-expression can be enjoyed. Yet its enjoyment requires the renunciation of the desire to be at home in the world of ordinary human intercourse and sympathy.

From a slightly different angle, we may bring together the meanings of the visiting-card incident through the interrelated terms of second-sight, double-vision, and two-ness. The consistent hyphenation of these notions might be taken to suggest a definitional identity; if so, the identity is dialectical:

- *Initial Affirmation: The Seventh Son and Second-Sight.* Black folks are gifted (and therefore capable of bringing gifts). One such gift is second-sight—

the ability to see beneath appearances, behind veils, to see what the others cannot see, including what white people cannot see of themselves.

• *Negation: Double-Consciousness.* The seventh son, transported across the crying waters of the Middle Passage, is placed in a white American world that denies him "true self-consciousness" but rather burdens him with a self-image reflected from the eyes (the "I") of the racial Other. Seen in that mirror, he is "less than"—worthy only of contempt and pity. Second-sight, a positive twofold aspect of selfhood, becomes double-consciousness, self-negating selfhood. In psychoanalytic terms, this alienated form of consciousness would be formulated as a Black Ego or I, who is always under the surveillance of a whitened-out Superego or Ego-Ideal. Or, following Robert Gooding-Williams, double-consciousness is "the false self-consciousness that obtains among African Americans just when they observe and judge themselves from the perspective of a white, Jim Crowing American world that betrays the ideal of reciprocal recognition due to a contemptuous, falsifying prejudice that misrepresents the reality of Negro life" (2003, p. 20).

• *Negation of Negation?: Two-ness as Problem and Potential Solution.* Two-ness is the ultimate individualization and internalization of the problem of the color-line, the Veil experienced as an interior division or, as Hegelians would say, diremption.[10] The hyphen in *African-American* can be used as a symbol or sign of this division. This internalized problem cannot be overcome by wishful thinking—by pretending to be just American, because being American includes the assumption of white supremacy and black inferiority, or by pretending to be just African, because the American world contains cultural prizes of great value. Only by affirming the hyphen itself, by shouldering the weight of two-ness, is there a possibility that the Negro's double self might be merged into a better and truer one. The realization of that possibility requires the recognition that *the African's internalization of American culture has been paralleled by the [white] American's internalization of African culture.* Two-ness must be acknowledged and sublated on both sides of the color-line. Only through this mutual acknowledgment can the Veil be lifted.

In the long meanwhile, the tale of vulnerability and mis-recognition that Du Bois tells of himself is ubiquitous in the annals of race relations. Think, for example, of the succession of such incidents described by Frantz Fanon in *Black Skin, White Masks,* including the characteristic moment, after he had given a lecture on Negro and European poetry, when a French acquaintance enthused, "At bottom you are a white man" ([1952] 1967, p. 38). Here we have an insult in the form of a compliment. Or there is the incident in *The Autobiography of Malcolm X,* when the young man is told by a respected teacher, "you've got to be realistic about being a nigger. A lawyer—that's no realistic goal for a nigger. You need to think of something you *can* be.

You're good with your hands. . . . Why don't you plan on carpentry?" (X and Haley 1965, p. 36). Guard lowered, blow received, all-the-more painful, perhaps, because no harm was (at least consciously) intended. To the contrary: The teacher thought he was giving good advice. (And, if called on to justify himself, he might have claimed that Booker T. Washington would have said much the same thing.) Thereafter Malcolm turned away from the color-line and its abrasions, until he returned years later as the white man's worst nightmare, the veritable embodiment of the righteous anger of black folk. Or there is the moment of experienced invisibility with which Ralph W. Ellison begins *Invisible Man*. Here the intent is plain enough. A white man calls a black man "nigger" and for once receives blows, head-butts and kicks to match the insult. "Apologize! Apologize!" the protagonist yells, but the white man "still uttered insults though his lips were frothy with blood" ([1952] 1989, p. 4). In this instance, the furious demand for recognition is taken almost to its limit, and to no avail.

Ellison introduces this incident with the comment, "It is sometimes advantageous to be unseen, although it is most often rather wearing on the nerves. Then, too, you're constantly being bumped against by those of poor vision" (ibid.). Chester Fontenot describes another experience of this kind. He and a friend, both black, each well-dressed and carrying briefcases, were conversing in a hotel lobby. They were approached by a middle-aged white male who asked if either of them was the hotel bellman. The two friends did not emulate Ellison's protagonist in responding to the question; but, reflecting on the event, Fontenot observes that the "sensation of being 'bumped against' by 'people with poor vision' expresses the dilemma of self-representation for African Americans" (Fontenot 2003, pp. 130–131). And it also can result in a settled desire to avoid such abrasive interactions. Michael Hanchard, as a preface to the articulation of what he terms an ethic of aversion, tells this story:

> I believe I stumbled upon one response to the quotidian forms of racism in daily black life in the United States at a dinner in downtown Manhattan, with a large group of friends and acquaintances at a restaurant on the West Side, between Chelsea and the Village. We were about an hour into our meal when a black gentleman came looking for someone in the party whom he was picking up. The hostess, a young white woman in her mid- to late twenties engaged the man in a very friendly, professional manner and implored him to come back at some point to have dinner and enjoy the restaurant's wondrous food and hospitality. The man, courteous, poised and well-dressed, was in his mid-20's. Educated at one of the nation's best business schools and then employed by one of the world's top brokerage firms on Wall St, he would be considered a statistical anomaly according to the oft-cited statistics about young black male underachievement in the United States. His response was slow but deliberate, with a curl of condescension at the right edge of his mouth.

"I'm sure, ma'am. The restaurant seems very nice and I'm sure the food is quite nice as well, but I do not normally associate with whites after-hours, after work." The woman looked stunned, her mouth dropped, her eyes widened, and after a long pause asked feebly, why, in a plaintive voice. To which he responded, "I simply don't. I get enough interactions with whites during my working hours and working days, which are quite long. No disrespect to you or to your restaurant, but the work day and work week is about as much from you people as I can stand." He picked up his companion and left, but not before wishing the woman a good night and best of luck. The woman looked to us for recognition and some solace. Most of the members of the table who were also black were equally surprised, though not stunned. After a pause, the conversation turned from job positions and the latest current events to interactions with whites in a professional environment. One by one, most people at the table partially concurred with the young man's sentiment, though not with the forthright expression of his sentiment. All agreed that while they had white friends with whom they interacted at work, their interactions with whites outside of work were far fewer. One person commented on the young man's honesty, his willingness to say what many blacks felt but dared not utter. (Hanchard 2006, pp. 103–104)

Hanchard uses this experience to highlight the appropriateness of an aversive response to the stresses and strains of interacting with white folks; and when we come to Du Bois's description of his own hauteur in the next chapter, we would do well to keep it in mind. But the young man was not following a prescription of aversion in the incident itself. Quietly and politely, he was being confrontational. He was disrupting the assumption of a shared civil space that was implicit in the hostess's routine courtesy and in the dining choice of Hanchard and his companions. This combination of confrontation and aversion was fundamental to the roles played by both Du Bois and Malcolm X, whatever their affective and stylistic differences.

In these instances, as in the one that initiates the voyage of discovery in *Souls*, we see the possibility of turning away. Even Ellison's protagonist, despite his rage, breaks off contact in the end. The battle for recognition is interrupted; wounded and angry, one lives to fight another day. But sometimes the terms of engagement preclude either fight or flight. Then the ritual of humiliation is carried through to completion. Ossie Davis offers a particularly painful example from his boyhood. He was six or seven years old when two (needless to say, white) policemen picked him up off the street, drove him to the police station, and held him there for about an hour. As he describes it:

Anyway, going along with the white game of black emasculation seemed to come naturally. Later, in their joshing around, one of them reached for a jar of cane syrup and poured it over my head. They laughed as if it was the funniest thing in the world, and I laughed, too. Then the joke was over, the ritual was complete. They gave me several hunks of peanut brittle and let me go.

I ate the candy right away and went home. I never told Mama or Daddy. It didn't seem all that important. For whatever reason, I decided to keep the entire incident to myself. They were just having fun at the expense of a little nigger boy. And yet, I knew I had been violated. Something very wrong had been done to me, something I never forgot. (Davis and Dee 1998, pp. 43–44)

The literature on the sexual abuse of children overflows with stories of this kind. The power imbalance precludes struggle and induces a kind of complicity. The feelings native to the situation—the terror, the rage, and the shame—are disavowed ("it didn't seem all that important"). It is not to be spoken about, not a story to pass on; it is to be forgotten. But it will not go away. It falls into the category of what, in *Beloved*, Toni Morrison names "rememories"—experiences that refuse to become memories; that live on, intruding on the present as if they had a mind of their own; ghosts. Or they become embedded in one's character structure. This is what Davis calls "niggerization": "The process of niggerization is always a two-sided one, shared by two consenting individuals, one black, one white. The price of consent exacted from the black person, however, can be his life, livelihood, and all that he holds dear" (ibid., p. 44)—including his (or her) essential innocence, autonomy, and self-respect. One might protest that there is a misunderstanding here, that what seems (and only seems) like consent is rather the price paid for survival. But for the victim of the abuse, the experience is one of self-betrayal. If s/he looks in a mirror, s/he sees Hegel's slave and not E. E. Cummings' Olaf, the conscientious objector. Henceforward the internal basis for rejecting defilement will be, to a greater or lesser extent, undermined. Self-doubt becomes one's constant companion until, perchance, the opportunity arises to stand one's ground in the place where it formerly gave way beneath one's feet.

Du Bois, northern born and bred, did not have his character formed by the necessity of accommodation to southern treatment. When he did go South, he was armed with a high self-confidence that precluded the niggerization that Davis so acutely depicts. Still, even in the northern reaches of the land of white supremacy, there was a price to be paid for pride of self and pride of race.

3

"Be Your Own Father"

And this above all: to thine own self be true,
And it must follow, as the night the day,
Thou canst not then be false to any man.

SHAKESPEARE, *Hamlet*

There is an ironic echo of Polonious's famous advice to his son in *Invisible Man*. The protagonist encounters a black physician who has been driven insane by the cruel irrationality of white reacism. Having witnessed the young man's naïve faith in father figures both white and black, he cautions him, "be your own father" (Ellison, p. 156). As we are about to see in this psychobiographical portrait of the hero-narrator of *Souls* as a young man, Time spoke these words to Du Bois in the same breath as "Renounce shalt thou, thou shalt renounce."[1] The question is, who was the boy who had that experience, and how did he come to be a man? Or—given that Du Bois himself is our only source of information on the subject—how do the autobiographical stories he tells help us to understand his role as the hero-narrator of *Souls*?

His Mother's Son
"In 1868, on the day after the birth of George Washington was celebrated, I was born. . . . The year of my birth was the year that the freedmen of the South were enfranchised" (Du Bois 1968 [hereafter *Autobiography*], p. 61).[2] Characteristically, Du Bois links his life-history to the social history of his people. In the same associative fashion, he links himself to a founding father—even *the* founding father—of the Republic. This might be seen as another instance of two-ness, pointing toward the white men in Du Bois's

paternal lineage and paralleling the relative lightness of his skin. It can also be read as expressing desire for a strong and admirable father, in contrast to his actual one.

Alfred Du Bois, his son would say, was "a dreamer—romantic, indolent, kind, unreliable. He had in him the making of a poet, an adventurer, or a Beloved Vagabond" (p. 71). His grandfather, Du Bois's great-grandfather, was James Du Bois, a wealthy physician of French Huguenot descent, a loyalist during the American Revolution who resettled from Poughkeepsie, New York, to a plantation in Haiti after independence. He sired two sons with a Haitian black woman, the elder of whom was Alexander, Alfred's father. Although Alexander was a prominent member of the African-American community in New Haven, Connecticut, Alfred was a rake and a rambler, who abandoned his wife and child when the latter was still an infant. Du Bois believed, or wanted to believe, that his father was effectively driven out of Great Barrington, Massachusetts, by the hostility of his mother's family, the Burghardt clan, and that he intended to have his family follow him (p. 72; see also Lewis 1993, pp. 20–23). This may well have been true. But it also fits the pattern, so often seen in situations of divorce, in which the child blames the custodial parent for the breakup of the marriage. Such a splitting of responsibility for the break, combined with idealization of the missing parent, serves the defensive function of shielding the latter from the child's anger and thereby preserving a positive internal representation of him. This pattern might fit Du Bois, with these two variations: Blame is shifted from his mother to her family, and the idealization of his father is notably mild. Be that as it may, he grew up a fatherless child. And it is a good guess that he filled the intrapsychic space left by his father's absence with images of admirable men, men with whom he could identify, and whom he could strive to emulate.

Along these lines we can understand his choice of Otto von Bismarck, first chancellor of the German Empire, for his Fisk commencement address: "Bismarck was my hero. He made a nation out of a mass of bickering peoples. He dominated the whole development with his strength until he crowned an emperor at Versailles" (*Autobiography*, p. 126). He continues: "This foreshadowed in my mind the kind of thing that American Negroes must do, marching forth with strength and determination under trained leadership." He was, of course, to be one of those leaders, a founding father of his people as well as (necessarily) father to himself.[3] This familial circumstance also comes to mind when we see him, now a student in Berlin, confiding to the privacy of his journal: "is [it] the silent call of the world spirit that makes me feel I am royal and that beneath my sceptre a world of kings shall bow. The hot dark blood of that forefather—born king of men—is beating in my heart" (quoted in Aptheker 1985, p. 28). Here we have heroic aspirations imaginatively transformed into a royal destiny, along with a mythical and mystical patrilineage to replace the broken one of his childhood.

The more immediate consequence of the absence of Du Bois's father was the intimacy of his relationship with his mother, Mary Silvina. "Mother was dark shining bronze, with a tiny ripple in her black hair, black-eyed, with a heavy, kind face. She gave one the impression of infinite patience, but a curious determination was concealed in her softness" (Du Bois [1920] 1969, p. 6; hereafter *Darkwater*). She was born into a respectable New England African-American family. The Burghardts, although veering over time toward a kind of genteel poverty, were land owners of long standing in Great Barrington. Yet it seems Mary Silvina was not quite at home with her family's provincial propriety. Du Bois records that she had a child out of wedlock, his half-brother Idelbert, who was the only "illegitimate child throughout the family in my grandfather's and the two succeeding generations" (*Dusk*, p. 11). When she did marry Alfred Du Bois, at age thirty-five, it was to an outsider of dubious values and credentials. When he departed, she elected or was persuaded to stay with her natal family rather than to follow him. Du Bois reports, "mother no longer trusted his dreams, and he soon faded out of our lives into silence" (*Darkwater*, p. 10). Thereafter she "worried and sank into depression" (*Autobiography*, p. 73). Yet she carried herself with stoic dignity: "She was silent before family criticism. She uttered no word of criticism or blame." For his part, Du Bois respected her silence: "I think I knew instinctively that this was a subject which hurt my mother too much to even mention" (ibid.).

Mary Silvina was a devoted mother who took pride in her son: "She did not try to make me perfect. To her I was already perfect" (*Darkwater*, p. 11). And, as we can see in his tactful restraint concerning her broken relationship with his father, Du Bois reciprocated her love and concern. By the time he reached high school, he notes, his mother had become a "widow with limited resources," resources limited in part by a stroke that severely impaired her ability to work. "But I was keen and eager to eke out this income by various jobs: splitting, kindling, mowing lawns, doing chores. My first regular wage began as I entered high school" (*Dusk*, p. 13). And he was more than a family provider. Later in life he "always had more friends among women than among men." This began, he goes on to say,

> with the close companionship I had with my mother. Friends used to praise me for my attention to my mother; we always went out arm in arm and had our few amusements together. This seemed quite normal to me; my mother was lame, why should I not guide her steps? And who knew better about my thoughts and ambitions? (*Autobiography*, p. 279)

It is not much of a stretch to see the young Du Bois as the man of the household he and his mother shared.

Here we have a version of the oedipal configuration, one in which the son replaces the father as consort of the mother as well as playing the role of father to himself. One cannot predict an individual's future from the psychodynamics of such an initial familial situation. Various roads lead out from it. But one of the archetypal paths did become Du Bois's: that of the questing hero. The son who shoulders the father's responsibilities is charged with the defense of his mother and with bringing the prize of victory home to her. Perhaps, as Du Bois says, the world he longed for, with its dazzling opportunities, were theirs, not his. Still, "they should not keep these prizes . . . ; some, all, I would wrest from them" (*Souls*, p. 10). And so he did, beginning with the academic achievements that gave his mother such pride (*Darkwater*, p. 12; *Autobiography*, p. 100). Then, as he came into a man's estate, he increasingly merged his personal quest into that of his race. He became not only the hero-narrator of *Souls* but also an intellectual knight in life-long service to the cause of black people.[4]

Although Du Bois is quite laconic in describing his life with his mother, it seems clear that he was secure in her unconditional love and that she highly valued his intellectual ability and attainments. Perhaps, too, he was heir to her ambitions—ambitions doubly out of reach for someone female and black. His fierce drive to excel and his consistent support for women's rights and opportunities would fit such a hypothesis. One might take a step further and see her as idealizing her exceptional child, conceivably in compensation for her own experiences of rejection and devaluation, If so, he lived up to the ideal, playing to perfection the part she and fate assigned to him. But his autobiographical reflections give us no basis for believing that Mary Silvina bent his character to her own purposes. To the contrary: Du Bois notes that his mother "was not talkative, but listened well" (*Autobiography*, p. 81). One pictures her as quiet, receptive, and restrained, gratefully accepting her son's devotion to her but allowing him the freedom of thought and action to become who he was, not who she needed him to be. Hence we may imagine that their relationship provided him with a capacious and reliable matrix of selfhood, an external lifeworld that could be replicated as an inner world of freedom and creativity. When in *Souls* he mentions the "wonderful tales that swam in [his] head" (p. 10), we might think of them as taking form in an interior transitional space, shaped by his mother's patient love and his own innate mental capacity.[5] The mutual recognition of mother and son thus results in the emergent free self-consciousness of the son.

The private space occupied by Du Bois and his mother and the even more private one of his inner world were not hermetically sealed, in part because Great Barrington was relatively forgiving in its imposition of racial codes. It was, he claims, a "boy's paradise." Its natural surround was "apparently the property of the children of the town"; and his "earlier contacts with playmates and other human beings were normal and pleasant" (*Dusk*, p. 13; see also *Autobiography*, pp. 74–75).[6] He was far from being a recluse, but rather was "a center and sometimes the leader of the town gang of boys" (*Darkwater*, p. 11). "I was only moderately good at baseball and football," he reports, "but at running, exploring, story-telling, and planning of intricate games, I was often if not always the leader" (*Dusk*, p. 15). His quite detailed recollections of friends and activities in his autobiography testify to the accuracy of this claim (*Autobiography*, pp. 83–88). And as a portent of things to come, he and a friend were "joint editors of . . . the high school [newspaper, the] *Howler*, gotten out by hand, and lasting only for two or three issues" (*Autobiography*, p. 84).

Thus, in his youth as in later life, Du Bois was certainly in the social world. Yet he was not entirely of it. In explaining why he was relatively unaware of racial prejudice early on, he says: "I presume I was saved evidences of a good deal of discrimination by my own keen sensitiveness. My companions did not have a chance to refuse me invitations; they must seek me out and urge me to come as indeed they often did" (*Dusk*, p. 14). He does not attempt to identify the root of this sensitiveness, but a desire to avoid rejection is patently involved. This, too, would become racialized, beginning with the visiting-card incident. In later life, he tells us, "I did not seek white acquaintances, I let them make the advances and they therefore thought me arrogant. In a sense I was, but after all I was in fact rather desperately hanging on to my self-respect" (*Autobiography*, p. 283). Or, to state his point the other way around, we would see him as trying to avoid experiences of contempt and humiliation, with their built-in consequence of reactive rage. No need to seek out the individual bases for the desire to avoid this ubiquitous form of racially determined mis-recognition and denigration. The Veil is always already there; it is only a question of when one first experiences it. As Du Bois reports in his autobiographical accounts, however, a felt need to avoid rejection and protect his self-respect predated his consciousness of prejudice.

We might speculate that Du Bois's sensitivity to the possibility of rejection reflects a vulnerability based in his familial circumstances. As noted, his mother had born a child out of wedlock; she had been effectively abandoned by her vagabond husband; and she was criticized by members of her family for these shameful failings. Du Bois was a fatherless child, a circumstance that can be a real as well as imagined source of embarrassment. At least, this is the usual price that children pay when the communal norm is intact families and theirs is broken. Quite apart from who he *really* was, he therefore may have been burdened with an underlying sense of deficiency. And if this was his experience, then it would help to explain his anticipatory sensitivity to insult. In any case, his vulnerability to possible rejection did not undermine an affirmative sense of self or preclude vigorous social engagement. It would not have occasioned a split in the self, a condition of two souls in one breast, but only the establishment of a protective barrier built between a private sphere with its imaginative riches and a public sphere with its possibilities of mis-recognition—rejection and potential humiliation. Moreover, because Du Bois early proved himself to be a capable and responsible employee and, even more, because he excelled academically, the sphere of vulnerability was limited to personal interactions unrelated to performance.

Then comes the visiting-card incident. Because the schoolroom had always been a zone of acceptance and affirmation, Du Bois was taken by surprise when his offer of the card is haughtily, humiliatingly rejected by the white girl. There the matter might have ended if race prejudice had not hung sullenly in the Great Barrington air. Now it became something more than an atmospheric condition. It had a presence and a name, it could be both seen and heard. Henceforward, when his "sharp senses" registered these denigrating attitudes, Du Bois reports, "I flamed! I lifted my chin and strode off to the mountains, where I viewed the world at my feet and strained my eyes across the shadow of the hills" (*Darkwater*, p. 12). There were "some days of secret tears" as well, but rather than being daunted, he was "spurred to tireless effort" (ibid., p. 11). Then,

> As time flew I felt not so much disowned and rejected as rather drawn up into higher spaces and made part of a mightier mission. At times I almost pitied my pale companions, who were not of the Lord's anointed and who saw in their dreams no splendid quests of golden fleeces. (p. 12)

No doubt, Du Bois's Zarathustrian mountain and higher spaces, his private region of blue skies, is in part a refuge from the contumely of white folk, defined negatively by their imposition of the Veil. But it is expressive as well as, and even more than, defensive. For Du Bois retreated into *his* own domain, his inner world and private sphere, the matrix of his selfhood that had been constituted through the deep mutuality of mother and son. There he could arm and rearm, prepare and repair himself in anticipation of the glorious strife that lay ahead.

Viewing Du Bois in this light, we might also see a related aspect of his personality as part of his knightly armor. "It was not good form in Great Barrington," he says, "to express one's thoughts volubly or to give way to excessive emotion." Shaped by his environment, he developed a certain aloofness and emotional restraint, which was later reinforced by "inner withdrawals in the face of real or imagined discriminations" (*Autobiography*, p. 93).

> The result was that I was early thrown in upon myself. I found it difficult and even unnecessary to approach other people and by that same token my own inner life perhaps grew richer; but the habit of repression often returned to plague me in after years, for so early a habit could not easily be unlearned. The Negroes in the South . . . could never understand why I didn't naturally greet everyone I passed on the street or slap my friends on the back. (Ibid.)

Although there is no reason to discount the impact of New England emotional restraint on the formation of his character, Du Bois is not entirely consistent in his depiction of the origins of his habitual reserve. When he was about fifteen, he paid a visit to his grandfather, Alexander Du Bois. There he witnessed a conversation between the elder Du Bois and a guest, culminating in a formal toast:

> I had never before seen such a ceremony: I had read about it in books, but in Great Barrington both white and black avoided ceremony. To them it smacked of pretense. We went to the other extreme of casual greetings, sprawling posture and curt rejoinder. The black Burghardts indulged in jokes and backslapping. I suddenly sensed in my grandfather's parlor what manners meant and how people of breeding behaved. (Ibid., p. 98)

Evidently social life in Great Barrington was not all New England restraint, not altogether lacking in backslapping familiarity. Rather, Du Bois's environment provided him with a range of cultural possibilities, some of which imperceptibly blended in with his personal predispositions (New England restraint) and some of which he quite self-consciously chose. Thus he obviously took to heart the meaning of good manners and the habits of good breeding that he saw exemplified by his grandfather, just as he later adopted the carriage and raiment of German university life. These choices, when combined with his more deeply rooted inwardness, gave him an unmistakable dignity, a dignity that was in itself an assertion of selfhood and a demand for recognition in "'nigger'–hating America" (ibid., p. 183).

As Du Bois himself indicates, there was also a price to be paid for his dignified reserve. His youthful need to be asked to participate became a difficulty in approaching people. More: He comments that he knew too few of his contemporaries well because "I was in reality unreasonably shy" (ibid., p. 284). One might fall back on the social determinacy of this aspect of his character when the interactions involved white folk. As he says, in these instances, "I was in fact rather desperately hanging on to my self-respect. I was not fighting to dominate others; I was fighting against my own degradation" (ibid., p. 283). Here his natural reserve was accentuated by a deeply rooted desire to avoid experiences of mis-recognition; that is, interactions with a potential for humiliation and the reactive rage that he felt to be beneath him. But his avoidance of intimate contact was not limited to white people. Commenting on himself as a teacher, he notes "I did not know my students as human beings; they were to me apt to be intellects and not souls. To the world in general I was nearly always the isolated outsider looking in and seldom part of that inner life" (ibid.).[7] "My own exercise," he adds, "was walking, but there again I walked alone" (ibid., p. 284). Alone, and at least at times with loneliness. The thought continues: "I knew life and death. The passing of my first-born son was an experience from which

I never quite recovered" (ibid.). We hear again echoes of the last of the sorrow songs mentioned in *Souls* ("let us cheer the weary traveller") and recall the feeling of isolation when Du Bois identifies himself as the wayfarer who "girds himself, and sets his face toward Morning, and goes on his way" (*Souls*, p. 164).

It is important not to conflate aloneness with loneliness. Du Bois had a gift for solitude; alone, he was at home with himself. But as the reference to the death of his son suggests, these inner recesses were not untroubled. In the depths of his soul, the waters—"voice of my heart . . . voice of the sea"—are crying (*Souls*, p. 9). Were these waters troubled only after his son's death? I would guess not. We remember that his mother, after her husband left her, "worried and sank into depression." She was stoic and uncomplaining, but her sorrow was palpable to her son. If his inner world, the home of his solitude, was formed in part by the internalization of the one he shared with her, would it not have contained her sorrow along with her love, her worries along with her determination and support of his own ambitions? Then, too, there was the impact of her death. His graduation from high school had been her "great day"

> and that very year she lay down with a sigh of content and has not yet awakened. I felt a certain gladness to see her, at last, at peace, for she had worried all her life. Of my own loss I had then little realization. That came only with the after-years. (*Darkwater*, p. 12)

As with the death of his son, Du Bois treats his mother's death as liberation. In her dying, she is set free from the sorrows and worries of her life within the Veil. We might also imagine, following the line of analysis begun by Freud in "Mourning and Melancholia" (1917), that her death consolidated her son's identification with her. If so, we would see in Du Bois a twofold melancholy, a submerged sea of grief fed by the waters of his sadness at the loss of his mother and by his identification with her sadness over her own losses. And perhaps this early sorrow emerged and merged with the later one when his son—Burghardt, bearing his mother's maiden name—slipped away into death's other kingdom.

Du Bois may not have known at the time how much he lost with his mother's death, but he did know that he was "more alone than I had ever dreamed of being" (*Autobiography*, p. 102). Solitude, shadowed by a degree of melancholy, was to be his companion from that time forward. But his mother's death had a further implication:

> Now it was the choking gladness and solemn feel of wings. At last, I was going beyond the hills and into the world that beckoned steadily. There followed the half-guilty feeling that now I could begin life without foresaking my mother. . . . This very grief was a challenge. Now especially I must succeed as my mother so desperately wanted me to. (Ibid.)

The expression, "choking gladness," first used by Du Bois in *Darkwater*, expresses by its very awkwardness the painful mixture of a certain joy in his mother's release from her earthly trials and his own sorrow at losing her. The complicating factor is that the liberation was not only hers but also his. She would "fly away home," in the words of an old gospel song, he would fly away *from* home. His gladness was in part relief at being released from the burden of caring for her. The "half-guilty feeling" could be managed, however, just because his mother "so desperately wanted" him to succeed, especially academically. Hence we are not surprised to find him, alone in Berlin on the occasion of his twenty-fifth birthday, beginning a meditation on his future with "a dedication of my small library to the memory of my mother" (ibid., p. 170). Later, in *Souls,* when we see him defending the right to the higher learning of the Talented Tenth of black folk, we might imagine him to be speaking for her as well.[8]

Race Man

Du Bois maintained his family connections in Great Barrington after his mother's death and his own departure for Fisk. His children were born there; his wife and son were buried there. But he was called beyond the hills and into the world. As we are now envisioning him, he was a man whose innermost self was formed through the internalization of the mutually loving and recognitive relationship of mother and son, combined with his own innate intelligence and imagination. Here he was at home and alone, in a place of refuge and creativity both deeply private and tinged with melancholy. In a more active and public mode, he was the fatherless son who must be father to himself, his mother's consort, the protector of her honor, and of his own. A proud man who believed himself to be deserving of recognition and who was determined to win life's prizes, he was vulnerable to experiences of insult and rejection. Although a dignified reserve and aloofness helped him to avoid encounters of this type, for an ambitious African-American in white supremacist America the avoidance could never be complete. The moments of painful mis-recognition must necessarily occur. Then he would flame and stride off to his mountain retreat—into the recesses of his mind above the Veil. But the anger would linger on as a disquieting temptation to revolt and revenge, and his blue skies would be darkened by disappointed hopes.

What, then, about the companion to the ongoing struggle for recognition, the imperative of renunciation? For viewed one way, the distinctive thing about Du Bois is his unwillingness to renounce the good things in life: "But they should not keep these prizes, I said; some, all, I would wrest from them"—in memory of his mother, for himself, for his race. He would overcome their resistance and command the recognition that they would not willingly grant him. But along with bearing the tearing pain of his unreconciled strivings and warring ideals, additional personal sacrifice would be required to secure these victories. In this he resembles the protagonist in his parable, "Of the Coming of John," when education robbed him of his youthful innocence:

> He grew slowly to feel almost for the first time the Veil that lay between him and the white world; he first noticed now the oppression that had not seemed oppression before, differences that erstwhile seemed natural, restraints and slights that in his boyhood days had gone unnoticed or greeted with a laugh. (*Souls*, p. 146)

Renounce, renounce, your racial innocence—this is the message of the color-line for those with ears to hear and eyes to see.

That is not all. Du Bois may not have become a Communist until late in his life, but it is as if he had read Karl Marx's eleventh thesis on Feuerbach before he was twenty: "the philosophers have only *interpreted* the world, in various ways; the point, however, is to *change* it" (Marx 1845, p. 145). Already at Fisk and then with increasing focus and dedication, he gave his life over to the task of changing his world. He might remind us of Hegel's world-historical individuals, the heroes who derive "their purposes and their vocation, not from the calm, regular course of things . . . but from that inner Spirit . . . which, impinging on the outer world as on a shell, bursts it to pieces" (Hegel 1956, p. 30). But winning *this* prize involves the renunciation of ordinary happiness: "They attained no calm enjoyment; their whole life was labor and trouble; their whole nature was nought else but their master-passion" (ibid., p. 31). Self-sacrifice is the hero's destiny. So, too, Du Bois, who obeyed the command, "*Thou shalt forego*" with but "small complaint." Yet one might say of him that self-denial was simultaneously self-fulfillment. He had from an early age a hunger for learning and for written self-expression, along with a gift of independent thought and a remarkable industriousness. As he said of himself, "I above all believed in work, systematic and tireless" (*Autobiography*, p. 124). He cultivated these propensities of his character, honed them and polished them, until he brought them all under his disciplined self-control. He was not only his own father but also his own man, the master of his master-passions. And when—negatively in the visiting-card incident and positively when he went south to Fisk—he became a Negro, his individual self-actualization became identified with the liberation of black folk. Seen this way, renunciation, the foregoing of the peace of mind and happiness accompanying the tending of private gardens, might be interpreted dialectically as the foundation of a noble, even stoic, austerity and self-restraint, and as the necessary mediation of Du Bois's racial project. If so, we would do well to keep in mind Jean-Paul Sartre's conceptualization of such projects. "Every man is defined negatively," Sartre claims, "by the sum total of possibles which are impossible for him; that is, by a future more or less blocked off" ([1963] 1968, p. 95)—in this instance, by being born into the prison-house within the Veil. The critical task is then to "lift the Veil and set the prisoned free" (*Souls*, p. 133), to negate this negation: for "man is characterized above all by his going beyond a situation, and by what he succeeds in making of what he has been made" (Sartre [1963] 1968, p. 91).

4

Humani Nihil A Me Alienum Puto

To this opinion I am given wholly
And this is wisdom's final say:
Freedom and life belong to that man solely
Who must reconquer them each day.

GOETHE, *Faust*

The foray into biographical matters in chapter 3 was not aimed at reducing the text to the personality of its author, but rather at bringing the author more fully into the text. This brief excursus on Du Bois's intellectual development has the same aim.

If we were searching the European philosophical and literary canon for Du Bois's elective affinities, Goethe would seem to be an obvious choice. When Du Bois was doing graduate work in Germany, he wrote a letter to the Fisk *Herald*, commending the study of Goethe for purposes of racial advancement (Lewis 1993, p. 139). And in *Souls*, he figures the conflicted souls of black folk in Faust's image. More generally, each man was a poet and a philosopher, a scientist and a Romantic. Each of them could say with Terence, "*humani nihil a me alienum puto*"—nothing human is alien to me.[1] Du Bois had reasons of his own to speak these words: "Black Africa influenced Rome. Many of her great men were called 'African' because of their birth, and some of these had Negro blood. Terentius Afer (Terence the African) was an ex-slave whose complexion was described by Suetonius as *fuscus*, or dusky" (Du Bois [1946] 1965, p. 144). But he would not deny Goethe's right to them, and he might even claim the great German as one of his spiritual fathers—a more worthy ancestor than the wayward Alfred Du Bois and a less conflicted one than the founding fathers of the

American Republic. But his lineage includes many other figures as well, and our present task is to provide some indication of how he molded them together through the force of his own intellectual passion.

A good starting point is Keith Byerman's claim that there is a persistent tension in Du Bois's work between "an empiricist mode of perception and an idealist system of morality" (1978, p. v). He characterizes this tension as dialectical, by which he means that the polarities interpenetrate in a productive or generative fashion. This is a plausible interpretation, but I would modify it in two ways. First, I believe it is more accurate to see the polarities in the dialectical relationship as scientific self-discipline and imaginative self-expression—a version, to put it differently, of the classical German philosophical antithesis of objectivity and subjectivity. Second, we might picture Du Bois's intellectual development as dialectical in a somewhat stricter sense, as proceeding from an immediate unity of these extremes through their diremption into antithetical objective (disciplined scientific) and subjective (imaginative) sides, before culminating in their reunification in a mediated, more determinate, form.[2]

Origins

In the beginning or, if one prefers, before it, there was the Word of God—the Old and New Testaments and the Congregational Church of Great Barrington. In the company of his mother, Du Bois was a churchgoer in his youth, and he characterizes himself as "still a 'believer' in orthodox religion" when he graduated from Fisk (*Autobiography*, p. 285). Although he became decidedly anticlerical and was a self-proclaimed agnostic in later years, the unifying Christian vision of this world and the next did not fade entirely away. Its emphasis on restraint, duty, and sacrifice were, so to speak, gospel to him; and the stories, parables, images, and language of the King James Version of the *Holy Bible* were constitutive of his literary style as well as his moral and ethical sensibility.

With a bit of literary license, one might say that Du Bois found the secular equivalent of the Bible in Thomas Babington Macaulay's five-volume *History of England from the Accession of James the Second*. When he was sixteen years old, he purchased the full set from a local bookseller on an informal installment plan. Macaulay's great work was anything but scientific, but it did combine a sweeping political and moral vision with a richly detailed narrative of English life. Then, at Fisk and later at Harvard came exposure to the works of Thomas Carlyle (see Arnold Rampersad [1976] 1990, pp. 66–67).[3] Perhaps Du Bois saw himself, or at least his aspirations, in Carlyle's conception of the Hero:

> Universal History, the history of what man has accomplished in this world, is at bottom the History of the Great Men who have worked here. They were

the leaders of men, these great ones; the modellers, patterns, and in a wide sense creators, of whatsoever the general mass of men contrived to do or attain; all things that we see accomplished in the world are properly the outer material result, the practical realisation and embodiment, of Thoughts that dwelt in the Great Man sent into the world: the soul of the world's history, it may justly be considered, were the history of these. (Carlyle 1966, p. 1)

A fitting prospect for Mary Silvina's beloved son, with his surging and noble ambitions! A bit more concretely, Carlyle offered Du Bois a conception of leadership that fit with his worship of heroes: "We must have more Wisdom to govern us, we must be governed by the Wisest, we must have an Aristocracy of Talent!" (Carlyle 1965, p. 34). We hear more than an echo of this view when Du Bois says of the Talented Tenth, "Can the masses of the Negro people be in any possible way more quickly raised than by the effort and example of this aristocracy of talent and character?" (Du Bois 1903b, p. 36).[4]

The point in grouping together Christian faith, Macaulay, and Carlyle is to suggest that early on Du Bois had access and susceptibility to an encompassing if not yet developed Weltanschauung. At Fisk, his interests multiplied. The curriculum included English literature (*Hamlet* is especially noted), Latin, German, French, Greek (including part of the *Phaedo*), philosophy, political science, history, mathematics, and the natural sciences (in Aptheker 1985, pp. 4–13). Within this diversity, however, philosophy was his first love. "I had hoped to pursue philosophy as my life career," he writes, "with teaching for support" (*Autobiography*, p. 133). And when he reached Harvard, study philosophy he did, with William James, Josiah Royce, and the young George Santayana. In their company, he was undoubtedly exposed to Hegel. Royce was a Hegelian. James, himself anti-Hegelian, was discursively engaged with Royce. Du Bois took a course from James focused on James Martineau's *A Study of Religion* (1888), which includes a brief discussion of Hegelian philosophy. He also took a course with Santayana on French and German philosophy that presumably ended with Hegel; and Santayana was especially interested in *The Phenomenology of Spirit* at this time (Zamir 1995, pp. 113–114, 247–249). Further, although Hegel makes only rare appearances in Du Bois's published work, one of these might be read as a latter-day comment on overcoming two-ness: "Race consciousness, race solidarity conceived along . . . broad outlines becomes not the enemy of labor solidarity, but the only path to it. They form a perfect Hegelian category: the thesis of Negro race consciousness; the antithesis; the union of all labor across racial, national, and color lines; and the synthesis; a universal labor solidarity arising through the expansion of race consciousness in the most exploited class of all labor" (1937, p. 207). So there is little reason to doubt that Du Bois made use of such a "Hegelian category" in articulating his conception of the struggle for an integral African-American identity.

On the other hand, there is no evidence that he evolved his own world-view through critical engagement with Hegel's, or that, as Shamoon Zamir (1995, p. 13) claims, he drew "heavily on the middle chapters of Hegel's *Phenomenology of Mind* . . . as a resource not only for his famous depiction of African-American 'double consciousness' but for his entire narrative" in *Souls*.[5] Du Bois makes no mention of having studied *The Phenomenology of Spirit* with Santayana but recalls with evident pride that he "sat in an upper room and read Kant's *Critique*" with him (*Autobiography*, p. 143). This experience is reflected years later (in 1933) when he wrote in *The Crisis* that "there are certain books in the world which every searcher for truth must know: the Bible, *Critique of Pure Reason, Origin of Species*, and Karl Marx's *Capital*" (in Lewis 1995, p. 538). As to double-consciousness, it is far more likely that Du Bois adapted it Emerson or from James, whose analysis of the "consciousness of self" in his *The Principles of Psychology* includes what we would now term split or multiple personality (James 1890, chap. 10).[6] Rather than straining to find a decisive impact of Hegel on Du Bois or to claim that the problematics of *The Phenomenology of Spirit* were imported into *Souls*, it therefore seems better to abide by a rule of interpretive parsimony and stick closer to the evidence at hand.

In taking issue with the Hegelianizing of Du Bois's emergent worldview, I do not intend to deny that his thinking "echoes the most prominent philosophers and poets writing in the European romantic tradition (such as William Blake, Samuel Taylor Coleridge, Friedrich Schiller, and George Wilhelm Friedrich Hegel" (Blight and Gooding-Williams 1997, p. 197).[7] But as I hear it, the echo was sounded in his own voice. To use a Nietzschean metaphor, Du Bois incarnated a will to power at once racial and individual. Whatever he made use of, he placed his own stamp upon; he led, he did not follow. From the first, Du Bois was—if we wish to categorize him at all—a Du Boisean.

Although Du Bois took evident pleasure in exploring such worlds of the mind, his philosophical and aesthetic preoccupations remained anchored in the this-worldly matter of race relations. While still at Fisk and in an application for a Harvard fellowship, he wrote: "I wish to take the field of *social science* under *political science* with a view to the ultimate application of its principles to the social and economic advancement of the Negro people" (in Aptheker 1985, p. 13). This project was not in the usual sense philosophical; but as he said in retrospect, he had "conceived the idea of applying philosophy to an historical interpretation of race relations" (*Autobiography*, p. 148). He continued: "In other words, I was trying to take my first steps toward sociology as the science of human action. It goes without saying that no such field of study was then recognized at Harvard" (ibid.). Despite the lack of such an academic field, his Harvard mentors provided him with both a push and a pull in its direction. On the one hand, James not only put before him the idea of philosophical pragmatism, but also told him candidly that there was "not much chance for anyone earning a living as a philosopher." On the other, Albert Bushnell Hart was forwarding a rigorously documentary approach to American history, and one that included a focus on the South and slavery (e.g., Hart 1891). Responding to this dual impetus, Du Bois turned his attention to what Byerman terms the empiricist mode of perception.

Intellectual Antipodes
On the surface, the movement away from philosophical speculation was accelerated when Du Bois reached Berlin. As Kenneth Barkin puts it, although "Berlin was full of Hegelians, . . . he chose to study political economy, or what would evolve into the discipline of sociology" (2000, p. 92). His mentors were Adolf Wagner and Gustav Schmoller, and especially the latter. Both were founding members of the Verein für Sozialpolitik (Association for Social Policy), which had the proximate aim of alerting "the educated public to the growing alienation of the worker from the mainstream of German life" (ibid., p. 88). Beyond that, the Verein "called for publicly funded work programs, municipal city planning, social welfare programs, and other social institutions to become actively involved in bringing about social improvements" (Lemke 2000, p. 54). Hence one might say that the Verein political economists were proclaiming that the problem of the twentieth century was the class-line, and they hoped to solve it by using the results of empirical research into the actual conditions of social life to influence state policy.[8]

Du Bois not only studied with Schmoller and Wagner; he also followed their example and became a member of the Verein (Aptheker 1973, p. 23). When he returned from Berlin, he brought with him the Verein program of policy-oriented social scientific research.[9] As Sieglinde Lemke puts it, "what Schmoller tried to do for Germany, Du Bois wanted to do for black America" (2000, p. 54). In combination with Hart's documentary approach to history, this orientation is evident in *The Suppression of the African Slave-Trade to the United States of America, 1638—1870* (1896; hereafter *Suppression of the African Slave-Trade*) and even more in *The Philadelphia Negro* (1899). Moreover, the sociological studies of Negro life and the annual conferences that Du Bois initiated at Atlanta University bear the mark of the Verein, which each year commissioned detailed scholarly work and held a conference on contemporary German social and economic problems (Barkin 2000, p. 94). This empirical work on race had a moral or political aim. One has only to read, for example, the final chapters of these two books to be reminded of their author's moral passion and commitment to the advancement of the Negro people. But this aim was to be realized by adhering to the most exacting standards of scientific objectivity. Early on in *The Philadelphia Negro*, Du Bois notes not only the problems of validation inherent in sociological research methods but also the danger that "some personal bias, some moral conviction or some unconscious trend of thought due to previous training" might distort the results ([1899] 1996, p. 3). Yet even if personal convictions do enter somewhat into the "most cold-blooded scientific research as a disturbing factor," a scrupulous adherence to standards of objectivity can yield results sufficiently "credible" so that they can "serve as the scientific basis of further study, and of practical reform" (ibid., pp. 3—4). Or as he put it years later in autobiographical comments recorded by Moses Asch, "The Negro problem was a matter of knowledge. . . . We were talking about it and we didn't know anything about it. . . . Just because a man was born in a milieu didn't mean he knew what all the other millions were doing. What we needed was an academic study of the American Negro" (Folkways Records 1961). Although there was no equivalent in the United States of the German state as an instrument of social policy, progress could be hoped for if educated and influential European-Americans were to replace their misperceptions of African-Americans with knowledge of the actual situation.

There is little to be seen in Du Bois's social scientific research of the other side of his developmental dialectic, his youthful philosophical and heroic aspirations. His values are, so to speak, close to the factual ground, indeed so close that the tension between science and morals has been reduced to the thin line of a fact-value distinction. But these larger aspirations, split off from his commitment to scientific objectivity, lingered in the background. He preserved among his papers (and cited in his autobiography) a piece of wild speculation from the late night of his twenty-fifth birthday. It is oddly reminiscent of the opening scene of *Faust*, in which the aging philosopher, alone at night in his study, calls forth the spirits to aid him in his attempt to solve the riddle of reality. So, too, the youthful philosopher: "be the Truth what it may I will seek it, on the pure assumption that it is worth seeking and Heaven nor Hell, God nor Devil shall turn me from my purpose till I die" (quoted in Aptheker 1985 p. 28). He continues:

> If I strive, shall I live to strive again? I do not know and in spite of the wild *sehnsucht* [yearning] for Eternity that makes my heart sick now and then— I shut my teeth and I do not care. *Carpe Diem!* What is life but life, after all. Its end is its greatest and fullest self—this end is the Good. The Beautiful its attribute—its soul, and Truth its being. (Ibid.)

Here in all its midnight sublimity we have a moment of pure philosophical romanticism. Tempted sometimes by a yearning for Eternity—death? escape from care?—Du Bois affirms life and action, *Carpe Diem!* Philosophical questions demand this-worldly answers. Or, as Faust says, reframing the Gospel of Saint John, "In the beginning was the *Deed!*" (Goethe, p. 46).

Du Bois, now striking a more Hegelian note, goes on to commit himself to his people and their destiny:

> I am firmly convinced that my own best development is not one and the same with the best development of the world and here I am willing to

sacrifice.[10] That sacrifice is working for the multiplication of Youth X Beauty and now comes the question how. The general proposition of working for the world's good becomes too soon sickly sentimental. I therefore take the work that the Unknown lay in my hands and work for the rise of the Negro people, taking it for granted that their best development means the best development of the world. (Quoted in Aptheker 1985, pp. 28–29)

The "Unknown" is more akin to the God of the Gospels than to Hegel's Absolute Spirit. Still, the way Du Bois links his personal striving to that of his people, and his people's striving to the best development of the world, has more in common with Hegel than with the anti-Hegelian empiricism of Schmoller and Wagner. Further, his willingness to sacrifice other possibilities of self-development at the altar of the Negro people might remind us of Hegel's world-historical individual, whether or not he actually had that heroic model in mind. We also might hear echoes of Hegel in the lines already cited in chapter 3, when the young man asks himself, "is [it] the silent call of the world spirit that makes me feel that I am royal and that beneath my sceptre a world of kings shall bow" (p. 28). But whether or not he is casting himself in a Hegelian role, it is undoubtedly a heroic one: "[I plan] to make a name in science, to make a name in literature, and thus to raise my race. Or perhaps to raise a visible empire in Africa thro' England, France, or Germany. . . . I will go unto the king—which is not according to the law and if I perish—I PERISH" (p. 29).[11]

"Strivings of the Negro People"

Thus we have an antithesis of disciplined social science and unrestrained spiritual striving, joined in the young man's joining of his own destiny to that of his race. But even before Du Bois put the finishing touches on *The Philadelphia Negro*, there were intimations of a new and highly original unity, a veritable sublation of this antithesis. In 1897, the *Atlantic Monthly* published his "Strivings of the Negro People," the essay that became the first chapter of *Souls*. Like the latter, it begins with his personalization of the problem of racial identity and the visiting-card incident; it contains the notions of two-ness, double-consciousness, and the Veil; and it sets up the historical problematic that will frame the narrative of the book (Du Bois 1897, pp. 194–198). As Lewis puts it, here Du Bois "projected his own personal dilemma—the gift or curse of marginality—on to the group, thereby psychoanalytically defining for at least a century the supposedly unique tension beneath African-American racial identity" (1993, p. 199). Although a distinctive authorial voice and a clear vision of the racial dilemma characterized both *The Suppression of the African Slave-Trade* and *The Philadelphia Negro*, neither of them centered on Du Bois himself, on his personal experience and self-definition. Now for the first time we glimpse Robert Stepto's hero-narrator, who veritably embodies the "tension beneath African-American identity," and who will give *Souls* its spiritual and aesthetic unity.

With "Strivings of the Negro People," Du Bois began a process of blending imaginative self-expression—his poetic and philosophical leanings, his gifts as a storyteller, and his musicality—with the self-discipline of the social scientist. *Souls* marks the culmination of that process, an extraordinary fusion of the subjectivity and objectivity of racial experience. In words that we are now better prepared to hear: "In its larger aspects [its] style is tropical—African. This needs no apology. The blood of my fathers spoke through me and cast off the English restraint of my training and surroundings."[12] Or as he asked rhetorically in *Dusk of Dawn*: "What is Africa to me? Once I should have answered the question simply: I should have said 'fatherland' or perhaps better 'motherland'" (*Dusk*, p. 116).[13] The feeling of royalty heard in "the silent call of the world spirit" now resounds from his ancestral African home.

Du Bois's casting off of "English restraint" in *Souls* was not, however, simply a matter of intellectual or artistic development. It also reflects, from among the events of those times, two in particular: the lynching of a man named Sam Hose and the death of his son Burghardt, both in 1899. Taken together, these events qualitatively intensified the feelings Du Bois expressed in the 1897 article. And he could not avoid connecting them, if only because they were linked both temporally and affectively.[14]

First the lynching of Sam Hose. As we know, violence, often actual and always impending, was an integral part of the system of white supremacy. It would be hard to exaggerate its brutality. "Between 1890 and 1917, to enforce deference and submission to whites, some two to three black Southerners were hanged, burned at the stake, or quietly murdered each week" (Litwack 1998, p. 284). That estimate, which Leon Litwack views as conservative, does not include "legal lynchings (quick trials and executions) and private white violence and 'nigger hunts'" (ibid.) or the race riots that increasingly became the response of whites to blacks in urban areas. So Sam Hose, who was lynched on April 23, 1899, not far from Atlanta, was one of the many victims of Southern treatment. He had been working for a planter named Cranford, had asked for his wages and permission to visit his ill mother. Cranford refused and they quarreled. The following day Cranford threatened Hose with a pistol while he was chopping wood. Hose, in self-defense, flung his ax at Cranford, killed him, and fled (ibid., p. 280).

The newspapers told a different story: Hose, "a monster in human form," had struck Cranford from behind while he was eating, pillaged the house, and then raped Mrs. Cranford repeatedly "within arm's reach of where the brains were oozing out of her husband's head" (quoted in Litwack, p. 280). He was apprehended and lynched, in the presence of over two thousand men and women, some of whom took a special excursion train from Atlanta to witness the spectacle. And a gruesome spectacle it was:

> After stripping Hose of his clothes and chaining him to a tree, the self-appointed executioners stacked kerosene-soaked wood high around him. Before saturating Hose with oil and applying the torch, they cut off his ears, fingers, and genitals, and skinned his face. While some in the crowd plunged knives into the victim's flesh, others watched "with unfeigning satisfaction" (as one reporter noted) the contortions of Sam Hose's body as the flames rose, distorting his features, causing his eyes to bulge out of his sockets, and rupturing his veins. (Litwack 1998, p. 281)

No spectacle is complete without souvenirs: "Before Hose's body had even cooled, his heart and liver were removed and cut into several pieces and his bones were crushed into small particles" (ibid.). There was a retail market for the bones.

Thus Hose, transformed from ordinary man to dangerous and rapacious beast by the rhetorical mobilization of white racist fantasies, became a sacrificial offering at the altar of white supremacy. Nietzsche's analysis of punishment as festival and ritual, as legitimated cruelty and as expression of *ressentiment*, comes forcibly to mind (Nietzsche [1887] 1967). More to the present point, the Hose lynching had a direct effect on Du Bois:

> At the very time when my studies were most successful, there cut across this plan which I had as a scientist, a red ray which could not be ignored. I remember when it first, as it were, startled me to my feet: a poor Negro in central Georgia, Sam Hose, had killed his landlord's wife. I wrote a careful and reasoned statement concerning the evident facts and started down to the Atlanta *Constitution* office. . . . I did not get there. On the way news met me: Sam Hose had been lynched and they said that his knuckles were on exhibit at a grocery store farther down on Mitchell Street, along which I was walking. I turned back to the university. I began to turn aside from my work. (*Autobiography*, p. 222)[15]

We can only imagine the intensity of rage and disgust that is expressed in Du Bois's turning back to the university; but later that year he characterized the lynching as a "crucifixion" (in Aptheker 1970, p. 775), and in *Souls* we have visible proof of his turn away from the stance of the "calm, cool, and detached scientist" (*Autobiography*, p. 222).

With the Hose lynching, a passionate and angered protest against racist injustice entered more decisively into Du Bois's work. Then, just one month later, on May 24, 1899, his son Burghardt died.[16] Anger was present in the experience of his son's death as well, when the "pale-faced hurrying men and women" in Atlanta glanced at the little funeral cortege and said derisively, "Niggers!" (*Souls*, p. 133). The horizontal plane of Du Bois's lifeworld was now decisively split by racist brutality and contempt, leaving him with the fierce pride and anger that animated his seeking of the political kingdom. But the deep wound of his son's death—the wound from which he "never quite recovered"—set the seal of melancholy on the vertical plane and left him with a dream of death's other kingdom, where not only Burghardt but also Mary Silvina awaited him. The dialectical unity of *Souls,* like the dialectical unity of Du Bois's soul, forms around this kernel of profound pain. If Africa and the blood of his ancestors speak through him, they merge with the mournful cry and voice of the sea. There is no end to the Middle Passage. Well we might assign to Du Bois Faust's great self-affirmation: "freedom and life belong to that man solely, who must reconquer them each day." But in so doing, we must be profoundly mindful of the dogged strength required to wage that daily battle.

5

Go Down, Moses

When Israel was in Egypt land,
Let my people go!
Oppressed so hard they could not stand,
Let my people go!
Go down, Moses,
way down in Egypt land.
Tell old Pharaoh,
Let my people go!

NEGRO SPIRITUAL

Our engagement with both *Souls* and its hero-narrator began with the visiting-card incident in "Of Our Spiritual Strivings." We viewed it as an experience of mis-recognition, or recognition denied, having—for Du Bois—an aesthetic/affective core of humiliating insult, suppressed anger, and an inward turning tinged with melancholy. We witnessed a lifeworld taking form around this moment, split horizontally and vertically by the Veil, within which the African-American struggle for recognition is both mediated and shadowed by the imperative of renunciation. As we come now to the reconstructive reading of the text, we pick up the story at this point of origination, beginning with a further thought about the image of the Veil.

The primary significations of the Veil are negative. Topographically, it occupies the same position as the "shades of the prison-house," with its walls "relentlessly narrow, tall, and unscalable to sons of night who must plod on darkly in resignation" (*Souls*, p. 10). It bars black folk from entry into the kingdom of cultural heaven; and, when they see themselves through it or in its shadow, they are yielded "no true self-consciousness." Taken this way, they are in the position of the children of Israel, when Moses returns to them after receiving the Lord's commandments on Sinai:

> And afterward all the children of Israel came nigh: and he gave them in commandment all the LORD had spoken with him in mount Si'nai. And *till* Moses had done speaking with them, he put a veil on his face. But when Moses went in before the LORD to speak with him, he took the veil off, until he came out. (Exod. 34:32–34)

In like fashion, the Israelites are commanded to hang a veil between "the holy *place* and the most holy,"—between the place of worship and the "ark of the testimony" (Exod. 23:33). By analogy, true knowledge, the holy of holies, is the possession of white folk; black folk see it, and see their own souls, only "darkly, as through a veil" (*Souls*, p. 14).

But as we know, the veil has a secondary meaning: "the Negro is a sort of seventh son, born within a veil, and gifted with second-sight in this American world" (*Souls*, p. 10). The veil is here a caul, a signifier of the magical powers of those born within it. From this perspective, it is white folk who stand at the foot of Mount Sinai, black folk who speak with the Lord face to face. It is the latter, in other words, who are the soul of the Republic:

> There are to-day no truer exponents of the pure human spirit of the Declaration of Independence than the American Negroes; there is no true American music but the wild sweet melodies of the Negro slave; the American fairy tales and folk-lore are Indian and African; and, all in all, we black men seem the sole oasis of simple faith and reverence in a dusty desert of dollars and smartness. (*Souls*, p. 16)

The "sons of the Fathers would fain forget" the great words on which the nation is founded (*Souls*, p. 45); they have become the worshippers of the golden calf. Only the spiritual strivings of black folk carry within them the promise of redemption.

These two meanings of the Veil are less contradictory than they might at first appear. Rather, they represent both the problem of the color-line and its solution. It is as if Du Bois were saying, a nation divided against itself cannot stand—two-ness is a matter of national and not just African-American identity. When the Veil is lifted, "two world-races may give each to each those characteristics both so sadly lack" (ibid.). Only then will America be made whole. Following Werner Sollors (1986, p. 49), we might be reminded of Paul's second letter to the Corinthians: The veil of Moses is "done away in Christ," and we see, no longer darkly, but rather "as in a glass the glory of the Lord" (2 Cor.: 3, 14—18). Someday.

In the meantime, black and white are not equally wanderers in the deserts of exile. Rather, if one wishes to place the African-American people within the Old Testament narrative, they have not yet been brought "forth out of the land of Egypt, from the house of bondage" (Deut. 8:12). And Du Bois, figured here as Moses, must descend into the Southern house of bondage, there to raise the ancient cry, "let my people go." Not surprisingly, the modern-day rulers of the "Egypt of the Confederacy" were no more likely than their ancient predecessors to heed the voice of prophecy (*Souls*, p. 81).

If, as I hope to show, *Souls* grows organically up from its aesthetic/ affective roots, it also grows out from the thematic seeds planted in "Of Our Spiritual Strivings." After introducing the image of the Veil, along with the double-consciousness and two-ness which are its psychological consequences, Du Bois portrays the Negro people as attaching their hopes to three successive panaceas: freedom, defined negatively as the end of literal slavery; the ballot and political power; and education. Education on its most practical side is conjoined to work and economic advancement. But none of these aims was realized. They fell victim to resurgent white supremacy and the cultural underdevelopment of a people who had been but recently enslaved. This does not imply that these goals were to be renounced; rather, they needed to be "melted and welded into one" (*Souls*, p. 15).

One such welding is *Souls* itself. Chapters II through X involve interlocking investigations of these aspects of the problem of the color-line and the possible solutions attached to them. Chapter II, "Of the Dawn of Freedom," takes up the issue at the time of emancipation and focuses on the Freedmen's Bureau. Du Bois treats the Bureau as a potential institutional solution to the problem, but with its potential unrealized. The failure was in part a function of weaknesses in the Bureau itself, but these might have been overcome "had political exigencies been less pressing, the opposition to government guardianship of Negroes less bitter, and the attachment of the slave system less strong" (p. 32). Then there might have been a permanent Freedmen's Bureau, a tutelary nation within a nation, a benevolent paternalism to replace the malevolent paternalism of slavery, which over time might have permitted Negroes to emerge as citizens of the Nation. This was not to be, and the problem of the color-line carries over into the next generations. Then a quite different paternal authority arises, offering an alternative solution: Booker T. Washington and his program of "industrial education, conciliation of the South, and submission and silence as to civil and political rights" (p. 34). Akin in this regard to the sons of founding fathers, Washington is portrayed as betraying the ideals of the people he leads. Hence his leadership is opposed, on the one side by those who would follow the road of revolt and revenge, on the other by the "thinking class of American Negroes" who hold fast to the principles of the Founding and insist on using all "civilized and peaceful" means in realizing them for the

Negro people (p. 43). Du Bois speaks for the latter, a rebellious son against a misguided and misguiding father—so to speak, a true son of the American Revolution.

"Of the Dawn of Freedom" and "Of Mr. Booker T. Washington and Others" can be fit together under the rubric of *politics*, and more specifically political leadership. They offer a critique of and an alternative to the existing modalities of African-American politics; and, barely beneath the surface, they announce Du Bois's own leadership bid. The following seven chapters are *cultural*, in the twofold sense of cultural cultivation and way of life. Chapters IV through VI are about education. "Of the Meaning of Progress" depicts Du Bois's youthful experiences as a teacher in Alexandria, Tennessee. It leads into "Of the Wings of Atalanta," with Du Bois now positioned as a professor at Atlanta University. He uses the myth of Atalanta to frame his upholding of the values of higher culture against the lure of crass materialism. Then comes Chapter VI, "Of the Training of Black Men," a systematic appraisal of black educational experience that provides a sociological grounding for the defense of higher education for African-Americans.

Chapters VII through IX explore economics and everyday life. They are arranged to parallel the three chapters preceding them. In "Of the Black Belt" Du Bois is our guide on a sociological carriage-ride through Dougherty County, Georgia. As in "Of the Meaning of Progress," we learn about everyday culture through stories of individual experience—snapshots of life's hardships deep within the Veil. This leads into "Of the Quest of the Golden Fleece," a mythically framed meditation on the effects, for ordinary black folk, of commercial greed and corruption. Building on the impressions gained in "Of the Black Belt," this chapter also complements the economic side of the analysis in "Of the Wings of Atalanta." "Of the Sons of Master and Man" mirrors "Of the Training of Black Men." Like Chapter VI, it is systematic and sociological, in the manner of Du Bois's German mentors and his own Atlanta University studies. Moreover, both chapters involve attempts to use sociological knowledge as vehicles of communication between black and white elites and thus carry forward Du Bois's adaptation of the program of the Verein für Sozialpolitik.

Chapter X, "Of the Faith of the Fathers," analyzes the black churches and black religious experience. It concludes Du Bois's exploration of the collective lives of black folk. He observes that the Negro churches were "really governments of men" (p. 122), echoing his earlier characterization of them in *The Philadelphia Negro*. There he had claimed that the Negro church was the "peculiar and characteristic product of transplanted Africans" and offered this concise account of its encompassing presence in African-American life: "Its tribal functions are shown in its religious activity, its social authority and general guiding and co-ordinating work; its family functions are shown by the fact that the church is a centre of social life and intercourse; acts as newspaper and intelligence bureau, is the centre of amusements—indeed, is the world in which the Negro moves and acts. So far-reaching are these functions of the church that its organization is almost political" ([1899] 1996, p. 201). Read this way, Chapter X balances the two political chapters (II and III) with which this, the larger part of *Souls*, begins. Further, because the churches are also the institutional setting for the "inner ethical life" of the African-American people, the political has been animated with, precisely, their "spiritual strivings." Thus the first part of the text has a strong resemblance to a dialectical relationship. We begin with the organized political life of the people and proceed through interpenetrating and opposed explorations of high and folk culture until we arrive at the religious (political and spiritual) life of the group.

As is evident, Chapters II through X of *Souls* stay largely on the horizontal plane of African-American life. The vertical plane is not absent, but it is the verticality of higher versus lower culture. Correspondingly, the disciplined sociological side of Du Bois's authorial persona, to be sure richly interpenetrated and enlivened by the imaginative one, grounds this part of the text. "Of the Faith of the Fathers," just because its core is the "inner ethical life" of black folk, effects the transition to the more personal, passionate, and painful chapters that follow. In Chapters XI through XIII, subjectivity (imagination and individuality) leads, objectivity follows. The vertical plane, now a *via dolorosa*, predominates; the horizontal plane is presupposed but not further investigated. If the specter of Sam Hose haunts the earlier chapters, the ghost of Burghardt haunts these. The world within the Veil becomes the valley of the shadow of death. When we exit from it, we have the sorrow songs on our lips.[1]

Betrayals

"Of the Dawn of Freedom"
In his synoptic interpretation of the period he would later term "Black Reconstruction," Du Bois functions as the voice of historical reason. The tone is temperate and fair-minded, as if the affairs of men were being viewed from on high. His perspective is not, however, value-neutral. The opening stanza, from James Russell Lowell's abolitionist *The Present Crisis*, evokes a situation of injustice: "Truth forever on the scaffold, Wrong forever on the throne" (*Souls*, p. 17). We are reminded of the epidemic of lynching that forced a redefinition of Du Bois's scientific mission. Still, Lowell writes, the "great Avenger" is only apparently absent:

> Yet that scaffold sways the future,
> And behind the dim unknown
> Standeth God within the shadow
> Keeping watch above His own. (ibid.)

God stands within the Veil *and* above the fields of human strife, judging the actions of men and women in the present and promising the future to those who have been and are being wronged. Du Bois makes Lowell's words his own and, by so doing, places himself on that same mountaintop.

From this vantage point, watching the clash of Union and Confederate legions, Du Bois echoes the question emergent in those days: "What shall be done with Negroes?" (ibid.). Throughout the chapter, black folk are placed in this, the object, position. Subjectivity and agency are almost entirely in the hands of the whites. Plainly, this cannot be the whole story, and later, in *Black Reconstruction in America* ([1935] 1992), Du Bois reverses perspective and centers the narrative in the actions of black people. Now, however, his view is that slavery was ill-preparation for freedom. It had been emasculating (*Souls*, p. 23) and dehumanizing. It "classed the black man and the ox together." Under its weight, "the black masses, with half-articulate thought, had writhed and shivered." As the Union armies advanced, they fled toward it, forming a "dark human cloud that clung like remorse on the rear of those swift columns" (p. 20). Then, when slavery abruptly ended, they "welcomed freedom with a cry"—but without clarity of purpose: "amid all crouched the freed slave, bewildered between friend and foe" (pp. 26–27). The ex-slaves required guidance, institutional support, and protection if they were to effect the transition from bondage to self-mastery.

We see here a vertical order anchored in the horizontal plane of sociohistorical reality. White people were obliged, as a matter of pragmatic necessity and moral responsibility, to be headmasters in a school of democracy for black people. Because they did not meet this obligation, their tutelary duties would be passed on to the Talented Tenth of black people themselves; but the distinction between elite and mass would remain. In any case, at the dawn of freedom, a transitional program and transitional institutions were required. The Freedmen's Bureau was a response to these exigencies and became "a full-fledged government of men. It made laws, executed them and interpreted them; it laid and collected taxes, defined and punished crime, maintained and used military force" (p. 26). Further, it "set going a system of free labor, established a beginning of peasant proprietorship, secured the recognition of black freedom before courts of law, and [to Du Bois, its greatest achievement] founded the free common school in the South" (p. 30). But, as noted above, its mission was prematurely terminated. A "social seer" might have imagined its continuation, a "permanent Freedmen's Bureau" rather than a temporary one, forming "a great school of prospective citizenship" that would have "solved in a way we have not yet solved the most perplexing and persistent of the Negro problems" (p. 32). But the facts were to the contrary; and the "passing of a great human institution before its work is done, like the untimely passing of a single soul, . . . leaves a legacy of striving for other men" (p. 33). Or, to state the matter more plainly, not only was its promise unfulfilled, its promises were broken: "despite compromise, war, and struggle, the Negro is not free." Instead he sits, "veiled and bowed," barred like the ancient Israelites from using the "King's Highway." And so Du Bois concludes the chapter as he began it: "The problem of the Twentieth Century is the problem of the color-line" (ibid.).

As indicated, the story Du Bois tells is social and historical. It begins in the early days of the Civil War and ends in 1870, and it is structured by the Bureau's response to the political, educational, and economic difficulties confronting the freed slaves. It is a tragic tale, with the untimely passing of the great institution paralleling and foreshadowing the even more untimely passing of Du Bois's first-born child. Or, looking backward, the missed opportunity signified by the demise of the Freedmen's Bureau parallels the tragic flaw in the nation's founding. "We must face the fact," Du Bois wrote in *The Suppression of the African Slave-Trade*, that the problem of slavery "arose principally from the cupidity and carelessness of our ancestors." Driven by greed and cozened by moral cowardice, they compromised with the slave system when it was in its infancy. Consequently, with

> the faith of the nation broken at the very outset, the system of slavery untouched and twenty years' respite given to the slave-trade to feed and foster it, there began, with 1787, that system of bargaining, truckling, and compromising with a moral, political, and economic monstrosity, which makes the history of our dealing with slavery in the first half of the nineteenth century so discreditable to a great people. ([1896] 1970, p. 198)

Some four score years later, another failure of political and moral will resulted in the death of the Freedmen's Bureau and the virtual re-enslavement of the Southern Negro. In each instance, a great error led on to profound misery; and in each instance, the "social seer" recognizes that another choice might have been made, another road taken.[2]

The view that the Freedmen's Bureau died prematurely is certainly an interpretation of the empirical record, a judgment that bears the mark of its author's melancholy. Still, it does not leave the plane of historical experience. By contrast, Du Bois's larger interpretive perspective does rise above *and* fall beneath it. In the former regard, his tone is distinctly prophetic.[3] As Keith Byerman observes, "he tells a nation of its sin and calls for repentance" (1978, p. 75). Joining his voice to Lowell's, he invokes a divine providence overseeing and judging the affairs of men. Or, speaking in his own: The "granting of the ballot to the black man was a necessity, the very least a guilty nation could grant a wronged race, and the only method of compelling the South to accept the results of the war" (*Souls*, p. 32). In the latter regard, there are ghosts that arise from their unquiet graves and walk among the living. For the dawn of freedom, no matter how stormy, is the end of days for the slave system. Du Bois selects two figures to symbolize its passing. They are the Adam and Eve in the genesis of the new order; and, like the Biblical originals, they bequeath a complex legacy to their children.

—the one, a gray-haired gentleman, whose fathers had quit themselves like men, whose sons lay in nameless graves; who bowed to the evil of slavery because its abolition threatened untold ill to all; who stood at last, in the evening of life, a blighted, ruined form, with hate in his eyes;—and the other, a form hovering dark and mother-like, her awful face black with the mists of centuries, had aforetimes quailed at the white master's command, had bent in love over the cradles of his children, and had closed in death the sunken eyes of his wife,—aye, too, at his behest had laid herself low to his lust, and borne a tawny man-child to the world, only to see her dark boy's limbs scattered to the winds by midnight marauders riding after "cursed Niggers." These were the saddest sights of that woeful day; and no man clasped the hands of these two passing figures in the present-past; but, hating, they went to their long home, and, hating, their children's children live to-day. (p. 27)

The gray-haired white man, an aging patriarch, is placed between deceased warrior fathers and deceased warrior sons. He has been ruined by war and by the emancipation of the slaves, and he is hate-filled. He is also the master who imposed his sexual will upon his female slaves. The black woman who quailed before his wrath and lay low to his lust is less person and more maternal presence—"a form hovering dark and mother-like, her awful face black with the mists of centuries." She is part the victim of white sexual assault, part the nurse of white babies, and (perhaps) part incarnation or apparition of mother Africa, the original life-giver to all black folk. We can also say she is the oedipal mother whose body is given over to the father and the pre-oedipal mother who is identified with nurture and nature. She, too, is hate-filled.[4] Her son in the story literally has been torn apart by white marauders; but as Du Bois has already told us, the surviving sons of these unions are torn apart by conflicting racial identities. And they carry on the family feud, bringing into future generations the hostility of master and bondswoman.

Thus the plane of historical experience in "Of the Dawn of Freedom" has a spiritual/moral dimension rising above it and archetypal desires pulsing below it. We could interpret the latter biographically, as the racialized oedipal ghosts of Du Bois's own family history. We might also say, with Marx and with greater historical pertinence, the "tradition of all the dead generations weighs like a nightmare on the brain of the living" (Marx 1852, p. 595). For Du Bois, powerfully and concisely, articulates one of the primal fantasies, indeed the primal scenes, of the American racial imaginary. The slave system was a hothouse of desire. Its asymmetrical power relations incited the enactment of unconscious fantasies. The white master lusts after the flesh of the black bondswoman. The black man is placed in the position of the son who helplessly witnesses the primal scene. At the same time and most perversely, the white master suspects and fears that the bondsman covets his mistress, perhaps also that she desires to take and be taken by him. But her transgressive desire, be it fact or fantasy, must not be thought or spoken, nor need it be. Far more economical to cast the slave in the role of Black Oedipus, the rebellious son who defies the Law of the Father, is guilty of lusting after forbidden fruit, and therefore—given the equivalency of thought and deed—is punishable for his violation of the incest taboo. When the midnight marauders dismember the tawny man-child, this racialized oedipal image is what drives them to madness—they, the valiant defenders of white Southern womanhood! We think again of poor Sam Hose, accused of raping the wife of the man he killed. These phantasmal/actual configurations of desire continue to play their fell part, long after the demise of the antebellum social relations that generated them.[5]

We see, then, that the dawn of freedom is haunted by ambiguities. Du Bois gave voice to them from the outset, not only in the verse by Lowell but also in "My Lord, What a Morning [Mourning]," the musical notation that heads the chapter. Heard one way, it is joyful and triumphant:

> You'll hear the trumpet sound,
> To wake the nations underground,
> Looking to my God's right hand,
> When the stars begin to fall.
> *Refrain:*
> My Lord, what a morning,
> My Lord, what a morning,
> Oh, my Lord, what a morning,
> When the stars begin to fall.

But as Eric Sundquist comments: "The hymn of resurrection can contain both 'morning' and 'mourning'—the first signifying the dawn of the new millennial day, when the dead are raised (or the enslaved are emancipated); the second signifying a transfigurative power in the act of mourning. [Here,] however, the ambiguity is particularly purposeful. Reconstruction has turned out to be a false dawn; instead, the song of joy has been transformed into a song of grieving once again" (1993, p. 498). We are reminded that Du Bois titled his "autobiography of a race concept" *Dusk of Dawn.*

"Of Mr. Booker T. Washington and Others"
Although the triadic configuration of racialized oedipal desire is absent in "Of Mr. Booker T. Washington and Others," the son's challenge to paternal authority underlies and animates the argument. Washington was only twelve years older than Du Bois; but in politics, age is a secondary matter.

Paternity follows from the occupancy of positions of power, and the Wizard of Tuskegee was "the one recognized spokesman of his ten million fellows, and one of the most notable figures in a nation of seventy millions" (*Souls*, p. 36). He was the inheritor of the race problem left unsolved by the premature demise of the Freedmen's Bureau and, most famously in his "Atlanta Exposition Address" of 1895, offered the solution of accommodation. Both sides, white and black, were to be the beneficiaries of this arrangement. The white South would be left in peace, free from black demands for civic and political equality; the black South would be left in peace, free from the animosity of white folk and free to advance itself bit by bit, until white tolerance became earned respect. Thus, to repeat those memorable words, "in all things purely social we can be as separate as the fingers, yet one as the hand in all things essential to mutual progress" (Washington 1895, p. 169). He went on to assure his white audience that "the wisest among my race understand that the agitation of questions of social equality is the extremist folly, and that progress in the enjoyment of all the privileges that will come to us must be the result of severe and constant struggle rather than of artificial forcing" (p. 170). And that struggle was to be waged close to the ground:

> Our greatest danger is that in the great leap from slavery to freedom we may overlook the fact that the masses of us are to live by the productions of our hands, and fail to keep in mind that we shall prosper in proportion as we learn to dignify and glorify common labour, and put brains and skill into the common occupations of life; shall prosper in proportion as we learn to draw the line between the superficial and the substantial, the ornamental gewgaws of life and the useful. (p. 168)

In a word, Washington advocated the renunciation of higher culture along with the renunciation of political power and civic rights. These were precisely the aspirations Du Bois refused to renounce, the very aspirations for which he was ready to renounce the tending of his own private gardens. Nor could he accept the role that Washington had arrogated to himself, of speaking for and exemplifying "the wisest" of the race. That seigniorial claim had necessarily to be contested, along with the substantive program that Du Bois believed to be not prudent accommodation but rather unmanly acquiescence to brutal and degrading white supremacy.

Just as problematically, Washington was demanding of black folk an acquiescence to his power paralleling his program of acquiescence to white power. He was stationed in the contradictory position of mediator between the races, at once the loyal son of the great white fathers and the father of loyal black sons. But to Du Bois, this loyalty, in the one case as in the other, spelled the death of self-determination, for black people as a collectivity, for himself as an individual. Hence the lines from Byron's *Childe Harold's Pilgrimage* that open the chapter:

> From birth till death enslaved; in word, in deed, unmanned!
> . . . .
> Hereditary bondsmen! Know ye not
> Who would be free themselves must strike the blow? (*Souls*, p. 34)

Although Du Bois was ambivalent about the kind of blow to be struck by the Negro sons of freedom against white supremacy, there can be no mistaking the challenge to Washington in these words. Or, striking a less martial note, there is the refrain of the accompanying musical notation from "A Great Camp-Meeting in the Promised Land":

> Oh walk togedder, children
> Dont yer get weary,
> Walk togedder, childron,
> Dont yer get weary,
> Dere's a great camp-meetin' in de Promised Land.

Sundquist interprets Du Bois's choice as an ironic comment on Washington's message of patience and perseverance. But he also notes that "the camp meeting might be the occasion for the transmission . . . of political ideals, plans for escape and revolt" (1993, p. 497). If we join the two meanings, we have a political statement that is in tune with the text: Washington's camp meeting must be replaced with another one—thinking ahead historically, like the one at Niagara in 1905.

It would take us too far afield to rehearse Du Bois's changing views of Washington, from his initial acceptance and praise for the stance adopted by the older man in the Atlanta Exposition Address through his confrontation with him in *Souls* to the increasing antagonism manifested in the Niagara movement and eventually in the founding of the National Association for the Advancement of Colored People (NAACP) (see Lewis 1993, especially chaps. 10 and 12). It is tempting, however, to see the two men as greeting the dawn of the twentieth century with a crossing of autobiographical swords. Washington's autobiography, *Up From Slavery*, was published in 1901. Du Bois responded with an article published in the July 16, 1901, issue of the *Dial*, referencing the autobiography but focused on Washington's role as race leader (in Sundquist 1996, pp. 245–247). This article, with its political cutting edge considerably sharpened, became the corresponding chapter in *Souls*. Viewing *Souls* as a whole from this angle, we can see it as presenting a contrasting portrayal of a race leader. Along related but more substantive lines, Arnold Rampersad suggests that *Souls* was a challenge to Washington's portrayal of slavery in his autobiography:

I would argue that the crucial element [of difference between the two men] involved Du Bois's acute sensitivity to slavery both as an institution in American history and as an idea, along with his distaste for Washington's treatment of the subject in *Up From Slavery*. To some extent Du Bois's book functions, in spite of its only partial status as an autobiography, as a direct, parodic challenge to certain forms and assumptions of the slave narrative . . . which had so aided Booker T. Washington's arguments. (Rampersad 1989, pp. 105–106)

Whatever the influence of Washington on the substance and style of *Souls*, Du Bois's rhetorical strategy in confronting the Wizard is simple and effective. As in "Of the Dawn of Freedom," he adopts a stance of judicious and fair-minded appraisal, which, in its assertion of the right to pass judgment, places him above the older man. At the same time he identifies himself with the "educated and thoughtful colored men" whose opinions had been silenced by the Tuskegee Machine (*Souls*, p. 36). He protests this silencing by appeal to basic democratic values: "Honest and earnest criticism from those whose interests are most nearly touched . . . this is the soul of democracy and the safeguard of modern society" (p. 37). Then, having established the right to judge Washington's leadership, he cuts the Wizard down to size by placing him in a patrilineage of Negro leadership extending from Cato of Stono, leader of a major slave rebellion in 1739, through Frederick Douglass, the "greatest of American Negro leaders" (p. 39). The roster includes men who were motivated by the feeling of revolt and revenge Du Bois manifestly rejects; but their very inclusion sharpens the image of manly self-assertion against which Washington is to be measured and found wanting:

Before 1750, while the fire of African freedom still burned in the veins of the slaves, there was in all leadership or attempted leadership but the one motive of revolt and revenge,—typified by the terrible Maroons, the Danish blacks, and Cato of Stono, and veiling all the Americas in the fear of insurrection.

[After the Revolutionary War] . . . the slaves in the South, aroused undoubtedly by vague rumors of the Haytian revolt, made three fierce attempts at insurrection,—in 1800 under Gabriel in Virginia, in 1822 under Vesey in Carolina, and in 1831 again in Virginia under the terrible Nat Turner. (pp. 37–38)

Although these insurrectionary leaders are dead and gone, they are not without living heirs:

One class [of critics of Washington] is spiritually descended from Toussaint the Savior, through Gabriel, Vesey, and Turner, and they represent the attitude of revolt and revenge; they hate the white South blindly and distrust the white race generally, and so far as they agree on definite action, think that the Negro's only hope lies in emigration beyond the borders of the United States. (p. 41)

Liberation through emigration is a vain hope, and rebellion is consigned to the antebellum past. Still, the rebellious ancestors are not condemned. At least implicitly, they wear the mantle of heroism. The "fire of African freedom . . . burned in [their] veins," and they succeeded in "veiling all the Americas in the fear of insurrection."[6] The Veil of white supremacy is countered with the veil of insurrectionary dread; and the ghosts of the rebellious Africans live on in racial memory, inspiriting their descendants. Although Du Bois may not number himself among these heirs of a rebellious past, he uses these modern extremists to express his own anger. This indirection would permit him to skewer Washington without appearing to be intemperate himself.

Thus framed, the "triple paradox" of Washington's program appears as a kind of impotency or auto-castration:

1. He is striving nobly to make Negro artisans businessmen and property-owners; but it is utterly impossible, under modern competitive methods, for workingmen and property-owners to defend their rights and exist without the right of suffrage.
2. He insists on thrift and self-respect, but at the same time counsels a silent submission to civic inferiority such as is bound to sap the manhood of any race in the long run.
3. He advocates common-school and industrial training, and depreciates institutions of higher learning; but neither the Negro common-schools, nor Tuskegee itself, could remain open for a day were it not for teachers trained in Negro colleges, or trained by their graduates. (p. 41)

Washington's program cuts out or off precisely those modes of action required for its realization. Hence it might seem that Du Bois aims merely at supplementing it. In like fashion, his manifest intraracial political goal is not to replace Washington but only to open up a space for shared racial leadership. But Washington had no intention of modifying his approach to the race problem nor of loosening his grip on the racial machinery. We might imagine him, in a most private conversation, dressing down the young Harvard upstart the way A. H. Bledsoe, the president of the College in *Invisible Man*, puts down the young protagonist: "I's big and black and I say 'Yes, suh' as loudly as any burrhead when it's convenient, but I'm still the king down here . . . This is a power set-up son, and I'm at the controls" (Ellison [1952] 1989, p. 142). Or, to shift from one imaginary register to another, we could picture Washington as the primal father of the Negro family. He would defend himself against any member of the brother-band who attempted to displace or diminish his power. And when Du Bois sought to make the older man's program a part of a larger whole, that was just what he was doing. Willy-nilly, he was claiming the mantle of racial leadership and forwarding another, more racially self-respecting approach to the problem of the color-line.

"Of Mr. Booker T. Washington and Others" is the most bare-bones (I almost said bare-knuckled) chapter in *Souls*. Du Bois sticks close to his argument and close to the ground. There is one moment, however, where personal pathos creates an opening to the upper reaches of his spiritual world. This is in response to a passage in *Up From Slavery*, where Washington describes a young man with some high school education "sitting down in a one-room cabin, with grease on his clothing, filth all around him, and weeds in the yard and garden, engaged in studying French grammar" (1901, p. 94). Du Bois comments: "So thoroughly did [Washington] learn the speech and thought of triumphant commercialism . . . that the picture of a lone black boy poring over a French grammar amid the weeds and dirt of a neglected home seemed to him the acme of absurdities" (*Souls*, p. 35). And yet: "One wonders what Socrates and St. Francis of Assisi would say to this" (ibid.). For these were men who shunned wealth as so many fetters and lived their lives in the service of higher intellectual and spiritual values. They embodied the ideal of renunciation. As Du Bois stated in a commencement address he delivered to high school students in 1907: "The life of St. Francis teaches us . . . that renunciation is the inevitable first payment for healthy social uplift, . . . a renunciation of dreams of great wealth and instead a contentment with humble means, along with deep unselfish devotion to a splendid cause" (Du Bois 1907, p. 300). Seen in this light, studying French signifies the calling of racial leadership along with the desire for high cultural achievement. How dare Washington deny to black folk the company and example of the saint and the philosopher . . . and so devalue the path Du Bois himself had determinedly followed! Which is to say, from Du Bois's perspective Washington's views of racial advancement were insulting as well as wrong-headed. They were something like an educational Jim Crow car and a blackface version of the "amused contempt and pity" against which he had defined himself. How could he not take them personally as well as politically?[7]

Vindicating Enlightenment

"Of the Meaning of Progress"
One of Washington's techniques for winning the favor and support of powerful whites was to provide them with the guilt-free pleasure of laughing at the stereotypical foibles of black folk. That some of his compatriots might find this objectionable or even humiliating was no concern of his. And he was adept at using this kind of ridicule to discredit the aspirations

of those who departed from the prescribed path of progress. At one point in *Up From Slavery*, he had paused to parody a certain type of "educated Negro, with a high hat, imitation gold eye-glasses, a showy walking-stick, kid gloves, fancy boots, and what not" (1901, p. 92).[8] Allowing for some exaggeration, he might have been describing Du Bois at Wilburforce, after his return from Berlin. Washington also derides students at a school in Washington, D.C., who—compared to students at Hampton—"knew more about Latin and Greek when they left school, but they seemed to know less about life. . . . Having lived for a number of years in the midst of comfortable surroundings, they were not as much inclined as the Hampton students to go into the country districts of the South" (ibid., p. 76). Yet Fisk students like Du Bois, who learned Latin and Greek, did exactly that. When he tells of us these experiences in Chapter IV of *Souls* and then goes on to defend higher education and high culture in the chapters that follow, we may understand him to be continuing the argument in "Of Mr. Booker T. Washington and Others," as well as carrying out the program suggested in "Of Our Spiritual Strivings."

We have already observed that "Of the Meaning of Progress" and "Of the Wings of Atalanta" follow an autobiographical line of descent and immersion, as Du Bois goes from being a Fisk student teaching in the Tennessee backcountry to his position as a professor teaching at Atlanta University. They also mirror each other, not only because the one setting is rural and the other urban, but because Du Bois is a primary school teacher of poor, uneducated people in the first and a university teacher of elite, educated people in the second. Taken together, they approximate to the ideal of "education of youth according to ability" (*Souls*, p. 42) Du Bois advanced against Washington—advanced, too, against the white supremacists who told black folk to "be content to be servants, and nothing more; what need of higher culture for half-men?" (p. 15). And when we hear him warning Atalanta against the temptation of those golden apples, we recognize that he is also warning black folk against Washington's commercialism, his "gospel of Work and Money," which serves "almost completely to overshadow the higher aims of life" (p. 40). Progress cannot be measured in dollars.

What, then, is the meaning of progress? The question was implicitly raised in "Of Our Spiritual Strivings" when Du Bois remarks that the disappointed hopes of the first years of freedom led to "the sobering realization of the meaning of progress"—no quick victories, no rapid passage into the promised land, but rather a long, hard climb. There is also an undoubted irony in his use of this expression, when the advance from slavery to freedom had so very nearly turned around into a retreat from freedom to slavery. Hence when he gives Chapter IV the title, "Of the Meaning of Progress," he is linking it to these questions and inflections, and continuing their exploration at the level of lived experience. One might get the opposite impression from the chapter's poetic invocation, which concludes "Nichte die zarte Jungfrau wähle / Nichte der Hirtin weiche Seele!" (p. 46). This is from Schiller's *The Maid of Orleans* (1801) and can be translated "Choose not a tender woman's aid / Not the frail soul of shepherd maid!" (in Martin, Swanwick, and Lodge, p. 94). Out of tune, one might think, with the homely tale Du Bois is about to tell. But the retention of the German sets the verse in an antiphonal relationship to the plainspoken black folk of Alexandria and simultaneously parallels the German-educated Du Bois's relationship to them. Further, the poem is about the simple country girl, Johanna, who heeds the call to bear arms in her country's fight for freedom. She speaks these words in a moment of doubt, after she has spared the life of an English warrior who touched her heart. And she dies in her country's service. Just so, the verse points us toward Josie, the heroine of Du Bois's tale, who "had about her a certain fineness, the shadow of an unconscious moral heroism that would willingly give all of life to make life broader, deeper, and fuller for her and hers" (*Souls*, p. 47) and who sacrifices herself for her family and dies of a broken heart. And it might be added that the musical notation, from "My Way Is Cloudy," fits Johanna or Josie equally well:

> Oh! Breth-er-en, my way, my way's cloud-y, my way,
> Go send them angels down,
> Oh! Breth-er-en, my way, my way's cloud-y, my way,
> Go send them angels down.

Needless to say, Josie is not the only one, in the Jim Crow South, for whom the way is cloudy.

"Of the Meaning of Progress" nestles comfortably into the overall geography of *Souls*, performing its double function of advancing Du Bois on his journey southward and revealing the obstacles that stand in the way of planting the tree of knowledge within the Veil. Leaving aside the explicit work of mourning that is "Of the Passing of the First-Born," it also stands out as the most moving of the stories he tells, and the one in which his personal presence combines most beautifully with the black folk who become present to us through him. Maybe this is because here he recaptures the spirit of his own youthful days, maybe also because here, and only here, he reveals himself as his mother's son. He describes setting out from Fisk in search of a rural school needing a teacher: "I learn from hearsay (for my mother was mortally afraid of fire-arms) that the hunting of ducks and bears and men is wonderfully interesting, but I am sure that the man who has never hunted a country school has something to learn of the pleasures of the chase" (p. 47). We remember Mary Silvina's love of learning and her pride in her son's academic achievements. She prepared him for the hunting of country schools, if not the hunting of bears and men. He was following the path she laid out for him as he "walked on and on" until he reached a backwoods area where "the coming of a stranger was an event, and men lived and died in the shadow of one blue hill"—where he happened to meet Josie, a "thin, homely girl of twenty, with a dark-brown face and thick, hard hair" (p. 47). She told him "anxiously that they wanted a school over the hill . . . that she herself longed to learn,—and thus she ran on, talking fast and loud, with much earnestness and energy" (ibid.). Unlike the quiet Mary Silvina, to be sure, but the lovingness with which Du Bois portrays her suggests that he found something of his mother's sad, worried, and devoted spirit in this "child-woman" above whom there "hovered like a star" the "longing to know, to be a student in the great school at Nashville" (p. 48).

Along related lines, we might step outside the narrative long enough to bring forward another piece of biographical information. In his autobiography, Du Bois comments that, when he arrived at Fisk, he "actually did not know the physical difference between men and women," nor how to "solve the contradiction of virginity and motherhood" (*Autobiography*, p. 280). He blames his ignorance, plausibly enough, on the sexual puritanism of Great Barrington. Just as plausibly, we may infer an inhibition of sexual curiosity as a defense against incestuous desire in a boy who played, in the absence of his father, something of the role of husband to his mother. Be that as it may, he lost his innocence and virginity in Alexandria, when he "was literally raped by the unhappy wife who was my landlady" (p. 280). Lewis believes the woman was Josie's mother and claims "we can decode her identity from a cryptic paragraph" (1993, p. 71). He doesn't indicate which paragraph this might be, however, nor how he decodes it. He claims Josie was a Dowell, which is plausible. Her home is described as a "dull frame cottage with four rooms," and Du Bois says that he "liked to stay with the Dowells, for they had four rooms and plenty of good country fare" (*Souls*, p. 49). He characterizes her mother as having a "quick, restless tongue" and as scolding her husband for being so "easy" (*Souls*, p. 47). Perhaps this fits with "the unhappy wife who was his landlady." Further, it is a conspicuous feature of his account that he omits mention of his regular domicile and speaks only of weekend visits with various families. And he reports the last names of several of the families he visited, but we are left to infer Josie's family name. These omissions would fit with a wish to drop a veil of privacy over his taboo sexual experience and so to drop it out of the story he is telling. In his autobiography the veil is lifted, but the anonymity of the woman is maintained. Perhaps. More to the present point, the initiation into sexuality by an older, married woman may help to account for the unique mention of his mother and the maternally shaded portrait of Josie.

But we have gotten ahead of the story. Having come to a community in need of a schoolteacher, Du Bois went to see the local commissioner, who accepted his certification and even invited him to dinner. "This is lucky," the young man thought; "but even then fell the awful shadow of the Veil, for they ate first, then I—alone" (p. 48). Dinner became the eating of humble pie, and he was expected to be grateful for having been given the opportunity.[9] That was the norm for black folk in the white South; but Du Bois was Northern born and bred. As he comments in his autobiography, the commissioner "would have been astonished if he had dreamed that I expected to eat at the table with him and not after he was through" (*Autobiography*, p. 116). Hence for him, social convention was mis-recognition, the painful and humiliating dropping of the Veil—all-the-more painful because he must necessarily swallow the commissioner's leavings along with his own feelings. Yet this deference, he would discover later on, was part and parcel of Washington's approach to the problem of the color-line. It is not to be wondered that Du Bois would not view acceptance of the "emasculating effects of caste distinctions" (*Souls*, p. 45) as compatible with the project of racial advancement.

In rural Tennessee, advancement did not come easily, with deference or without it. School attendance would fall off, perhaps because economic necessity intervened. Du Bois would be told by a father, the "crops needed the boys," or by his wife, "Lugene must mind the baby" (p. 49). At other times skepticism about the value of education would cause the absences:

> When the Lawrences stopped, I knew that the doubts of the old folks about book-learning had conquered again, and so, toiling up the hill, and getting as far into the cabin as possible, I put Cicero's "pro Archia Poeta" into the simplest English with local applications, and usually convinced them—for a week or so. (Ibid.)

We might imagine Washington chuckling to himself, "Cicero indeed!" But he would be missing both Du Bois's irony and the fact that the young teacher was only trying to open the doors to basic literacy. Still, the antiphonal relationship between the highly literate author of *Souls* and the largely illiterate folk who populate the narrative could also be interpreted as an instance of two-ness, of a clash of cultures between Du Bois and these rural Tennesseans, as well as within the man himself. Then Washington, more soberly and with greater justice than in his mocking devaluation of *trivium* and *quadrivium* (the classical arts and sciences) might claim that two-ness is the fate only of self-alienated Negroes, the ones who have attenuated ties to their racial roots. Up to a point, Du Bois might recognize himself in Washington's criticism. In "Of Our Spiritual Strivings," he offers several examples of the contradictions of double aims that follow from double-consciousness. One of these is the "would-be black *savant* [who confronts] the paradox that the knowledge his people required was a twice-told tale to his white neighbors, while the knowledge that would teach the white world was Greek to his own flesh and blood" (p. 11). Although Du Bois would not speak of himself as a "would-be black *savant*," the dilemma he depicts there does speak to his own, and especially at this time. But then, again, what would the meaning of progress be if racial roots can bear plants no taller than shrubs and cotton?

The barriers the young educational missionary encountered are more clearly seen if we put programmatic matters to one side and return to Josie. She came to school at first and "studied doggedly" (p. 48). But she was also invaluable, almost a second mother, to the members of her family:

> Best of all I loved to go to Josie's and sit on the porch eating peaches, while the mother bustled and talked: how Josie had bought the sewing-machine; how Josie worked at service in winter, but that four dollars a month was "mighty little" wages; how Josie longed to go away to school, but that it "looked like" they never could get far enough ahead to let her. (p. 50)

Here it is plain that the young woman's ambitions were sacrificed to the well-being of the family.[10] Not Time, but her own heart said to her, "Entbehren sollst du, sollst entbehren." Still, when Du Bois left Alexandria after his second summer of school teaching, it may have seemed that the renunciation was not final. When he returned for a visit ten years later, he found out that it was. "We've had a heap of trouble since you've been away," Josie's mother told him (p. 51). First one of her brothers got into an altercation with a white man and—as such things go—landed in jail. Her other brother would visit him, and then one night "Josie emptied her purse, and the boys stole away." After that, she "grew thin and silent, but worked the more . . . shivered and worked on, with a vision of schooldays all fled, with a face wan and tired,—worked until, on a summer's day, some one married another; then Josie crept to her mother like a hurt child, and slept,—and sleeps" (p. 51). For this brave child-woman, dying from heartbreak was the ultimate reward for open-hearted self-sacrifice. Mary Silvina escaped this fate, perhaps because she had her wondrous son to console her. Yet she may have been in the back of his mind when he asked himself, "sadly musing" as he rode in the Jim Crow car back to Nashville, "How shall man measure Progress there where the dark-faced Josie lies? How many heartfuls of sorrow shall balance a bushel of wheat?" (p. 53). "Man shall not live by bread alone," Jesus replied to the tempter (Matt. 4:4), and so might Du Bois to Washington.

In the last scene of *The Maid of Orleans*, Johanna, mortally wounded, is reconciled with and recognized by those for whom she gave her life. The light of heaven shines on her and she says:

See you the rainbow yonder in the air?
Its golden portals heaven doth wide unfold,
Amid the angel choir she radiant stands,
The eternal Son she claspeth to her breast,
Her arms she stretcheth forth to me in love.
How is it with me? Light clouds bear me up—
My ponderous mail becomes a winged robe;
I mount—I fly—back rolls the dwindling earth—
Brief is the sorrow—endless is the joy! (In Martin, Swanwick, and Lodge, p. 133)

I wonder if there was a moment for Josie, amidst the sadness of her dying, when she glimpsed the rainbow above the Veil and felt the love of heaven in her mother's arms.

"Of the Wings of Atalanta"
Reflecting on the mix of "life and love and strife and failure" in Josie's world, Du Bois wonders if it amounts to "the twilight of nightfall or the flush of some faint-dawning day" (*Souls*, p. 54). The "or" is not to be taken literally. Du Bois is notable for articulating historical ambiguities and contradictions; we have here not substantive opposition but rather rhetorical apposition. From another perspective, however, the either/or does have substantive meaning. Although, as we have just seen, he is keenly aware of the situational constraints on choices of action, he also endows human individuals with a high level of agency, a great capacity to affect their own destinies. Hence when we find him, now stationed on the hills overlooking Atlanta, saying that the city is "new Lachesis, spinner of web and woof for the world" (p. 55), it brings to mind the myth of Er in Plato's *Republic*, in which Lachesis tells the assembled souls as they are about to be reborn:

> Souls of a passing day, here beginneth another cycle of mortal life that leads to death. No Destiny shall cast lots for you, but you shall all choose your own Destiny; let him that draws the first lot choose a life, and thereto he shall cleave of necessity. But Virtue knows no master; as each honors or despises her he shall have more or less of her. (Quoted in Rouse 1956, p. 419)

The people of Atlanta (of the South, of the United States) must choose to give highest honors to material gain *or* spiritual and intellectual growth, "the Gospel of Work befouled by the Gospel of Pay" (*Souls*, p. 55) *or* the holy trinity of "Truth, Beauty, and Goodness" (p. 57). (For a moment Atlanta disappears and we are back in Berlin: "What is life but life, after all. Its end is its greatest and fullest self—this end is the Good. The Beautiful its attribute—its soul, and Truth its being." The scene fades and we are back at Georgia.) By their choices, they will further determine the meaning of progress.

"Of the Wings of Atalanta" was written for *Souls* and, as already noted, it parallels "Of the Quest of the Golden Fleece." The latter, combined with "Of the Black Belt," was originally one article, "The Negro As He Really Is." The use of mythological framing, along with Du Bois's division of the article into two parts, shows that the parallelism is intentional and not just a matter of interpretive reconstruction. The two mythologically framed chapters are also mirror images of each other. "Of the Wings of Atalanta," both topographically and argumentatively, places intellectual values above material ones. It is also a plea for interracial collaboration in building this higher culture. Thus the concluding lines from the poem by John Greenleaf

Whittier that heads it: With the end of slavery, "They are rising—all are rising—/ The black and white together" (p. 54). The simplicity of this verse, attached to an encomium of the university, continues the antiphony of the previous chapter, where the verse in German is attached to an elegy of everyday living and dying. The lyrics of the accompanying musical notation, from "The Rocks and Mountains," also suggest the antithesis between higher learning and the soul-deadening pursuit of wealth and the sins of interracial strife: "The trumpet shall sound and the dead shall raise / Rocks and mountains don't fall on me; And go to mansions in-a-sky / Rocks and mountains don't fall on me." Those who heed the trumpet's call will reach the mansions of higher learning; those who don't will fall beneath the rocks and mountains.

By contrast, "Of the Quest of the Golden Fleece" examines the consequences of inverting that order of valuation and giving in to the lust for material gain. "The Brute" declares, in the poetry of William Graham Moody, that for the "cunning and few / Cynic favors I will strew / I will stuff their maw with overplus until their spirit dies." Simultaneously from the "patient and the low / I will take the joys they know." And then "Madness shall be on the people, ghastly jealousies arise / Brother's blood shall cry on brother up the dead and empty skies" (p. 89). If the wings of Atalanta are broken and the skies above the Veil, avoided, become a void, then the madness of an unbounded, greedy desire for gain will reign. People, no longer remembering they cannot live by bread alone, will destroy each other in their hunger for it. Instead of black and white rising together, they will mutually fall.

For the moment, the depressing prospect of cupidity triumphant is held in check as Du Bois, from his station at Atlanta University, first argues against the overvaluation of material wealth and then for the benefits of cultural enlightenment. In both instances, his stance is intellectually aristocratic. One is reminded of the ordering of values and social classes in *The Republic*, where wisdom-loving kings and courageous warriors rule over the farmers and craftsmen, with their desire for gain and material satisfaction. Not that, for either Plato or Du Bois, the necessities of life should be ignored. Both would agree with Aristotle that there is a natural and just art of acquisition that aims at the satisfaction of needs (*Politics*, book 1, chap. 8). But this form of acquisition must be distinguished from chrematistic, its perversion, in which wealth becomes an end in itself (chap. 9). In like fashion Du Bois acknowledges that "work and wealth are the mighty levers to lift this old new land [of the South]" (*Souls*, p. 56). "Yet the warning is needed lest the wily Hippomenes tempt Atalanta to thinking that golden apples are the goal of racing, and not mere incidents along the way." "Golden apples are beautiful," he adds: "I remember the lawless days of boyhood, when orchards in crimson and gold tempted me over fence and field" (ibid.). This somewhat ironic admission of youthful lust might be read against Paul in

I Corinthians (13:11): "When I was a child, I spake as a child, I understood as a child, I thought as a child; but when I became a man, I put away childish things." Those who have grown in wisdom know how to control and limit their desires, so that the race may be fairly run.

Another kind of nostalgia colors Du Bois's comparison of the Old South to the New: "She [Atlanta/Atalanta] forgot the old ideal of the Southern gentleman,—that new-world heir of the grace and courtliness of patrician, knight, and noble; forgot his honor with his foibles, his kindliness with his carelessness, and stooped to apples of gold,—to men busier and sharper, thriftier and more unscrupulous" (*Souls*, p. 56). And as the Southern gentleman disappears, so does his Negro complement, "the faithful, courteous slave of other days, with his incorruptible honesty and dignified humility" (p. 57). Later, in "Of the Sons of Master and Man," he notes with a certain regret the passing of the time when "through the close contact of master and house-servant in the patriarchal big house, one found the best of both races in close contact and sympathy" (p. 107). It is hard to resist the thought that the sympathy was more on the side of house-servant than the master, and that a better course would have been to follow Marx in writing the poetry of the future rather than of the past (1852, p. 597)—that is, fully to recognize the progressive meaning of the bourgeois destruction of "all feudal, patriarchal, idyllic relations" (Marx and Engels 1848, p. 475). That not being the case, we might think Du Bois is leaning on the ancient principle of warfare, the enemy of my enemy is my friend. The Lost Cause of the Old South stands in a critical relationship to the triumphant commercialism of the New. Recognizing the virtues of the one is to condemn the venalities of the other. Still, we may be permitted a moment of uneasiness when the author of *The Suppression of the African Slave-Trade* sees traces of the "grace and courtliness of patrician, knight, and noble" in the men who perpetuated and benefited from that grim traffic in human flesh.

Although we may be uncomfortable when Du Bois dignifies members of the Southern slavocracy, we know that he does not restrict the patent of nobility to upper class white folk or even to high-minded intellectuals, black or white. Black folk like the heroic Josie are, rather, the soul of the Republic; and his fears concerning the corrosive effects of money worship are even greater for them than for their pale-skinned counterparts: "In the [antebellum] Black World, the Preacher and Teacher embodied once the ideals of this people,—the strife for another and juster world, the vague dream of righteousness, the mystery of knowing; but to-day the danger is that these ideals, with their simple beauty and weird inspiration, will suddenly sink to a question of cash and a lust for gold" (*Souls*, p. 57). Then America, white as well as black, would truly have lost its soul and the possibility of redemption.

Given the seductive power of cash and the lust for gold, guardians must be found for the homely virtues of black folk. These can only be their educational leaders, the builders and immediate beneficiaries of the Negro colleges of the South: "Here, amid a wider desert of caste and proscription, amid the heart-hurting slights and jars and vagaries of a deep race-dislike, lies this green oasis, where hot anger cools, and the bitterness of disappointment is sweetened by the springs and breezes of Parnassus" (p. 59). And here we find Du Bois. Perhaps with the rebuke of Washington still echoing in his ears, he sends forth his proud affirmation of classical education:

> Nothing new, no time-saving devices,—simply old time-glorified methods of delving for Truth, and searching out the hidden beauties of life, and learning the good of living. The riddle of existence is the college curriculum that was laid before the Pharaohs, that was taught in the groves by Plato, that formed the *trivium* and *quadrivium*, and is to-day laid before the freedmen's sons by Atlanta University. And this course of study will not change. . . . [T]he true college will ever have one goal,—not to earn meat, but to know the end and aim of that life which meat nourishes. (pp. 58–59)

One eats to live, not lives to eat. As in the instance of *The Republic*, there is a rightful ordering of human values. The needs of the body and the desiring faculty of the soul are met in the lower domain of Becoming, those of the spirited and rational faculties of the soul in the upper one of Being. Those with the capacity to experience the True, the Beautiful, and the Good ascend from one to the other. So, too, in *The Souls of Black Folk*. The text itself is arranged to suggest this ascending line, with the critique of the lust for gold preceding the affirmation of higher education. Beginning in the agora (marketplace), we end on the acropolis, where the temple is dedicated to Athena, the goddess of wisdom.

The Negro colleges, these "Sanctuar[ies] of Truth and Freedom and Broad Humanity," did not grow spontaneously, as if they were native plants bursting unguided from Southern soil. They had to be laboriously cultivated by those who were willing to "spread with their own hands the Gospel of Sacrifice" (p. 59). Progress in Du Bois's sense means renunciation for those dedicated to achieving it. Personal sacrifice is the middle term linking an initial situation in which the spiritual aspirations of black folks are limited by the impenetrable Veil of race prejudice to an imagined culmination in which there would be colleges "that yearly send into the life of the South a few white men and a few black men of broad culture, catholic tolerance, and trained ability, joining their hands to other hands, and giving this squabble of the Races a decent and dignified peace" (p. 61). The Veil would fall and mutual recognition would replace the de facto relations of lordship and bondage that darkened the dawn of freedom.

'Tis a consummation devoutly to be wished! Yet Du Bois seems to acknowledge, if indirectly, the two major barriers to having this dream come true. The first is the Veil itself, which was, after all, put in place by a few white men, even if its more vile manifestations were the work of many. Du Bois does not minimize this obstacle; indeed, the four chapters that follow "Of the Wings of Atalanta" can be read as both documenting the difficulties of interracial communication and attempting to surmount them. By his own account, however, the difficulties seem almost insurmountable, especially if recognition is needed from the sons of the former masters.

The second barrier is—to use the metaphor—the lure of Hippomenes' golden apples. Aside from the happy fit of Atalanta and Atlanta, Du Bois no doubt chose the myth because it could serve as a cautionary tale. Atalanta not only loses the race and in turn her virginity by her inability to forgo the apples; she also loses her humanity. She is, as Du Bois puts it, led into "lawless lust with Hippomenes" (p. 58).[11] Venus had given the young man the apples and devised the plan through which he would win Atalanta as his bride. But Hippomenes commits the cardinal sin of hubris. He acts as if the victory were his alone and gives no thanks to the goddess. Offended, she leads the couple to defile a divine sanctuary by their lust, for which they are punished by being turned into lions. "Heed my warning," we might hear Du Bois saying, "lest you lose yourselves in bestial appetite!" Still, the manifest moral of the story is not necessarily its meaning. Atalanta could no more resist the lure of Hippomenes' apples than Adam could resist biting into the apple offered to him by Eve. In the one case as in the other, innocence is lost. When Du Bois ends the chapter saying "fly, my maiden, fly, for yonder comes Hippomenes," isn't he as much as acknowledging that the apples of gold are as irresistible as the forbidden fruit in the "orchards in crimson and gold" of his boyhood?

"Of the Training of Black Men"

As we know, by the time Du Bois came to writing *Souls*, his faith in dispassionate social science research as a vehicle for interracial communication had been shaken by the sheer brutality of white supremacy. Still, although now with a more polemical thrust, he retained a commitment to the Verein program. This is evident in "Of the Training of Black Men," where he uses sociological data on Negro educational achievement to continue the argument that was preliminarily stated in the chapter on Atlanta and Atlanta University. As before, he is contending against white prejudice concerning the intellectual abilities of Negroes and (as he views it) Washington's complicity with these prejudicial beliefs. And as before, he reminds us of Plato in his affirmation of spiritual values. The opening verse is from *The Rubaiyat of Omar Khayyam:*

> Why, if the Soul can fling the Dust aside,
> And naked on the Air of Heaven ride,
> Were't not a shame—were't not a Shame for him
> In this clay carcase crippled to abide? (p. 62)

We think of the *Phaedo*, which Du Bois read at least in part when he was at Fisk (Aptheker 1985, p. 10). There Plato sharply separates soul from body, elevating the value of the former over that of the latter. Then in *The Republic* he builds a model of the just society around this conception of the self. In like fashion, Du Bois builds a sociological model of Negro education and life around the hierarchical ranking of cultural values he has already established.

Du Bois begins with a reframing of the problem of the color-line. He identifies three streams of thinking—we might say of theory and practice—flowing from "the shimmering swirl of waters where many, many thoughts ago the slave-ship first saw the square tower of Jamestown" (*Souls*, p. 62). We remember that *Souls* begins with the crying waters of the sea and of the poet's heart, which evoked for us the Black Atlantic. Here we pass from poetry to history, to European expansion generally and the Middle Passage in particular. The former, European expansion, carries in its stream the thought of "human unity," albeit with the afterthought that the unity is created through "force and domination,—the making of brown men to delve where the temptation of beads and red calico cloys" (ibid.).[12] The latter, the stream flowing from the "death-ship" of the slave trade, is the thought of the Old South, "the sincere and passionate belief that somewhere between men and cattle, God created a *tertium quid*, and called it a Negro" (ibid.). We know, as does Du Bois, that this is a rationalization for slavery and segregation, not the reason for their existence. But rather than naming it as such, he undercuts it with the master's afterthought that "some of them with favoring chance might become men." Hence defensive measures must be taken. The masters "build about them walls so high, and hang between them and the light a veil so thick, that they shall not even think of breaking through" (p. 63). The existence of the Veil, maintained by force and fraud, gives the lie to the "sincere" beliefs of these Southern gentlemen. And yet, their beliefs are not without effect on these veiled souls. Although the third stream of thought is the assertion of human rights and a plea for recognition by black folk, its afterthought is the haunting question, "suppose, after all, the World is right, and we are less than men?" (ibid.). Hence the appropriateness, as a counter to this self-doubt, of the lyrics of the musical notation for the chapter: "Way over in E-gypt land / You shall gain the vic-tory . . . March on, and you shall gain the victory." If black folk struggle forward toward freedom and enlightenment, they will succeed at last.

Like the initial statement of two-ness and double-consciousness, which this formulation builds on and extends, Du Bois here provides an aesthetically exquisite synopsis of a world founded on domination. Because European civilization is spread through conquest, each social relationship that it engenders is self-contradictory. These relationships are ordered one inside the other, with the two-ness of African-American identity at the center. Or we may think of the overall relationship as a dialectical triad, with the universality of world culture linked to the individuality of African-American identity through the particularity or negative moment of the death-ships of the slave trade. Either way, the heart of the matter is first the actual and then the virtual enslavement of black people.

What is to be done, Du Bois asks, about this situation, so that black folk may contribute to American civilization rather than be excluded from it, help to realize the principles on which the nation is founded rather than to be the "afterthought" that contradicts them? He gives the obvious answer: education. But what kind of education, and who is to educate the educators? For, on the one hand, we have the now-familiar issue of industrial education, which Washington proposes as the only practicable solution to the problem and which Du Bois sees as only a partial solution at best. And, on the other hand, there is the reality of racial separation, which Washington affirmed in his Atlanta Exposition Address and which Du Bois must, if reluctantly, accept. This separation is "so thorough and deep that it absolutely precludes for the present between the races anything like that sympathetic and effective group-training and leadership of one by the other, such as the American Negro and all backward peoples must have for effectual progress" (p. 66). As was true in the days of the Freedmen's Bureau, tutelage is required for racial advancement. But with segregation and Jim Crow solidly in place, the education of black people must be by black people. And if Southern universities are unwilling or unable to perform the task of teaching the teachers, this pedagogical function must also be performed by black folk.

Three more specific issues are implicit in this framing of the problem of the color-line and the educational approach to its solution: what would happen if black people are deprived of the educational opportunities they need and deserve; are black people capable of educational achievement, and especially of the education required of educators; and how does one justify, in the context of cultural backwardness, an institutional commitment to knowledge the value of which cannot be measured in dollars and cents?

Du Bois's approach to the first issue reflects the continuing influence of his German mentors. We remember that the Verein für Sozialpolitik sought to appeal to the rational self-interest of the educated classes by alerting them to the alienation of German workers and the dangers to social stability that would result if steps were not taken to integrate the proletariat into the mainstream of German life. In like fashion Du Bois appeals to the "saner selfishness, which Education teaches men" (p. 63). The South has available to it "a stalwart laboring force, suited to the semi-tropics." Refusal to "use and develop" this force risks "poverty and loss" (ibid.). Or worse: "no secure civilization can be built in South, with the Negro as an ignorant, turbulent proletariat" (p. 71). "Well and good," the enlightened Southerner might respond, "train your people for 'proletarian' life, as your German friends might put it; make them 'laborers but nothing more' (ibid.). Be careful not to stimulate the very 'turbulence' you warn us against." But this Bookerite approach, Du Bois responds, will not keep the peace. Higher education is imperative:

> By taking away their best equipped teachers and leaders, by slamming the door of opportunity in the faces of their bolder and brighter minds, will you make them satisfied with their lot? or will you not rather transfer their leading from the hands of men taught to think to the hands of untrained demagogues? (Ibid.)

There is a fork in the road, a choice to be made between responsible and irresponsible racial leadership. College-educated Negroes, "with their larger vision and deeper sensibility, . . . have usually been conservative, careful leaders. They have seldom been agitators, have withstood the temptation to head the mob" (p. 70). Committed to the "higher individualism which the centres of culture protect," they have risen above "our modern socialism, and out of worship of the mass" (p. 73). They are keepers of the peace, not fomenters of unrest.

Because he renounced the path of revolt and revenge along with that of accommodation and acquiescence, these peacekeepers would include Du Bois himself. Yet his renunciation was not quite whole-hearted. Paralleling or perhaps cutting across the two-ness of his cultural identity, he was both impelled toward and morally repelled by anger as a wellspring of action. This anger recurrently surfaces in *Souls*, but always as the emotion of someone other than Du Bois himself. At the same time, this use of displacement as a way of controlling the anger engendered by white supremacy opened the way to its polemical employment. Du Bois holds before his white readers the specter of the "untrained demagogues," ill-educated, intemperate, and irresponsible rabble-rousers who will be born from the frustrated ambitions of those with a capacity to excel. Led by such men, the mass of black folk "must more and more brood over the red past and the creeping, crooked present, until it grasps a gospel of revolt and revenge and throws its new-found energies athwart the current of advance" (p. 72). The rational self-interest of ruling elites dictates the cultivation of black educational capacities. Moreover, Du Bois does not condemn his people for harboring these outraged feelings. Rather, in an imagined dialogue between ordinary Negroes and white southern gentlemen, he acts as their advocate:

> Even today the masses of Negroes see all too clearly the anomalies of their position and the moral crookedness of yours. You may marshal strong indictments against them, but their counter-cries, lacking though they be in formal logic, have burning truth within them which you may not ignore, O Southern Gentlemen! If you deplore their presence here, they ask, Who

brought us? When you cry, Deliver us from the vision of intermarriage, they assert that legal marriage is infinitely better than systematic concubinage and prostitution. And if in just fury you accuse their vagabonds of violating women, they also in fury quite as just reply: The wrong which your gentlemen have done against helpless black women in defiance of your own laws is written on the foreheads of two millions of mulattoes, and written in ineffaceable blood. And finally, when you fasten crime on this race as its peculiar trait, they answer that slavery was the arch-crime, and lynching and lawlessness its twin abortion, that color and race are not crimes, and yet they it is which in this land receives most unceasing condemnation, North, East, South, and West. (Ibid.)

Again we have, as in "Of the Dawn of Freedom," the white man's sexual violation of black women, with its legacy of mulatto children, along with the criminal violence of slavery and white supremacy. But the scene has shifted. Archetypes set in a broad historical landscape have been replaced by judges and advocates in what amounts to a courtroom confrontation. Du Bois appears as a lawyer for the defense. He presses the counterclaims of black people against the condemnation of their white accusers. He does not quite identify himself with these rebuttals—"I will not say such arguments are wholly justified"—but he places very little distance between himself and the people he is representing: "I do say that of the nine million of Negroes in this nation, there is scarcely one out of the cradle to whom these arguments do not daily present themselves in the guise of terrible truth" (ibid.). Continuing in this vein, we can hear him saying to white folk and white Southerners in particular, "Get your business right, because the day of judgment is coming." If the sins of the fathers are expiated, if black folk are enabled to follow the high road of education, then all will be well. If the high road is closed off, then the low road will be taken. Thus moral judgment and rational self-interest, principle and prudence, are mutually reinforcing.

Given that it is in the best interest of white folk as well as black to hold open the doors of educational advancement, are black folk capable of walking through them? Again following the model of the Verein für Sozialpolitik and relying on the data he generated through the Atlanta University conferences, Du Bois makes his case by presenting the actual, highly impressive empirical record of black educational achievement (pp. 70–72). This record does not, in itself, justify the devotion of resources to the classical curriculum. If we combine the data of black educational accomplishment with the prior argument concerning the results of frustrating intellectual aspirations, however, higher education can be defended on pragmatic grounds. The people who lived and are living by the Gospel of Sacrifice, who have forsaken ordinary pleasures to establish and maintain the black colleges, along with those who have graduated from them, will feel deprived and become embittered if they are robbed of the fruits of their labor. Further, as Du Bois previously argued against Washington, "neither the Negro common-schools, nor Tuskegee itself, could remain open a day were it not for teachers trained in Negro colleges, or trained by their graduates" (p. 41). Children advance in learning from primary schools to universities, but the knowledge required for teaching them descends from the universities to the primary schools. Stated differently, university training is the root of education, the common and industrial schools are the "foliage" (p. 67). Then, too, it is precisely the higher knowledge that consorts with the "higher individualism," and that, shared by black and white alike, makes possible effective interracial communication and cooperation. Healing America's racial wounds will demand "broad-minded, upright men, both black and white" (p. 71)—"a few white men and a few black men of broad culture, catholic tolerance, and trained ability" (p. 61).

Still—turning to the matter of justifying these elevated cultural pursuits— pragmatic considerations are not the be-all and end-all for Du Bois. Just as his night-thoughts in Berlin fly beyond the boundaries of disciplined social science, so here in *Souls* his investment in intellectual values far exceeds the price at which they could be converted into worldly goods. Above the field of such practical strivings, "there must come a loftier respect for the sovereign human soul that seeks to know itself and the world about it; that seeks a freedom for expansion and self-development; that will love and hate and labor in its own way, untrammeled alike by old and new" (p. 73). We think, of course, of Socrates, who heeded the oracle that commanded, "know thyself," or perhaps of Faust's ultimate wisdom: "freedom and life belong to that man solely, who must reconquer them each day." And in the ongoing creation of this realm of freedom, "the longings of black men must [also] have respect":

> the rich and bitter depth of their experience, the unknown treasures of their inner life, the strange rendings of nature they have seen, may give the world new points of view and make their loving, living, and doing precious to human hearts. (Ibid.)

In this spiritual Callipolis, there can be no color-line, no Jim Crow cars or humiliating refusals of the gifts of black folk. Recognition must be granted as recognition is deserved, all the more because, within the Veil, it is withheld. For these dark-hued seekers of knowledge, in "these days that try their souls"—as for the youthful Du Bois, in that "wee wooden schoolhouse" of long ago—"the chance to soar in the dim blue air above the smoke is . . . boon and guerdon for what they loose on earth by being black" (ibid.).

Souls begins with the moment when Du Bois first experienced the Veil and the desire to fly above it, when the pain of being denied recognition generated both the desire to excel (to avenge the humiliating insult not by returning it but rather by demonstrating his superiority to those claiming to be his superiors) and the yearning to live in his own world, free from the slings and arrows of the one into which he was born. Now, as we near the conclusion of his story about the education of black folk, the trope of blue skies brings us back to that opening scene, or rather brings that scene forward. His personal experience becomes explicitly exemplary; what is true of him is true of the Talented Tenth of the African-American people. It does not thereby cease to be personal. The last scene of this act finds him in his library, maybe the one in his study at Atlanta University, maybe the one in his own mind:

> I sit with Shakespeare and he winces not. Across the color line I move arm in arm with Balzac and Dumas, where smiling men and welcoming women glide in gilded halls. From out the caves of evening that swing between the strong-limbed earth and the tracery of stars, I summon Aristotle and Aurelius and what soul I will, and they come all graciously with no scorn nor condescension. So, wed with Truth, I dwell above the Veil. (p. 74)

We recognize the space of Du Bois's meditation, the one his mother permitted him, where he could be at home with himself and where his fathers were of his own choosing. The English poet, French novelists, Greek and Roman philosophers—none of them wince at his presence, scorn him, or condescend to him. Unlike the white girl who rejected his visiting-card and her many successors, these spiritual ancestors do not reject his overtures of friendship and desire for communion. One is reminded of Niccolò Machiavelli during the period of his exile from Florence:

> When evening comes I return home and go into my study, and at the door I take off my daytime dress covered in mud and dirt, and put on royal and curial robes; and then decently attired I enter the court of the ancients, where affectionately greeted by them, I partake of that food which is mine alone and for which I am born; where I am not afraid to talk with them and inquire the reasons for their actions. (Quoted in Ridolfi 1963, p. 152)

Du Bois like Machiavelli, Machiavelli like Du Bois—each man sought refuge and solace from a world too much with him, temporary escape from the prison-houses and battlefields of practical affairs.

Still, such libraries of the mind cannot be hermetically sealed. For Du Bois, the shadow of the Veil enters even here and falls across the pages on his desk:

> Is this the life you grudge us, O knightly America? Is this the life you long to change into the dull red hideousness of Georgia? Are you afraid lest peering from this high Pisgah, between Philistine and Amalekite, we sight the Promised Land? (*Souls*, p. 74)

Looking out and down from his spiritual sanctuary, Du Bois executes a glissade from the secular to the sacred. When he introduced the theme of education as the key to liberation in "Of Our Spiritual Strivings," he noted that it seemed to be "the mountain path to Canaan . . . steep and rugged, but straight, leading to heights high enough to overlook life" (p. 13). Now he stands like Moses on Pisgah, the mountain heights from which the great liberator and lawgiver saw the land he would not be allowed to enter. From this elevated position, Du Bois can see a new Promised Land. Will black people be able to cross over into it, against the will of the knightly white Americans who patrol its borders and despite the temptation of, if not a golden calf, Atalanta's golden apples? A question for which there is only one answer: "Way over in E-gypt land / You shall gain the vic-tory . . . March on, and you shall gain the victory."

Platonic Heights, Feminine Depths

Before we descend with Du Bois from his spiritual home above the Veil into the nether regions of the Black Belt, let's pause briefly to take up two (as we will see, related) issues: the matter of his "Platonic" inclinations and questions concerning the feminization of blackness.

As to the first issue, it is not the case that Du Bois was Platonist, any more than he was a Hegelian or a Goethean.[13] He has, rather, affinities with all three, in part because they are among his varied spiritual ancestors and in part because, whatever the lineage of influence, he shares with them habits and patterns of thought. From Goethe he explicitly borrowed the Faustian themes of a soul divided against itself and the imperative of renunciation. He also modulated and adapted them, so that the one could serve as a psychological foundation for his conception of racial identity and the other as a characterization of the great weight carried by those men and women who dedicate themselves to the upward progress of the black race. A Hegelian spirit animated the intellectual milieu when Du Bois was at Harvard, and traces of the dialectic can be found in *Souls*. But beyond the matter of influence or lineage, it does not distort the text to make interpretive use of the problematics of recognition and a stripped-down version of dialectical development in interpreting it.

In like fashion, we can make use of Platonic themes. As we have already seen, Du Bois was unquestionably conversant with Plato. As noted above, he studied the *Phaedo* at Fisk; his library contained a copy of the *Republic* (Du Bois 1980, reel 89); Zora, the heroine of his first novel, *The Quest of the Silver Fleece*, brings a copy of the *Republic* with her when she returns to the South with the aim of educating young black folk ([1911] 2004, p. 399); and we have seen that he refers to both Socrates and Plato in *Souls*. But the affinities are stronger than these pieces of circumstantial evidence and direct reference would suggest. The vertical dimension of the text has at least a family resemblance to the division of social and intellectual labor in the *Republic*. In

Callipolis, Beauty City—the ideal polis—the education of the craftsmen and farmers consists of cultural conditioning and practical training; that is, the equivalent of the common school and industrial training favored by Washington and endorsed by Du Bois as the way of teaching "workers to work" (*Souls*, p. 61). But for those with noble souls and hence the potential for being warriors and philosophers, higher education is required, so that they may ascend into the intellectual realm where the best of them may come to know the Good. These wisest of the wise, the true philosophers, are the rulers of the polis. The warriors assist them and, together, they are the guides and guardians of the hoi polloi, the common people. In the Du Boisean republic, there are no warriors—rather brave leaders dedicated to defending the rights of black folk from the depredations of the white supremacists. But the members of the Talented Tenth are akin to Plato's philosophical rulers. They, too, must ascend the ladder of learning both to fulfill themselves and to guide their people. The guidance they provide is more democratic than in the Platonic instance. They aim to uplift people rather than to keep them in their place. But their role is unquestionably tutelary. In "The Talented Tenth," published the same year as *Souls*, Du Bois puts it this way:

> Can the masses of the Negro people be in any possible way more quickly raised than by the effort and example of this aristocracy of talent and character? Was there ever a nation on God's fair earth civilized from the bottom upward? Never; it is, and ever was and ever will be from the top downward that culture filters. The Talented Tenth rises and pulls all that are worth saving up to their vantage ground. (1903b, p. 36)

The reference to an "aristocracy of talent and character" suggests that Du Bois had Carlyle in mind; but Plato would recognize his values in this model of political and cultural pedagogy. And despite his emphasis on pulling upward "all that are worth saving," for Du Bois as for Plato there must always be the Few who are excellent and the Many who are not.

There is a long history of justification for such hierarchical and aristocratic conceptions of social relations and a variety of democratic criticisms of them.[14] Perhaps the criticism that cuts closest to the Du Boisean bone is the way in which this elitist tendency can consort with a residual overvalorization of the culture of white folk. We have already seen that it leads him into a somewhat sentimental and romantic view of social relations in the patriarchal big house of the Southern plantations, with the "best of both races in close contact and sympathy"; and we might call to mind Malcolm X's polemical depiction of House Negroes identified with their masters and Field Negroes who oppose them as a corrective for this interpretation of the matter. We might also summon Du Bois as a witness against himself: "slavery was the arch-crime. . . . [T]he wrong which you gentleman have done against helpless black women in defiance of your own laws is written on the foreheads of two millions of mulattoes." If these slave-masters were indeed the best of their race, they hardly deserve the aristocratic warrant Du Bois seems prepared to grant them. And on the other side of the color-line, what does it say about the integral culture of black folk if those who have been imbued with the high culture of the white world are the best of their race? In raising this question, I do not intend to deny the overwhelming problems of underdevelopment that were the legacy of slavery nor, as Du Bois argued, the need for something like a long-lived Freedmen's Bureau. Nor, of course, can there be any question of the right of black folk to commune with Shakespeare and Balzac, Aristotle and Aurelius. But the valorization of high culture over low carries with it a parallel judgment of individuals and collectivities. At its extreme, there are moments in *Souls* when it even seems that language and individuality are derivatives of the world culture. Escaping slaves formed a "dark human cloud that clung like remorse" to the Union legions, at times "almost engulfing and choking them." The black slave woman who figures in the racialized primal scene is "a form hovering dark and mother-like," in contrast to the more defined "grey-haired gentleman" who is her white counterpart. During the years before the Civil War, the number of enslaved Africans increased exponentially: "like a snake the black population writhed upward" (*Souls*, p. 76). The Southern cotton fields seem like "the foam of billows" across a "Black and human Sea" (p. 89). The American descendants of Europeans are never characterized in such barely human or, at best chthonian, figurations; and even the chapter headings place the words of white folk above the wordless music of black folk, uncomfortably paralleling the Platonic elevation of mind over body.

It will not do to overextend this line of interpretation. We know there is a countervailing tendency in *Souls* to valorize black folk culture and to see in it a spirituality superior to the greedy materialism of the white world. As to the songs, it was an audacious challenge to the white cultural dominance of the period to pair them with the poems. Despite these valuations, however, it is hard to shake the sense that the "higher individualism" (p. 73) is inflected white and set against the depths of black soul and spirit. Viewed this way—that is, through the optic of the Platonic tendency in Du Bois's theory of culture—two-ness has a vertical as well as a horizontal dimension. Just so, it involved a degree of alienation from the ordinary black folk with whom he also identified. This can be seen in "Of the Meaning of Progress" or, in a different way, in relation to Washington, who could claim for himself the mantle of black racial authenticity against the de-racialized Du Bois. As Rampersad puts it, "Washington's philosophy, for all its materialism, philistinism, and pessimism, reposed whatever confidence it had in the people themselves. In so doing, it was at once a native American ideology, whereas Du Bois' complainings rang of European and 'bookish' exoticism out of place in the New World" ([1976] 1990, p. 87). Or, going beyond

Rampersad's scholarly restraint, we might imagine the Wizard, or I suppose his ghost, reading the part of *The Autobiography of W. E. B. Du Bois* where its author states of his experience in going south to Fisk, "hence-forward I was a Negro." "One doesn't become a Negro," thinks the older man, snorting derisively, "you are one or you aren't, and I guess we know where to place you!" To which Du Bois might reply: "Your either/or is beguilingly simple, but in the real world things are more complex. Where would your Tuskegee be without people like me? What about your wife, who 'read Virgil and Homer in the same class room with me' (in Paschal 1971, p. 50)? Perhaps it is easier for you, believing you can just *be* a Negro. But we—the Negro people—must become who we are. We, too, must be able to say, *humani nihil a me alienum puto*. If achieving this goal means that we must renounce the peace of mind of an essentialized racial identity and bear the burden of two-ness—bear even the distancing consequences of ascending the divided line along with the lacerating division of the color-line—so be it." Yet Washington, confident in the knowledge that he had come up from slavery rather than descending into "a region where the world was split into white and black halves," would not necessarily be silenced.

We can hear echoes of this spectral debate between the aspiration to excel and claims of racial authenticity down to our own times. They would fade away in the absence of white supremacy. But, however cracked, the sounding board of valorized whiteness remains, reverberating with the drumbeats of prejudice, quite sufficient to "deafen us to the wail of prisoned souls within the Veil, and the mounting fury of shackled men" (*Souls*, p. 64). From this perspective, it is a secondary matter whether one comes to the giving of the Word from the top down or the bottom up. The prisoned souls will find a way to speak and the shackled men a way to express their fury.

It might be granted that the problem of Du Bois's political and cultural "Platonism" is built into *Souls*. More speculatively, we might see traces of gender hierarchy along this vertical dimension. The twofold figuration of the race as deeply spiritual and not individuated could be viewed as a feminization of blackness, with masculine intellect and individuality rising above it. This would fit, in a most uncomfortable way, with the old charge against the NAACP that it consisted of "white heads and black bodies." Or, without altering the structure, one could attempt to reverse its values. In this vein, Cynthia Schrager argues that blackness in *Souls* occupies "a position analogous to that of the 'feminine' in sentimental culture" and that, as such, it functions as a "'posture of dissent' against the materialism of American culture" (1996, p. 554). This is consistent with Du Bois's worry that, if unguarded, black ideals, "with their simple beauty and weird inspiration, will suddenly sink to a question of cash and a lust for gold" (*Souls*, p. 57). Byerman, too, sees a feminization of the black masses in *Souls*, adding that "this feminizing of the race is part of Du Bois's family romance, in which he himself and those like him play the role of strong son preserving the racial mother from the depredations of the father" (1994, p. 18).

We adopted and extended Byerman's argument linking race and Oedipus in our earlier exploration of Du Bois's familial relationships. More generally, I find it difficult to think race matters without an understanding of racialized oedipal or, if one prefers, oedipalized racial, relations. This orientation framed the interpretation I offered of the brilliantly sketched drama of the white patriarch, black maternal presence, and tawny man-child in "Of the Dawn of Freedom." But if there is a feminization of blackness in *Souls*, its origins would lie, not in the oedipal triangle, but rather in pre-oedipal processes of masculine individuation. Returning to the model of masculine gender development introduced in Chapter 1, man is, inconveniently for him, born of woman. In the beginning, he is in her and of her. Her heartbeat is the rhythm of life, the pulse of her blood is his first song. Passing through the chasm of birth, he lives within a mother-world, experiences there the most sublime pleasure and the most abysmal pain. At first there is no language, no clear boundary between self and (m)other, indeed no clear sense of the mother as an other. There is rather a sensuous and sensual surround, wordless but not soundless, musical especially if the mother croons to him but even if she doesn't.

Time passes, boundaries begin to emerge, language marks their emergence. The boy begins to experience himself as a self, separate from his mother, who by that very fact also begins to be experienced as a self. Soon enough his selfhood will be identified with masculinity and dis-identified with the feminine matrix from which it emerged. He is not-her and, from now on, he will have two, sometimes interpenetrated and sometimes opposed, figures of the maternal: the preindividuated magical and musical matrix of his selfhood and the woman who is destined to be his first and most enduring object of sensual desire. Hence he will experience, usually unconsciously, a two-ness of both self and other.

Assume, then, a black boy born of a black mother. Especially in a racialized society, he will have a background sense of the black race as maternal presence, the matrix and spiritual wellspring of the self. In this respect we may speak of a feminization of blackness. Does this mean that masculine individuality and linguistic capability will be raced white or not-black? Plainly not. Rather, the boy who emerges from the mother-world is met by his black father. Although his father is his rival in the oedipal drama in which his mother plays her role as object of desire, he is also the man with whom he can identify. He will enter the world of black men through this paternal identification. Alternatively, if his father is absent, he may enter black manhood through the side-door of identification with other black boys or other black elders. Thus where normative masculine gender identity is built around a disconnect between the pre-oedipal and oedipal stages, black identity bridges and links them. It is continuous, not discontinuous. Hence we may speak of a masculinization as well as a feminization of blackness.

One may plausibly assign to Du Bois the pre-oedipal feminization of blackness briefly sketched above, and therefore imagine a maternal penumbra surrounding his characterization of the spiritual depths of the race. We might even say that the spirit of the black mother-world, by its very depth, rises above the plane of mundane and narrowly rational concerns. Heraclitus comes to mind: "You will not find the boundaries of soul by travelling in any direction, so deep is the measure of it" (quoted in Burnet 1930, p. 138). Still, the valorization of a feminized blackness does not truly escape the boundaries of the masculine imaginary. The idealization of the feminine and the maternal is an integral part of the Romantic tradition within which Du Bois located himself, and within which individuality and high intelligence are gendered masculine.[15] This not to deny, however, that an identification of black spirituality and the feminine/maternal is a resource that can be drawn upon in the struggle against white supremacy.

When we turn from the pre-oedipal to the oedipal aspect of the tale, we'd have to say that, for Du Bois, masculine individuality does have a tincture of whiteness. In becoming his own father, he identified strongly with the great men who walked on the stage of European civilization. Yet it is not the case that his masculine identity was established with the reading of Macaulay. Whatever the difficulties created by his father's absence, his masculinity predated the crystallization of his racial identity. But race and gender did converge in the moment when the Veil fell. In the visiting-card incident it was, after all, a girl who rejected him and withheld recognition of his selfhood. Being black had resulted in a negation of masculine selfhood, and that negation must somehow be negated. The image arises of a blackness that is, to speak ironically, whiter than white—of a black self that surpasses its white rivals, and that contains within itself the individuality which is, for *them*, the unearned reward for being born white. There is then a two-ness at once raced and gendered, a tension that manifests itself in a cultural Platonism, on the one hand, and a desire to plunge into the redemptive spiritual depths of the black race, on the other. And precisely this dual self will enter the racialized oedipal arena to challenge the white fathers who violate the Law and to defend black mothers and children against such violations.

In the Shadows of Slavery

"Of the Black Belt"

The three chapters on education follow Du Bois south, from Tennessee to Georgia. But the geographical descent is offset by cultural ascent. The section ends on Parnassus if we speak Greek, Pisgah if we speak Hebrew. As we now turn from educational to socioeconomic matters, the geographical descent is continued and matched by a cultural one. In the latter regard, *we* might imagine the philosophical hero-narrator returning from the sunlit world where Truth, Beauty, and Goodness can be clearly seen to the shadowy cave of political conflict and mundane affairs. Du Bois himself effects this descent along a biblical path. "Of the Training of Black Men" ends on "high Pisgah." The epigraph for "Of the Black Belt" is from the first verse of "The Song of songs, which *is* Solomon's" (Song of Sol. 1:1). The bride speaks:

> I *am* black but comely, O ye daughters of Jerusalem,
> As the tents of Kedar, as the curtains of Solomon.
> Look not upon me, because I *am* black,
> Because the sun hath looked upon me:
> My mother's children were angry with me;
> They made me the keeper of vineyards;
> *But* mine own vineyard I have not kept. (Song of Sol. 1:5–6)

We call to mind the Maid of Orleans who leads us into "Of the Meaning of Progress," hence also Josie, who well might say, "because I *am* black, because the sun hath looked upon me." Here the bride guides us down from the mountain overlooking Canaan into the vineyards—not, however, those of the Promised Land. Instead we find that we've returned to the house of bondage, to the "Egypt of the Confederacy" (*Souls*, p. 81), where black folk are only rarely free to keep their own "vineyards." The "dull red hideousness of Georgia," glimpsed from above when Du Bois was in his inner sanctum, now surrounds us: "Out of the North the train thundered, and we woke to see the crimson soil of Georgia stretching away bare and monotonous right and left" (p. 74). The metaphor of the Georgia earth has become the fact of it, and the cultural descent has been geographically extended. We travel on until we reach Dougherty County, the heart of the Black Belt. As when we were taken to Alexandria, Tennessee, here we will be in the company of ordinary black folk. Listening to the bride, we will know better than to look down on them because they *are* black.

In their company, are we also in a mother-world? Perhaps so. Both of the chapters in which we share the everyday lives of black folk begin with the presence of a woman. There is a difference. In "Of the Meaning of Progress," she is the virginal Saint Joan, who signifies Josie, a real, individuated woman. Further, Du Bois presents himself as his mother's son, and the narrative consists in good part of family portraits. The chapter is certainly about black folk, but the focus is on the young teacher and these families rather than on "the race"—on existence rather than essence, so to speak. We also remember that he lost his virginity to an older woman one of those summers. If the feminization of race (supposing it to exist) is rooted in the mother-world, it may be that the youthful protagonist of this story had not yet fully emerged from this matrix of identity and therefore could not comfortably reimmerse himself in it. By contrast, the black and comely woman in the Song of Solomon is a bride, and a most sensual one. There is no individual counterpart to her in "Of the Black Belt"; she seems rather to signify the essence of the experience that lies ahead. And the protagonist of this chapter is not secured within a network of familial relations. He more nearly resembles a sojourner, going forth into a mystic region of blackness, a stranger in a strange land. One might be tempted to figure him as Marlow, following the river into the heart of African darkness. But even putting to one side the exotic Africanism in Joseph Conrad's tale, that temptation surely must be resisted. Du Bois encounters neither Kurtz nor Kurtz's jungle, but rather a people oppressed by slavery—de jure then and de facto now. He is far more Moses than Marlow and maybe, for *this* moment, more Solomon than Moses. We might figure him as the bridegroom, come to sing the praises of his bride. She has been reviled by her mother's children and made to be the keeper of vineyards not her own, because the sun has looked upon her and she *is* black. She he would wed; losing himself in her, he will be found. Having gone south, now continuing the descent, joined to his people, he *is* black.

But who is *she?* If she is found in the Black Belt, is she daughter or mother? The musical notation for the chapter is from "Bright Sparkles in the Churchyard." The lyrics of the song add a maternal tone to the sensual femininity of the Song of Solomon. The titular bright sparkles—for example, broken glass placed on a grave—are an African survival in African-American culture (Sundquist 1993, p. 510), while the theme is the resurrection after death, a rebirth into sublimity figured as maternal solicitude:

> In de heaven, once, in de heaven, twice,
> In de heaven she'll rejoice.
> Mother, rock me in de cradle all de day (4x).

Again following Sundquist, the mother can be variously understood as the church (as in Mother Zion, an African Methodist Episcopal Zion church), as the slave mother from whom children may be torn away, or as a figure for the African homeland (p. 509). It seems unlikely that Du Bois was intending to evoke a religious institution as a signifier of the lifeworld of black folk. But taking the Song of Solomon and the Sorrow Song in conjunction, we have license to experience a feminized blackness as its matrix.

Whether or not Du Bois intended to identity the lifeworld of black folk with the feminine and maternal images and intonations that lead into "Of the Black Belt," he plainly intends to give the narrative a hypnotic, spellbinding quality. The mood as we concluded "Of the Training of Black Men" was elevated and luminous; now, as we penetrate more deeply into Dougherty County, it is unsettling, dark, and melancholy. But the chapter is not simply, or even primarily, a mood piece. It is structured so that we travel into this place of mystery and out of it again, while substantively the affective tonalities amplify, rather than subvert or replace, the historical and socio-logical argument Du Bois is making. For he aims at exposing the reader to the realities of Negro life in the Black Belt, and to show that it is a way of life constricted not only by the inherent harshness of subsistence farming but also by the mendacity of white folks.

As in "Of the Dawn of Freedom," Du Bois balances the slave past and a hoped-for free future on the fulcrum of the problematic present. He is looking for signs of a new day amid the visible wreckage of the old, and he finds them in the form of black-owned farms that are well-tended and prosperous. These give him "a comfortable feeling that the Negro is rising" (*Souls*, p. 84). But the weight of the evidence is on the other side. The stories of successful enterprise are few in comparison to those of black folk eking out a meager existence on the basis of tenant farming, sharecropping, and manual labor, bearing the burdens of virtual re-enslavement, on the one hand, and new forms of economic exploitation, on the other. Just after Du Bois passes the well-tended acres that left him feeling optimistic, he comes to rows of old cabins, "cheerless, bare, and dirty," and to a young black man, recently married:

> Until last year he had good luck renting; then cotton fell, and the sheriff seized and sold all he had. So he moved here, where the rent is higher, the land poorer, and the owner inflexible; he rents a forty-dollar mule at twenty dollars a year. Poor lad!—a slave at twenty-two. (p. 84)

Then there is the preacher's wife, "plump, yellow, and intelligent." She and her husband own their house, but no land: "We did buy seven acres up yonder, and paid for it; but they cheated us out of it" (p. 88). A ragged fel-low standing nearby tells of working for the same man who cheated them, of being paid in worthless scrip, and then having the sheriff take his mule, corn, and furniture. "Furniture?", asks Du Bois, "but furniture is exempt from seizure by law." The man replies, "Well, he took it just the same" (ibid.). In a variety of forms, dispossession is the name of the game. Thus, even al-lowing for the signs of better times coming, the overall picture is of ordinary people struggling to survive in a situation combining very nearly the worst of the old and new regimes. No wonder that the mood of the Black Belt is oppressive, mournful, and suffused with a bitter and biting anger.

The anger is familiar. "A little past Atlanta, to the southwest, is the land of the Cherokees, and there, not far from where Sam Hose was crucified, you may stand on the spot which is to-day the centre of the Negro problem,— the centre of those nine million men who are America's dark heritage from slavery and the slave-trade" (p. 75). Knowing Du Bois as we do, we are not surprised to find the center of the Negro problem identified not only with slavery and the slave trade but also with the lynching of Sam Hose. Indeed,

Hose is mentioned in each of the three chapters devoted to the sociology of black Southern life. His presence tells us that we will not be permitted to forget the outright brutality of Jim Crow as we explore its more insidious effects. White prostitutes harbored a "worthless black boy" too openly, so "he was hanged for rape" (p. 83). A struggling farmer stops Du Bois "to inquire after the black boy in Albany, whom it was said a policeman had shot and killed for loud talking on the sidewalk."

> And then he said slowly: "Let a white man touch me, and he dies; I don't boast this,—I don't say it around loud, or before the children,—but I mean it. I've seen them whip my father and my old mother in the cotton-rows till the blood ran; by—" (p. 85)

Memories of violence past live on and blend with violence present. People remember a plantation owner named Joe Fields—"a rough old fellow he was, and had killed many a 'nigger' in his day" (p. 78). "I've seen niggers drop dead in the furrow, but they were kicked aside, and the plough never stopped," another man tells Du Bois. "And down in the guardhouse, there's where the blood ran" (p. 82). All this Du Bois reports calmly, within the flow of the narrative, and in an understated, matter-of-fact fashion. Just so, he conveys to the reader the everyday nature of such violent assaults, the way in which they were woven into the fabric of life within the Veil.

The emerging picture, as we travel the roads through Dougherty County, is of black folk pinioned between past and present, on the one hand, force and fraud, on the other. But this picture does not tell the whole story. Struggling against "a sort of dull determined heat that seems quite independent of the sun," it takes Du Bois some days before he is sufficiently acclimated to set out from Albany (p. 78). When he does, in a horse-drawn carriage with a local resident as driver and guide, he is soon overtaken by a "resistless feeling of depression" akin to the heat. Near one house a "half-desolate spirit of neglect born of the very soil" has settled in, and the cotton-gins and machinery have "rotted away." Continuing, he passes remnants of plantations, houses half in ruin, uncared-for fields. "The whole land seems forlorn and forsaken." Ten miles go by, with no white face to be seen but only those of the black tenants, who remain here because they must (ibid.). His mind begins to drift. "This, then, is the Cotton Kingdom,—the shadow of a marvellous dream. And where is the King?" (p. 79). He is gone, it seems. Perhaps not entirely: "wherever the King may be, the parks and palaces of the Cotton Kingdom have not wholly disappeared." Then again, where slave-barons drove their coaches in the "merry past," all "is silence now, and ashes, and tangled weeds" (ibid.). Further along what appeared to be a village comes into view. Seen close up, it is the ruins of a plantation, occupied by a few struggling black souls. "I could imagine the place under some weird spell," Du Bois tells us, "and was half-minded to search out the princess" (p. 80). But if she had ever been there, she, like the King, had departed. Her place and his had been taken by the "Wizard of the North—the Capitalist," who had "rushed down in the seventies to woo this coy dark soil" (p. 81). But he, too, fled, undone by the thievery of his agents. "So the Waters-Lorings plantation was stilled by the spell of dishonesty, and stands like some gaunt rebuke to a scarred land." And Du Bois, himself spellbound, ends that day's journey; "for I could not shake off the influence of that silent scene" (ibid.).

Using himself as the vehicle, Du Bois has exposed us to something like an inverse enchantment, a hypnotic despondency or melancholia. It seems to have arisen from the fusion of two or three sources. There is, first, the lot of black folk, the profoundly painful impression of so many people struggling against a defeat so certain it seems like fate. There are the exceptions, those who are outwitting and outworking Jim Crow; but for the great majority, the prospects are bleak indeed. Our minds are drawn back to Josie, destined to die of heartbreak, and we wonder how many Josies are being broken in Dougherty County. Second, there are the ghosts of the Cotton Kingdom, a spectral royalty haunting the ruined halls and neglected roadways of their great estates. Du Bois does not wish us to experience regret at the passing of the "richest slave kingdom the modern world ever knew" (p. 82). For along with its grandeur "there was something sordid, something forced,—a certain feverish unrest and recklessness; for was not all this show and tinsel built upon a groan?" Built on such foundations, it "must in time sway and fall" (ibid.). Still, its visible and decaying incarnations are like intrusions of the dead into the land of the living. Perhaps the impression would not be so overwhelming were it not for the near-tropical fecundity of this part of the county—a superabundance, an overgrowth of life that incarnates the death of the old order as surely as its deserted edifices. It is as if Du Bois, not quite prepared for what he was to encounter, had ridden into a living kingdom of death, so overwhelming in its morbidity that he needed to beat a temporary retreat to regain possession of his own mind.

This day's ride is the lowest point—the most depressed point—we reach as we traverse the horizontal plane of *Souls*. It does not have the spiritual depth we experienced in "Of the Meaning of Progress," although Josie did come to mind along with the images of hard-pressed black folk. Nor does it convey the sharp feelings of sorrow that permeate the more personal chapters. And if it is a maternal depth, it is one that takes life rather than giving it, a dying mother-world in which the children are likewise doomed. Read this way, we have a feminization of experience that contrasts starkly with the generative sensuality of the bride in the Song of Solomon. Might we then see the woman black and comely as expressing Du Bois's hope for his people, the abyss of Dougherty County his worst nightmare? Was he haunted by the question "What if I am witnessing the past incarnate not only in the present but also in the future?" Ample reason, then, for a "resistless feeling of depression." Yet resist it he does. When the journey continues, the spell has been broken, and Du Bois is once more the acute sociological observer and analyst of the lives of black folk. But the experience—whether remembered or imaginatively elaborated—is not extraneous to the overall argument of *Souls*. If Dougherty County is the "centre of the Negro problem," then the core elements of the problem are precisely the hardship of subsistence farming, the infuriating and frustrating impact of the systematic force and fraud of Jim Crow, and—as a consequence—the depressive miasma that permeates everything and very nearly everybody, sapping the will and reinforcing the existing order of things. This is the heart of the Southern darkness. It will not do to stand by, however, waiting for it to pass, perhaps comforting oneself with the thought that the darkest hour comes just before the dawn. If there is to be a genuine dawn of freedom, it will be the work of those who, undaunted, "spread with their own hands the Gospel of Self-Sacrifice" . . . and of those who, too proud or hard to accept the fate intended for them, bend their backs to the task of turning even the "dull red hideousness of Georgia" into the Promised Land.

"Of the Quest of the Golden Fleece" / "Of the Sons of Master and Man"
In the following two chapters, there is a steady ascent from the low point in "Of the Black Belt." We remain in the South and, in "Of the Quest of the Golden Fleece," even in Dougherty County. But we return to Du Bois's native ground of systematic sociological argument and, in "Of the Sons of Master and Man," explicitly to the project of mutual recognition, that is, of uniting "intelligence and sympathy across the color-line" (p. 119).

As we observed earlier, "Of the Quest of the Golden Fleece" is the counterpart to "Of the Wings of Atalanta." The golden apples of the earlier chapter become the golden fleece of the later one, the wealth of Mammon becomes the wealth of King Cotton. Whittier is replaced by Moody, the interracial harmony that high culture might engender ("they are rising—all are rising—the black and white together") is replaced by the brutish antagonism of low culture, where "brother's blood shall cry on brother up the dead and empty skies" (p. 89). The lyrics of "Children You'll be Called On" continue the martial theme: "Children, you'll be called on / To march in the field of bat-tle / When this warfare'll be ended / Hal-le-lu." But unlike in "Of the Wings of Atalanta," here, the poetic frame of the chapter seems somewhat misaligned with the content, or at least remains external to it. The image of a modern Jason whose "quest for the golden fleece in the Black Sea" results in fratricidal madness certainly fits the Middle Passage, slavery, and the Civil War; and one might fairly claim that the Brute, a combination of King Cotton and Capitalism, tears apart the bonds of sociality, subjecting rich and poor alike to a war of all against all. The plantation past lives on in the industrializing present, greed of one kind is transmuted into greed of another, and poor black folk are the victims of both. Yet, as we are about to see, this is not the argument that Du Bois is actually making. By contrast, the three lines of verse from Elizabeth Barrett Browning precisely capture his intent in "Of the Sons of Master and Man": "Life treads on life, and heart on heart; / We press too close in church and mart / To keep a dream or grave apart" (p. 105). Likewise, the musical notation, from "I'm a Rolling," may be read as a plea for interracial solidarity: "O brothers, won't you help me to pray? (2x) / "Won't you help me in the service of the Lord?" (see Sundquist 1993, p. 505). Although the chapter details the effects of racial segregation—primarily on black people but also on white—the poetry expresses the belief or faith that people are people, that we are too alike to be kept forever apart. Fittingly this chapter ends with another three lines of verse, from Alfred, Lord Tennyson: "That mind and soul according well, / May make one music as before, / But vaster" (*Souls*, p. 119).

If these chapters on the sociology of everyday life end on a high note, they begin on a low one. The overriding impression that emerged from our passage through Dougherty County in "Of the Black Belt" was of the poverty of black folk. Following the thread of Du Bois's argument, we already have some idea about why this should be the case; and so do most Southern white folk. But the ideas of the latter are quite different from the ones Du Bois has articulated and exemplified:

> To the car-window sociologist, to the man who seeks to understand and know the South by devoting the few leisure hours of a holiday trip to unravelling the snarl of centuries,—to such men very often the whole trouble with the black field-hand may be summed up by Aunt Ophelia's word, "Shiftless!" (p. 100)

Why are black people poor? Comes the answer, they're just plain lazy. All three of the chapters on everyday life have as one of their aims the refutation of this charge. Du Bois does not deny that some Negroes are in fact shiftless. But he does deny that this characterization applies to members of the race generally, and he insists that the capacities and incapacities of black agricultural workers be historically and sociologically analyzed.

Not surprisingly, Du Bois adduces three general constraints on the efficacy of black labor. There is, first, the debilitating effects of slavery. Black workers "have been trained for centuries as slaves. They exhibit therefore, all the advantages and defects of such training; they are willing and goodnatured, but not self-reliant, provident, or careful" (p. 107). Hence, second, careful tutelage was required at the dawn of freedom. After all, it doesn't require "any fine-spun theories of racial differences to prove the necessity of group training after the brains of the race have been knocked out by two hundred and fifty years of assiduous education in submission, carelessness, and stealing" (p. 108). But this responsibility the nation shirked.

Nor did black people receive economic compensation for those centuries of bondage:

> Free! The most piteous thing amid all the black ruin of war-time, amid the broken fortunes of the masters, the blighted hopes of mothers and maidens, and the fall of an empire,—the most piteous thing amid all this was the black freedman who threw down his hoe because the world called him free. What did such a mockery of freedom mean? Not a cent of money, not an inch of land, not a mouthful of victuals,—not even ownership of the rags on his back. Free! (p. 95)

The ex-slaves were thrown into the world without resources or the training required to secure them. No wonder that, in a place like Dougherty County, most black folk are poor and ignorant, and ignorant in ways that go beyond illiteracy: "They are ignorant of the world, of modern economic organization, of the functions of government, of individual worth and possibilities,—of nearly all those things that slavery in self-defense kept them from learning" (p. 93). Thus we have not only poverty and ignorance but also a viciously circular relationship between them. And, third, these already crushing burdens were increased by the exploitation of former masters, landlords, and merchants. Unprotected by "the best elements of the South," black people became "in law and custom the victim of the worst and most unscrupulous men in each community" (p. 109).

Yet we might ask Du Bois, how could it be otherwise? By his own account, the patriarchal relationships that brought the best of both races together have passed away, along with the slave system within which they were embedded. They have been replaced by the characteristic relationships not just of capitalism, but of unregulated capitalism—akin to that of "England of the early nineteenth century, before the factory acts" (p. 108). The "captains of industry" who are coming to dominate Southern life, unrestrained by trade unions, labor laws, or the mores of the old regime, have neither "love nor hate" for their workers; with them "it is a cold question of dollars and dividends" (ibid.). Golden apples and golden fleeces are the order of the day, and those who hunger for them and don't question their value have the Brute on their side. It seems quixotic to believe that modern reincarnations of traditional Southern gentlemen could wrest social control from their hands—even leaving aside the question of whether these new world heirs of old-world aristocracies would exercise that control to the advantage of black folk. But as we know, Du Bois was attempting to bend the approach of the Verein für Sozialpolitik to his own purposes. He was appealing, over the heads of these captains of industry, to those individuals capable of recognizing a broader self-interest than dollars and dividends.

From another angle, the old regime was reincarnated in the new. Literal slavery was a thing of the past and universalized wage-slavery a thing of the future. In between was a socioeconomic system that might be characterized as neofeudal. Again using Dougherty as his database, Du Bois depicts an emergent class structure consisting of a "'submerged tenth' of croppers, with a few paupers; forty percent who are metayers and thirty-nine percent of semi-metayers and wage-laborers . . . [along with] five-percent of money-renters and six percent of freeholders,—the 'Upper Ten' of the land" (p. 101). The submerged tenth includes the "dissatisfied and shiftless field-hand" that the white Southerner uses to epitomize the race. In a way that is achingly familiar to us in our own time, a small part of the black population is used to vilify the whole. At the other extreme are those who, against all odds, manage to rise above the status of metayer. Their position is always precarious; for even those who manage to become free-holders "have little to tide over a few years of economic depression, and are at the mercy of the cotton-market far more than the whites" (p. 103). But they do exist, and Du Bois aims at making their achievement visible, just as he seeks recognition for the Talented Tenth of educated black folk. In between are the metayers and semi-metayers, peasants who are bound to the land by contract and who, while seemingly working for themselves, are really working for their landlords. Their condition resembles that of tenant farmers in France before the Revolution (p. 102), and this comparison is very much to the point. The poverty of black people does not require explanation by "fine-spun theories of racial differences" nor is it unique to them. Viewed in comparative sociological perspective, it is the historical rule rather than the racial exception. Combine the unregulated capitalism of early nineteenth century England with the feudal relations of prerevolutionary France, impose it on people who have been subjected to "two hundred and fifty years of assiduous education in submission, carelessness, and stealing," and the result is predictable. What then requires explanation is not the poverty and ignorance of the many but the economic and educational achievement of the few.

In short, starting from the low point of the submerged tenth, perhaps shuddering a bit at the memory of that day spent amid the melancholy ruins of the Cotton Kingdom, Du Bois leads us upward, if not to high Pisgah, at least to the foothills of economic progress. This is the major topographical feature in "Of the Quest of the Golden Fleece." The same vertical dimension structures "Of the Sons of Master and Man," and, as we've already seen, the two chapters contain overlapping economic analyses. The later chapter has a broader purview, however, as well as a higher reach. It begins with a reprise of its opposite number, "Of the Training of Black Men." Again the frame is the spread of European civilization, progressive no doubt in one regard but also accompanied by "war, murder, slavery, extermination, and debauchery" (p. 105). The task of "all honourable men of the twentieth century" is to ensure that "the survival of the fittest shall mean the triumph of the good, the beautiful, and the true" and not a continued reign of "greed and impudence and cruelty" (p. 106). The chapter, like so much of *Souls*, is a plea to these "honourable men" both black and white, a plea couched in the language of sociological research. Although the "average American scientist" deems it beneath his dignity to study the "actual relations of whites and blacks in the South," the "enormous race complications with which God seems about to punish this nation" lend urgency to the endeavor (ibid.). Not much time, Du Bois implies, for America to compensate for its sins. More concretely, his focus is on the absolute division between the races that characterizes the New South, a version of the color-line that leaves each race ignorant of the realities of the other and imposes on black folk the necessity of pulling themselves up by their own bootstraps—while white folk and the institutions expressing their interests continually push them back down.

Du Bois takes up in turn proximity of dwelling places, economic relations, politics and voting, Negro criminality and—as remedy for criminality and as prerequisite for effective citizenship—education, and less tangible matters of public opinion. Read one way, his analysis is an amicus curiae brief in support of his case against Washington or (we might suppose) against the court's ruling in *Plessy v. Ferguson:* For all the talk of separate fingers on one hand, black folk get the back of the hand; separate is inherently unequal. But *Brown v. Board of Education* was a half-century into the future and the NAACP, which initiated the case, did not yet exist. Hence Du Bois could not hope for a change in the de jure or de facto situation of racial segregation and white supremacy. He is left pleading a much weaker case; that is, for a change of elite public opinion, with the hope that such a change would have trickle-down effects for the larger black community. And that plea seems most unlikely to be heard. As he observed when arguing for the necessity of voting rights for black folk, "the best opinion of the South to-day is not the ruling opinion." Black folk are not the beneficiaries of the "guidance of the best," but rather of the "exploitation and debauchery of the worst" (p. 112). This is, after all, the South where "Sam Hose was crucified" (p. 75)—Sam Hose, whose death was the consequence of a typical dispute between master and man (p. 99); Sam Hose, a field-hand who in white public opinion belongs in the "same despised class" as the poet Phillis Wheatley (p. 118). Moreover, Du Bois was already finding that "there was no such demand for scientific work of the sort that I was doing, as I had confidently assumed would be easily forthcoming" (*Autobiography*, p. 222). Atlanta was not Berlin. But what other options were there? God might look disapprovingly upon the sins of the American fathers, but He was not sending down plagues or killing *their* first-born sons. Nor would it do to take the law in one's own hands. The path of revolt and revenge was both impractical and morally abhorrent. What else could be done but to work for leadership alliances across the color-line? Looking ahead, wasn't the NAACP just such an alliance? Or, sticking to cases, wasn't *Souls* just such a determined attempt to build a "union of intelligence and sympathy across the color-line" (*Souls*, p. 119)?

This last twist of Du Bois's tale is not the last word on the question of black liberation. Marcus Garvey and *his* heirs, to say nothing of Du Bois himself in his later years, would call into question the conception of elite/mass relations that underlies this approach to politics and that constitutes, sociologically, the vertical dimension of *Souls*. Nor are we about to forget that a combination of elitism and romanticism sometimes inclined Du Bois to a nostalgic view of the Southern past. Yet his romanticism was also the vehicle for his passions and his poetry, for that larger spiritual sensibility that made of *Souls* something far more than a social scientific study of the color-line. Moreover, the issue is not so simple as replacing a valorization of elites with a valorization of the masses, of substituting one kind of romanticism for another. There is a genuine, practical problem of elite/mass relations in processes of social transformation. Which is only to say, Du Bois may have been one-sided in his approach to black liberation, but this doesn't mean he was wrong-headed. And quite apart from these pragmatic concerns, we are not forgetting that, along with his love of the cultural heights of Europe, he had an equal attraction to the spiritual depths of Africa. In this regard he departed dramatically from the model of his German mentors, who most assuredly were not bone of the bone and flesh of the flesh with the working class. Just because, from his Fisk days on, he was rooted in African-American culture, his aristocratic tendencies were balanced by democratic ones.

The Religious Ties That Bind

"Of the Faith of the Fathers"
In the "Forethought" to *Souls*, after noting the content of the chapters we have been considering, Du Bois states: "Leaving, then, the world of the white men, I have stepped within the Veil, raising it that you may view faintly its deeper recesses,—the meaning of its religion, the passion of its human sorrow, and the struggle of its greater souls" (p. 5). Hence it would seem that I do not have authorial license for the division of the text between macrospheric and microspheric levels, which I have proposed and utilized. Instead, apparently following Du Bois, we'd have to say that we have been in "the world of the white man" up to this point and now, with the chapter on religion, are stepping within the Veil.[16] But this cannot be the case. Du Bois says that "Of the Meaning of Progress" and "Of the Wings of Atalanta" show "in brief outline the two worlds within and without the Veil" (ibid.); nowhere are we more inside the Veil than in "Of the Black Belt"; and relations between black folk and white—the problem of the color-line—are constituent elements of every chapter of the book. Because we cannot imagine

Du Bois not to have known this, the more plausible interpretation of the passage in question is that in *Souls* as a whole we have stepped within the Veil, and that the Veil is now being raised so that the reader may see into its "deeper recesses." For it is certainly the case that, beginning with Chapter X, "Of the Faith of the Fathers," we are entering more deeply into a spiritual domain. Du Bois powerfully evokes the experience of down-home worship, through the analysis of which we touch upon the core of African-American identity. But the mode of presentation is sociohistorical. As in several of the earlier chapters, the reader is told that here one finds numerous "attractive lines of inquiry"; that is, that the religious life of the Negro is of "deep interest to the student of his development, both socially and psychologically" (p. 121). Once again, Du Bois is appealing for understanding across the color-line. Moreover, his interpretation of the sacred is decidedly secular. We might say—remembering his mentor William James—that he places before us one of the varieties of religious experience without asking us to believe in it. Finally, he stays in his role as observer and interpreter, or at most participant/observer. Although he emphasized at the outset his kinship with those who live within the Veil, the focus remains on *their* experience, not his. In the three chapters that follow, the focus is reversed. Thus, as I've already suggested, "Of the Faith of the Fathers" brings one narrative line to an end and initiates the next.

The original title of Chapter X, when published in article form, was "The Religion of the American Negro." The new title reframes the exposition. On the one hand, it emphasizes Du Bois's concern with the spiritual ancestry of black folk. But why, then, the faith of the *fathers*? Perhaps the choice simply reflects a patriarchal cast of mind or is meant to parallel the fathers of the early Christian church. Closer to home, it evokes the Founding Fathers, along with the "sons of the Fathers" who would "fain forget" the principles of the Declaration of Independence (p. 45). Read this way, it subtly implies a separate and co-equal founding for African-Americans; and this reading is reinforced by the emphasis Du Bois places on the African origins of Negro religion. In so doing he carries forward the idea that America must come to recognize the fact that its culture blends the spirit of "two world-races," indeed that its soul—its "wild sweet melodies" and its capacity for "simple faith and reverence"—is most of all the gift of black folk (p. 16).

If its title lends the chapter a patriarchal cast, the opening two verses from Fiona MacLeod's "Dim Face of Beauty" bestow a feminine one:

> Dim face of Beauty haunting all the world,
> Fair face of Beauty all too fair to see,
> Where the lost stars adown the heavens are hurled,—
>   There, there alone for thee

> May white peace be.
> . . . .
> Beauty, sad face of Beauty, Mystery, Wonder,
> What are these dreams to foolish babbling men
> Who cry with little noises 'neath the thunder
>   Of Ages ground to sand,
>   To a little sand.

"Beauty, sad face of Beauty, Mystery, Wonder" is set in contrast to the foolish babbling men who know her not and, by virtue of this opposition, is gendered feminine. This gendered divide is even more evident in the verse Du Bois doesn't cite:

> For here where all the dreams of men are whirled
> Like sere torn leaves of autumn to and fro,
> There is no place for thee in all the world,
>   Who driftest as a star,
>   Beyond, afar. (MacLeod 1913, p. 166)

Beauty is celestial, akin to the eternal feminine; men are terrestrial. She is, moreover, akin to Fiona MacLeod herself, the imagined or experienced inner feminine voice and consciousness of the poem's author, William Sharp. Was Du Bois gesturing toward this other instance of two-ness? I don't know. It would be fitting if he were, given the place occupied by the sad Mary Silvina in his inner world. However that may be, the verses evoke a feminized beauty and spirituality as the essence of African-American religious experience.

Du Bois characterizes the accompanying spiritual, "Steal Away," as "the song of songs" (*Souls*, p. 158). The lyrics contain the archetypal ambiguity of the faith of the fathers: the coded message of escape from slavery in this world and the manifest message of escape into the next:

> Steal away, steal away,
> Steal away to Jesus!
> Steal away, steal away,
>   home,
> I ain't got to stay here.
> My Lord calls me,
> He calls me by thunder,
> The trumpet sounds within my soul,
> I ain't got long to stay here.

Combining *this* song of songs with MacLeod's "Dim Face of Beauty" we are once again drawn toward an eternal feminine.

Fittingly, Du Bois begins with his first experience of a Negro revival, already briefly mentioned in "Of the Meaning of Progress" (p. 50). Walking toward the meeting, he and his companions heard first a "rhythmic cadence of song,—soft, thrilling, powerful, that swelled and died sorrowfully in our ears" (p. 119). There are echoes of the melancholy mood of "Dim Face of Beauty," but also a different rhythm and a feeling of anticipation. Arriving, he felt the "air of intense excitement that possessed the mass of black folk": "A sort of suppressed terror hung in the air and seemed to seize us,—a pythian madness, a demoniac possession, that lent terrible reality to song and word" (p. 120). We recognize the pull of group emotion in this depiction, the way in which it heightens affect and lowers individuated rationality. Channeling this emotion, giving voice to the spirit, is the preacher. In response, the people "moaned and fluttered": "then the gaunt-cheeked brown woman beside me suddenly leaped straight into the air and shrieked like a lost soul, while round about came wail and groan and outcry, and a scene of human passion such as I had never conceived" (ibid.). Du Bois was immersed in a flood of feeling, released by the woman's orgasmic shriek. How can one resist the temptation of saying that, at this moment, he abruptly lost his spiritual virginity? Berkshire lad that he was, he was quite unprepared for such spiritualized sensuality, just as he was unprepared for the physical sensuality of the landlady who "raped" him and relieved him of his sexual virginity. They opened him up, those summers in Alexandria, body and soul. But they did not undermine his preexisting character. Du Bois was first and foremost a highly individuated and disciplined intellectual. His response to his religious experience was to theorize it.[17]

The core elements of the "religion of the slave" were, as we have just seen, the Preacher, the Music, and the Frenzy (ibid.). The Preacher was heir to the African priest or medicine man: "He early appeared on the plantation and found his function as the healer of the sick, the interpreter of the Unknown, the comforter of the sorrowing, the supernatural avenger of wrong, and the one who rudely but picturesquely expressed the longing, disappointment, and resentment of a stolen and oppressed people" (p. 123). When Christianity took hold—amply commingled with "heathen rites" and "Voodooism"—he became the founding father of the Negro church. The Music, "sprung from the African forests . . . was adapted, changed, and intensified by the tragic soul-life of the slave, until, under the stress of law and whip, it became the one true expression of a people's sorrow, despair, and hope" (p. 120). The Frenzy or "Shouting" is a version of the divine madness that is "as old as religion, as Delphi and Endor" (p. 121). It was and is produced when "the Spirit of the Lord passed by, and, seizing the devotee, made him mad with supernatural joy" (ibid.). Du Bois doesn't explicitly link it to Africa, but he does sharply separate it from the Christian experience of Great Barrington or of "Suffolk in olden time" (p. 119). Taking these elements together, we have something like the African essence of African-American identity, an identity that takes form in the shadow of slavery:

> The Negro has already been pointed out many times as a religious animal,[18]—a being of that deep emotional nature which turns instinctively toward the supernatural. Endowed with a rich tropical imagination and a keen, delicate appreciation of nature, the transplanted African lived in a world animate with gods and devils, elves and witches; full of strange influences,—of Good to be implored, of Evil to be propitiated. Slavery, then, was to him the dark triumph of Evil over him. All the hateful powers of the Under-world were striving against him, and a spirit of revolt and revenge filled his heart. He called up all the resources of heathenism to aid,—exorcism and witchcraft, the mysterious Obi worship with its barbarous rites, spells, and blood-sacrifice even, now and then, of human victims. Weird midnight orgies and mystic conjurations were invoked, the witch-woman and the voodoo-priest became the centre of Negro group life, and that vein of vague superstition which characterized the unlettered Negro even today was deepened and strengthened. (pp. 124–125)

There is more than a hint of exoticism in Du Bois's evoking of African origins, reminiscent of the orientalism so famously analyzed by Edward Said. In another register of meaning, we might recall Nietzsche's famous distinction between the fecund and overpowering "witches' brew" of the Dionysian and the enlightened individuality of the Apollonian. Another instance of two-ness perhaps: The Apollonian individual yearns to lose himself in the Dionysian abyss of sensuality and passion—and, dreading the loss of himself, pulls back into the safety of self-possessed artistic expression (Nietzsche [1872] 1956, pp. 38–41). The hyphenated nature of his identity is then expressed as a balancing act on a tightrope or a dance at the edge of a volcano. Or, in a psychoanalytic register, we have in slavery a darkened mother-world, one in which the children are in fact enslaved by and at the mercy of a malign power. Lacking power themselves, they resort to splitting and magical thinking in a desperate attempt to gain a semblance of control over that which they cannot control—a semblance that, like the Apollonian, will constitute a boundary around and successful defense of selfhood. Closer to home, and with the extremes attenuated, we have the tension between spiritual immersion and contained selfhood that Du Bois experienced at the revival meeting, a two-ness reflected in the way he now places himself at more than one remove from his transplanted African ancestors.

From one perspective—probably not the author's but also not one that decenters the text—this passage can be seen as paralleling the racialized primal scene in "Of the Dawn of Freedom." There we had a family drama: the gray-haired gentleman, ruined, with hate in his eyes; the dark and motherlike form, her awful face black with the mists of centuries; the midnight marauders who are the old man's legitimate heirs; and the tawny man-child who, in his vulnerability to lynching and his desire for revenge, will ensure that the story lives on. This was the new beginning that determined the contemporary shape of African-American life. Now we are presented with its original genesis, the passage from freedom to slavery that is mirrored in the later passage, however torturous, from slavery to freedom. We might even see these two great mytho-poetic moments as pilings or pillars, upon and between which Du Bois has reconstructed the world within the Veil. At an even deeper level, in the chapters that lie ahead, we plunge almost out of history and into the recesses of Du Bois's own soul. But at the present moment, we have reached a kind of bottom, a "before" in the diachronic ordering of things that constitutes the "beneath" in the synchronic one.

On this virtually anthropological foundation, Du Bois builds up a history of religious experience that expands to encompass the broader trends in black life. First comes a synoptic treatment of the institutional development of the Negro churches, from their plantation beginnings to great black churches—such as the African Methodist Church, "the greatest Negro organization in the world" (*Souls*, p. 124)—of the modern period. He then turns to the "inner ethical life" of the people, describing the transition from the rebellious religiosity of the transplanted Africans to the "passive submission" and "religious fatalism" of "newly learned Christianity" (p. 125).[19] Freedom would be found in the next world, not in this one. But the faith of the masters, intended by them as an instrument of control and domestication, was subverted by the slaves. The "black millions" heard the call of the abolitionists and made of freedom a decidedly this-worldly goal. So, as we know, "when Emancipation finally came, it seemed to the freedmen a literal Coming of the Lord" (p. 126). When the "inevitable Age of Reaction swept over the nation," it brought with it a painful reanimation of the dual trends of black religious life; that is, the tendency toward rebellion and defiance, on the one hand, and toward at least apparent acquiescence and accommodation, on the other. Hence the ambiguity of the religious ties that bind—that simultaneously bind black folk together and place them in a bind.

Now, suddenly, we find ourselves brought back to the point from which we began in "Of Our Spiritual Strivings." Tied to the "Negro Problem" as securely as Prometheus to his rock, black folk live a "double life" that imposes on them a "painful self-consciousness, an almost morbid sense of personality, and a moral hesitancy which is fatal to self-confidence" (p. 127). The result? "Such a double life, with double thoughts, double duties, and double social classes, must give rise to double words and double ideals, and tempt the mind to pretence or to revolt, to hypocrisy or radicalism" (ibid.). Du Bois, knowing his own two-ness, containing in himself the unreconciled strivings of being Negro and American, stands between the political extremes—between the radicals of the North and the compromising hypocrites of the South (p. 128). Thus stationed, as if between two shallow and impassable tributaries of a great stream, he can feel the "unguided might of powerful human souls who have lost the guiding star of the past and are seeking in the great night a new religious ideal" (p. 129). When it is found, "the pent-up vigor of ten million souls shall sweep irresistibly toward the Goal, out of the Valley of the Shadow of Death, where all that makes life worth living—Liberty, Justice, and Right—is marked 'For White People Only'" (ibid.). Jim Crow will flee, even from Dougherty County, and it will no longer be necessary to tell the pharaohs of the Egypt of the Confederacy, "let my people go!"

6

My Home Is Over Jordan

I'm just a poor wayfaring stranger,
Traveling through this world of woe.
But there's no sickness, toil, or danger,
In that bright world to which I go.
I'm going there to meet my Mother,
She said she'd meet me when I come.
I'm only going over Jordan,
I'm only going over home.
I'll soon be free from every trial,
My body asleep in the old graveyard.
I'll drop the cross of self-denial,
And enter on my great reward.

"WAYFARING STRANGER," TRADITIONAL

The return to the notion of double-consciousness toward the end of "Of the Faith of the Fathers" is both theoretically and aesthetically elegant. In "Of Our Spiritual Strivings" (Chapter I) its meaning was general and abstract (abstract in the sense of unfilled)—descriptive, to be sure, but in a prospective fashion. By Chapter X, it has been identified with the opposing political attitudes (hypocritical compromise, revolt and revenge) against which Du Bois has defined the emancipatory struggle, and which his definition of the struggle is meant to supersede. It has lost none of its general meaning. It continues to signify the two-ness, the internal split in African-American identity, that derives from the imposition of the Veil. But now it has been concretized, filled with the particularities of African-American life. It expresses the dualities of culture (e.g., high culture versus folk culture,

education versus economics) that have been elaborated and displayed between its initial and present articulations. Hence there is an almost irresistible temptation to play Hegelian and say that double-consciousness has
been unfolded dialectically; that is, from potentiality to actuality, and in just
such a way as to contain its own process of development. And when we
attend as well to the manifold poetic threads that are woven into and bind
together this tapestry of African-American life, we cannot help but think
that a cunning of reason was guiding Du Bois's hand, helping to create the
manifold of effects that so marvelously constitute the unity of the text. Or,
more soberly, we could say that Du Bois's manifest intention of unifying
the narrative was strengthened by the underlying coherence of his vision
of African-American life and the synoptic (integrative) power of his native
and cultivated intelligence.

Along these same dialectical lines, it is easy enough to see in *Souls* a system of racial and class relationships developing and unfolding historically,
progressing from the point of African origin through a prolonged phase of
alienation and leading toward the time when "Liberty, Justice, and Right"
will not be marked "For White People Only." To be sure, such a totalizing
view does not adequately recognize the way in which Du Bois's imaginative and often lyrical orchestration of personal, existential, geographical,
and topographical elements reproduces a lifeworld. Yet the influence of his
training in systematic historical sociology is evident throughout, and it con-
strains the more personal and self-expressive side of his authorial persona.
Correspondingly, he appears only occasionally as an actor in the drama he
is staging: as a New England schoolboy, as a young teacher in rural Tennessee
(who is exposed for the first time to down-home religion), as a professor at
Atlanta University, and as a sociological investigator of daily life in the Black
Belt. One might even say that he is as much or more the *Demiurge* of the
world he re-creates as he is the hero-narrator of the tale he tells. And if one
were to rejoin that the organic quality of the narrative is in good part a function of his aesthetic/affective sensibility, we could say, with equal fairness,
that this sensibility is the medium through which the organic lifeworld of
African-Americans is represented.

Chapters XI, XII, and XIII form a mirror image of the ones preceding
them. Individuals take center stage, the lifeworld of black folk becomes the
setting within which their tales are enacted. Instead of the sensibility of the
author functioning as a vehicle for displaying the facts of the racial matter, the facts of the racial matter function as a medium through which we
experience the sensibility of the author. If Du Bois resembles a *Demiurge* in
the larger narrative of *Souls*, he fully occupies the role of hero-narrator in
the more intimate and personal one. More simply, the emotional restraint
of the sociologist now gives way to the pain and passion of the man. The
hurt, anger, and melancholy that have only rippled through the landscape
of African-American life up to this point, breaking into its surface here and

there like waters from a subterranean river, now flow freely—as we might have guessed they would: "And the heart shall be weary and wonder and cry like the sea / All life long crying without avail / As the water all night long is crying to me" (p. 9).

To say that the two parts of *Souls* mirror each other is not to say that they are only externally or arbitrarily related. The Veil signifies them both, with the first part of the text occupying its outer reaches and the second part its inner recesses. They are joined by a twofold reflective process: the internalization of social relations, resulting in Du Bois as the individual incarnation of the problem of the color-line; and the reciprocal movement, the projection of his personality outward, so that the topography of African-American life takes form as the structure of his character writ large. More simply stated, there is the unifying presence of the man himself, who appears in both parts as a kindred spirit to the wayfaring stranger of the old folk song. Alone he experiences the white girl's insult, alone he travels to rural Tennessee, alone he sits in his study at Atlanta University, virtually alone (accompanied only by his driver) he travels through the world of woe that is Dougherty County. The solitude is unbroken in the second part, with the important exception of the feeling of shared grief in "Of the Passing of the First-Born." But even this chapter ends in a soliloquy, as Du Bois seeks to find meaning in and consolation for his loss. In like fashion, Alexander Crummell, at once alter ego and departed father, is portrayed as carrying the burdens of his spiritual and racial pilgrimage on his own shoulders, often rebuked and scorned but seldom aided or comforted. Finally there is John Jones—bound by ties of love to mother and sister, to be sure, but otherwise with no companion to ease the pain of double-consciousness. He dies alone. In these ways the aloneness of the first part slips into the loneliness of the second and, just so, reminds us that the affective difference between them is one of accent and not of essence. Hence we might say that, between the two parts of *Souls*, there is "a *difference* which is no *difference*, or only a difference of what is *self-same*" (Hegel [1807], 1977, p. 99).

The point can be stated differently. "Of the Faith of the Fathers" ends by characterizing the world of the present, riven by the Veil, as "the Valley of the Shadow of Death." This is the land through which we've traveled. The shadow shrouds, perhaps not with equal density, both the hollows of the Black Belt filled with a "resistless feeling of depression" and the hills of Atlanta where the University proudly and gloriously stands. The darkness was there from the beginning, from the time when the "death-ship" sailed with its captive human cargo from Africa to the Americas (*Souls*, p. 62). Veil/Vale/Valley: African-Americans live in the shadow-land of death. Yet death itself, although often referenced, struck only once or twice as we walked the lonesome valley. Perhaps we experienced it most painfully in the sad moment in "Of the Meaning of Progress" when Josie "crept to her mother like a hurt child, and slept—and sleeps" (p. 51). And we should pause for a moment to acknowledge another loss to that small rural community: "Uncle Bird told me how [one night] 'Thenie came wandering back to her home over yonder, to escape the blows of her husband. And the next morning she died in the home that her little bow-legged brother, working and saving, had bought for their widowed mother" (p. 53). The pain of such losses does not, however, center the text in these chapters, while death is our constant companion in the chapters that lie ahead. We are present to bear witness to the passing of each of the three protagonists. In two of the three cases, the passing is untimely, thus reflecting at the level of the single soul the demise of the Freedmen's Bureau—the passing of that great human institution before its work was done. As it was in the beginning of our journey, so shall it be in the end.

So Many Rivers to Cross

"Of the Passing of the First-Born"
The lynching of Sam Hose is one of the links between Du Bois as the author of *Souls* and Du Bois as its hero-narrator. So, too, is the death of young Burghardt. As we have noted, the two events are linked temporally and affectively; but in the latter regard, they are mirror images. Du Bois's reaction to the lynching combines anger and disgust; if there is a feeling of sadness, it is an echo, not the affective tone, of his response, When his son dies, Du Bois's sadness is nearly overwhelming; anger at the contumely of white people is present, but as counterpoint, not as the main theme. Appropriately, therefore, "Of the Passing of the First-Born" begins with the last verse of Algernon Swinburne's "Itylus":

> O sister, sister, thy first-begotten,
> The hands that cling and the feet that follow,
> The voice of the child's blood crying yet,
> *Who hath remembered me? who hath forgotten?*
> Thou hast forgotten, O summer swallow,
> But the world shall end when I forget. (*Souls*, p. 130)

We might read the verse as addressed to Du Bois's wife, Nina, whose grief at Burghardt's death surpassed even his own. They have lost their first-begotten child, whom they will never forget. The feeling of loss is amplified by the musical quotation, which is from "I Hope My Mother Will Be There." We might imagine that Du Bois identifies himself with his son and wishes for both of them the solace and comfort of a mother's love. One wonders, however, if the Greek myth of Itylus, who was murdered by his mother Aedon, was playing in the back of his mind. Here is how Penelope tells the story in the *Odyssey*: "As when Pandareos' daughter, the greenwood nightingale, / perching in the deep of the forest foliage sings out / her lovely song, when springtime has just begun; she, varying / the manifold strains of her voice, pours out the melody, mourning / Itylos, son of the lord Zethos, her own beloved / child, whom she once killed with the bronze when the madness was on / her" (Lattimore 1965, p. 295). Aedon killed her child in a state of derangement and was transformed by Zeus into the mournful nightingale. Did Du Bois see in Nina Aedon's grief? He tells us of her devotion to her son: "No hands but hers must touch and garnish those little limbs; no dress or frill must touch them that had not wearied her fingers; no voice but hers could coax him off to Dreamland, and she and he spoke some soft and unknown tongue and in it held communion" (*Souls*, p. 131). And he captures in words of compassion the pain of her loss: "in the chamber of death writhed the world's most piteous thing—a childless mother" (p. 132), thus inverting and intensifying the image of the motherless child. But did he also feel, in that human, all-too-human and familiar masculine way, that she was to blame—that she, who took upon herself the full responsibility for her son's care, should have taken better care that no ill befall him?[1]

We are not entitled to speculate further along these lines. Du Bois's love for his wife and the mother of his child is explicit and includes a grateful recognition that his connection to his son came "through her" (p. 131). He had been predisposed to see in his son primarily the extension and magnification of his own redemptive mission. He begins the chapter by replacing the text of the telegram announcing the boy's birth with a paraphrase of Isaiah's prophecy of the Messiah, "Unto you a child is born" (p. 130). But Nina was the mediator through whom he joined his idealizing identification with Burghardt to love for him:

> So sturdy and masterful he grew, so filled with bubbling life, so tremulous with the unspoken wisdom of a life but eighteen months distant from the All-Life,—we were not far from worshiping this revelation of the divine, my wife and I. . . . [And I] saw the strength of my own arm stretched onward through the ages through the newer strength of him; saw the dream of my black fathers stagger a step onward in the wild phantasm of the world; heard in his baby voice the voice of the Prophet that would rise within the Veil. (p. 131)

It is easy to imagine that, for this too-brief moment, Du Bois recaptured something of the magic of his own mother-world, suffused as it had been with Mary Silvina's idealizing love for her perfect child. He and Nina loved their son as deeply as his mother had loved him. And he would have experienced the additional satisfaction of being for Burghardt the father he himself had never had.

Yet even in this blessed time, Du Bois felt the burden of race. There was, as a characterological and situational given, his acceptance of the imperative of renunciation. David Lewis reports that Du Bois "had to leave Burghardt's

management to Nina much more than he wanted to, since the demands of
class lectures, conferences, magazine deadlines, the final *Philadelphia Negro*
chapters, and the ambitious new Atlanta University Studies left him only
minutes each day to spend with the baby" (1993, p. 212). Still, this work was
intrinsically gratifying; he was built to do it. Moreover, he now had the additional impetus of laboring in the interest of a better future for his son; and
he could imagine young Burghardt as the inheritor of his life's work. Accordingly this sacrifice was willingly made. But there was also the weight
of double-consciousness:

> Why was his hair tinted with gold? An evil omen was golden hair in my life.
> Why had not the brown of his eyes crushed out and killed the blue?—for
> brown were his father's eyes, and his father's father's. And thus in the Land
> of the Color-Line I saw, as it fell across my baby, the shadow of the Veil.
> (*Souls*, p. 131)

The baby is innocent, unaware of the fallen world surrounding the prelapsar-
ian garden his parents have created for him: "He knew no color-line, poor
dear,—and the Veil, though it shadowed him, had not yet darkened half his
sun" (p. 133). But his father had tasted the bitter fruit of the tree of knowledge and could not help seeing in the body if not yet the soul of his son the
two-ness with which he, himself, has been afflicted.

Then one night Burghardt's "little feet pattered wearily to the wee white
bed" (p. 131). He had fallen ill with what proved to be diphtheria. "Joy and
sleep slipped away" and the voice of Time became a "Voice at midnight," intoning a different message of renunciation, "crying, 'The Shadow of Death!
The Shadow of Death!'" (p. 132). The Valley of the Shadow of Death, primarily evoked as metaphor for life within the Veil in the preceding chapter, has
become literal and personal. Correspondingly, the renunciation voluntarily
undertaken in the hope of building a better world for all the dark-skinned
children has been infiltrated by the necessity of renouncing the hopes and
love he placed in his own beautiful child. "I shirk not," Du Bois truly tells us.
"I long for work. I pant for a life full of striving. I am no coward, to shrink
before the rugged rush of the storm, nor even quail before the awful shadow
of the Veil" (p. 132). But Death, it seems, was "jealous of [his] one little coign
of happiness" and stole into his refuge from the storm, his private world of
peace and love. The meaning of self-sacrifice was inverted. In this most intimate of places, in the deeper recesses of his own soul, willing sacrifice *for* the
future had been replaced by the unwilled sacrifice *of* the future.

Death, merciless, would not be denied. Burghardt's parents watched
helplessly as his last day slipped away:

> He died at eventide, when the sun lay like a brooding sorrow above the
> western hills, veiling its face . . . and the trees, the great green trees he loved,
> stood motionless. I saw his breath beat quicker and quicker, pause, and then

his little soul leapt like a star that travels in the night and left a world of darkness in its train. (p. 132)

Sometimes Du Bois's evocative reach exceeds his grasp; not this time. His pain, and Nina's, is palpable. The sun's face is veiled in sorrow and his son's soul departs from his body in a last breath, leaving the parents who so loved him in the darkness of their loss. His mother, we are given to believe, sees all the way to the other side, "beyond the stars": "He will be happy There; he ever loved beautiful things" (p. 133). His father, thinking himself "far more ignorant, and blind by the web of . . . [his] own weaving," sits alone and says to himself: "If still he be, and he be There, and there be a There, let him be happy, O Fate!" (ibid.).

The meaning of renunciation slipped off its axis, deepened and darkened by Burghardt's death; but the experience of withheld recognition was quite unchanged. White racism observed no period of mourning. We remember the "pale-faced hurrying men and women" of Atlanta who only glanced at the funeral cortege and said, "Niggers!" (p. 133). Du Bois attempts to use that moment and the larger social reality it exemplifies to give himself a certain grim consolation. He felt an "awful gladness" in his heart, perhaps an anguished echo of the "choking gladness" he felt when his mother died. His soul whispers to him, "Not dead, not dead, but escaped; not bond, but free" (ibid.). His son will never know the fall from grace, the "studied humiliations" of life within the Veil—no rejected visiting-cards, no Jim Crow cars, no injury to "that wild pride of being which his father had hardly crushed in his own heart" (ibid.).

The bitter draught of death-as-liberation did not quite do the work of numbing the father's pain. Du Bois can imagine his son carrying the burdens of race bravely, better indeed than he himself, and living to see the great day when the Veil is lifted. But that future is foreclosed. If, therefore, the future for all those other children is not to be foreclosed, he must continue on the path of self-sacrifice, bearing the added weight of the one sacrifice unwillingly made. And he, too much the philosopher to share his wife's simple faith, has only a "perhaps" and the wishful thought of a father and son reunion to help him bear it: "Perhaps now he knows the All-love, and needs not to be wise. Sleep, then, child,—sleep till I sleep and waken to a baby voice and the ceaseless patter of little feet [, no longer wearied,]— above the Veil" (p. 134).

Maybe, too, we are meant to hear the consoling words of the Sorrow Song with which Chapter XI begins, "I Hope My Mother Will Be There":

> I hope my mother will be there,
> In that beautiful world on high.
> That used to join with me in pray'r,
> In that beautiful world on high.

> Oh I will be there Oh I will be there
> With the palms of victory,
> crowns of glory you shall wear
> In that beautiful world on high. (p. 130)

There he, leaving earthly woe behind, might crown the young prince with the laurel his too-short life denied him.

"Of Alexander Crummell"

Burghardt died far too soon; Alexander Crummell died full of years. The affective quality of the two eulogies is therefore quite different. The child dying before his father feels like a violation of the natural order of things. Hence Du Bois's age-old lament, "If one must have gone, why not I?" (p. 134). Hence, too, on the morning of the young boy's burial "it seemed a ghostly unreal day" (p. 133). A degree of dissociation is common with the loss of a loved one, but it is intensified when time is so badly out of joint. Conversely, there is consolation in the thought that things are as they ought to be when the father's time of dying precedes the son's. The penultimate verse of Tennyson's "The Passing of Arthur," which heads "Of Alexander Crummell," captures this sense of completeness:

> Then from the dawn it seemed there came, but faint
> As from beyond the limit of the world,
> Like the last echo born of a great cry,
> Sounds, as if some fair city were one voice
> Around a king returning from his wars.

In like fashion, the musical quotation from "Swing Low, Sweet Chariot"— "the cradle-song of death which all men know" (p. 158)—conveys the sense of the circle of life rounded in a welcome homecoming.

These are not the only feelings we find in "Of Alexander Crummell." Du Bois retraces the painful path of renunciation and denial of recognition that Crummell followed—renunciation of the familiar sort, but a lack of recognition with the extra sting that comes with being a prophet not honored in his own time and country: "He did his work,—he did it nobly and well; and yet I sorrow that he worked alone, with so little human sympathy. His name today, in this broad land, means little, and comes to fifty million ears laden with no incense of memory or emulation" (p. 141). In memorializing his son, Du Bois laments the shattering of a prophetic dream; in memorializing Crummell, he offers recognition to a man who, too little recognized, dedicated his life to making the dream come true.

Du Bois met Crummell for the first time when the celebrated cleric and intellectual came to speak at the Wilberforce commencement of 1895. The younger man was immediately responsive to his "simple dignity" and "unmistakable air of good breeding." "Instinctively," Du Bois reports, "I bowed before this man, as one bows before the prophets of the world" (p. 135). His reverence for Crummell stands in stark contrast to his defiance of Booker T. Washington. The Wizard was all-too-willing to pander to those "sons of the Fathers" who would "fain forget" the values of the Declaration of Independence (p. 45). His was the magic of manipulation and the backroom deal. But Crummell was the real deal: "Some seer he seemed, that came not from the crimson Past or the gray To-come, but from the pulsing Now" (p. 135). He was the father one is rightly commanded to honor, Washington a father who had forfeited such respect. Hence, as Manning Marable claims, Crummell "became Du Bois's 'spiritual father,' the personification of the young scholar's image of what all Afro-American intellectuals should be" (1986, p. 34).[2] Or as Lewis puts it, "Unlike Alfred Du Bois, about whom the son now probably knew most of the unsavory truth, Crummell was an authentically patriarchal force—austere yet compassionate, admonitory yet trustworthy" (1993, p. 168). And not only a paternal presence: "Du Bois sensed that Crummell's demons, personal, professional, and racial, were very much like his own" (ibid.). Thus Crummell is a complex and composite figure—a historical personage, to be sure, but also a symbolic father, an ego-ideal (a model of the African-American intellectual), and an alter ego.

Of these significations, the historical Crummell is the least visible. He is covered over by the mantle of the prophet and cast in the role of spiritual pilgrim in an allegory of racial progress. With this veiling in mind, Eric Sundquist comments that Du Bois's "tribute to Crummell . . . remains a partial curiosity because it has little to say about Crummell's thought as such, and even the sketch of his career is thin" (1993, p. 517).[3] But Du Bois was writing a eulogy. He was not engaging in political or intellectual contestation, as he was with Washington, but rather giving one of the race's "greater souls" its due. Moreover, he was treating Crummell as a racial symbol, as one of the exemplary souls of black folk. Like to like, as the expression goes: "the priest 'did his work nobly and well,' just as Du Bois had done, denying himself loves, friendships, and conventional satisfactions in order to pursue his calling to uplift a people through knowledge" (Lewis 1993, p. 168). Both men dedicated themselves to spreading "with their own hands the Gospel of Sacrifice" (*Souls*, p. 59). Du Bois thus found it easy to identify with Crummell, to place himself empathically in the older man's position. The result is an elegiac biography etched in the glass of autobiographical imagination. "Of Alexander Crummell" is appropriately placed between "Of the Passing of the First-Born," which is historical and autobiographical, and "Of the Coming of John," which might be read as a fictionalized "autobiography of a race."[4]

The story Du Bois tells is framed by two sets of metaphors with Christian resonances, suitable for allegorizing a man of the cloth. Crummell's early life is characterized by his triumph over the temptations of Hate, Despair, and Doubt. His later life is marked by his passage through the Valley of Humiliation and the Valley of the Shadow of Death. At the same time, and in more mundane terms, the tale is a familiar one of fathers and sons—this time of Du Bois's spiritual father struggling to define himself against and liberate himself from both his own father and the fathers of the church. Hence it is quite properly viewed as a further, more specific, investigation of "the faith of the fathers."

Crummell was born in New York State in 1819. His mother was free born; his father was African and kidnapped into slavery. In Du Bois's telling, "the great black father whispered mad tales of cruelty" into the ears of his son (p. 135). His father's bitterness was the son's inheritance, and so "the temptation of Hate grew and shadowed the growing child" (ibid.). His experience was not and is not unique: "in this wide land to-day a thousand thousand dark children brood before this same temptation, and feel its cold and shuddering arms" (p. 136). We remember the "black boys" who sink into "silent hatred of the pale world about them and mocking distrust of everything white" (p. 10). Hence there lay before him, to use the now-familiar expression, the path of revolt and revenge. Like Du Bois, Crummell turned away from it, aided in his resistance by the kindly intervention of abolitionists who helped him along his educational way. These white fathers offset to a significant degree the bitterness of his black father. Still, the "shadowy, formless thing—the temptation of Hate . . . —did not wholly fade away, but diffused itself and lingered thick at the edges" (p. 136). It would be there waiting for him when the fathers of the church proved to be men of little faith.

As he came to be a man, a "voice and vision" called Crummell to be a priest, "a seer to lead the uncalled out of the house of bondage" (p. 137). Du Bois, although not conventionally religious, knew this experience: "I therefore take the work that the Unknown lay in my hands," he told himself that night in Berlin, "and work for the rise of the Negro people, taking it for granted that their best development means the best development of the world" (quoted in Aptheker 1985, pp. 2829). Each in his own way was prepared to heed the voice of Time when it demanded, "Entbehren sollst du, sollst entbehren." Each was prepared to follow where Moses had led.

But where the doors of the universities had opened to Du Bois, the doors of the priesthood were closed to Crummell: the bishops of the Apostolic Church of God told him, "the General Theological Seminary of the Episcopal Church cannot admit a Negro" (*Souls*, p. 137). This was the temptation of Despair; that is, that he would be denied the opportunity to fulfill his prophetic destiny. He fought against this temptation and, again with the help of white men, won out against it. He succeeded in becoming a priest, although the shadow lingered: "even then the burden had not lifted from that heart, for there had passed a glory from the earth" (p. 137). This was his experience of the Fall, of the loss of innocence, paralleling the moment in Du Bois's young life when the white girl's refusal of his visiting-card caused the Veil to fall, or rather to become visible. Perhaps they seem to be differently weighted, a child's experience of refused recognition and a grown man's initial exclusion from his chosen vocation. But Du Bois links them together by reference to Wordsworth's "Intimations." In his own case he invokes the moment when "Shades of the prison-house begin to close / Upon the growing boy" (in George 1904, p. 354). In Crummell's, he invokes the sad knowledge that "where'er I go . . . there hath past away a glory from the earth" (ibid.). Henceforward, each one lives with the knowledge that recognition can be denied at any time—not as a matter of personal failing, but rather because, as Louis Armstrong sings, "my only sin is in my skin" (in "(What Did I Do to Be So) Black and Blue"; Razaf and Waller 1929). Perhaps one can swallow the anger that accompanies the anticipation or actuality of insult; but a bitter aftertaste must surely remain.

Crummell's third trial was the temptation of Doubt. He secured his own congregation in Providence, Rhode Island, but was unsuccessful in sustaining and building it. It was not the voice of Time he now heard, but a mocking voice that asked him, "Oh, colored folks? . . . What do you *expect?*" (*Souls*, p. 138). Thus he was led to "doubt the worth of his life-work,—to doubt the destiny and capability of the race his soul loved because it was his" (ibid.). Self-doubt in this double sense was his unwelcome fellow traveler, and not his alone. Prejudice does not build self-assurance but rather engenders "self-questioning, self-disparagement, and the lowering of ideals" (p. 15)—"an almost morbid sense of personality and a moral hesitancy that is fatal to self-confidence" (p. 127). Almost inevitably, in the minds of black men who bend their minds and wills toward the attainment of "Liberty, Freedom, Opportunity," comes the afterthought: "suppose, after all, the World is right and we are less than men? Suppose this mad impulse is all wrong, some mock mirage from the untrue?" (p. 63). Then the self-sacrifice involved in racial leadership would be pointless and the choice of a spiritual vocation a folly.

Du Bois pictures Crummell as passing through a dark night of the soul. He closed the church door, "sank upon the steps of the chancel, and cast his robe upon the floor and writhed" (p. 138). Our minds might be drawn back by the commonalities of language to the "chamber of death" of young Burghardt, wherein "writhed the world's most piteous thing—a childless mother." Pain does create a link between the one moment and the other; yet a path was open for Crummell that was not available for the grieving Nina. He accepted his failure without losing faith in his mission and, having survived the trial of Doubt, requested a congregation in a city—Philadelphia—with a more substantial Negro population. But a greater trial lay just ahead. He was given a letter of introduction to Bishop Henry Onderdonk, ironically enough a brother of Bishop Benjamin Onderdonk who had refused him admission to the General Theological Seminary. Du Bois pictures Crummell mounting "six white steps" to confront this dignitary—"corpulent, red-faced, and the author of several thrilling tracts on Apostolic Succession" (p. 139). Facing the "thin, ungainly Negro," the Bishop intoned: "'I will receive you into this diocese on one condition: no Negro priest can sit in my church convention, and no Negro must ask for representation there'" (ibid.).

Here we have the classic instance of racial mis-recognition: The self-satisfied white father of the church sits in judgment on the sincere young black cleric and bars him, because he is of the race of Ham, from the rights and rites of Christian freedom. At that moment Crummell stands at the entrance of the Valley of Humiliation, into which he must descend if he wishes to profess his faith in Philadelphia, that city of brotherly love! Du Bois imagines him there, "the frail black figure, nervously twitching his hat before the massive abdomen of Bishop Onderdonk," imagines his eyes wandering to the "swinging glass doors" of a bookcase, within which he might find the "Lives of the Martyrs" and "The Whole Duty of Man." The one doorway represents the other, and he must decide whether to enter. Which way lies martyrdom; what is the whole duty of man? Just then he notices that:

> A little blue fly is trying to cross the yawning keyhole. He marches briskly up to it, peers into the chasm in a surprised sort of way, and rubs his feelers reflectively; then he essays its depths, and finding it bottomless, draws back again. The dark-faced priest finds himself wondering if the fly too has faced its Valley of Humiliation, and if it will plunge into it,—when lo! it spreads its tiny wings and buzzes merrily across, leaving the watcher wingless and alone. (Ibid.)

Like Robert Bruce, defeated in battle, self-doubting and alone but taking inspiration from a spider that again and again struggles to complete its web, Crummell looks away from the man who is devaluing him and sees in the humble, undaunted, and instinctively wise fly his own course of action: "I will never enter your diocese on such terms" (p. 140).

The mise-en-scène is archetypal, and Du Bois means it to be so. "A million swarthy men," he says, would bear "the oppressor's wrong, the proud man's contumely" if "they but know that this were sacrifice and not some meaner thing" (ibid.). But it *is* some meaner thing and accordingly the meanings of renunciation multiply. The vocation of racial leadership requires it, in the plain sense of self-sacrifice as a path to the greater end of collective self-actualization. But Onderdonk was demanding something closer to self-immolation; that is, the sacrifice of self-respect. Confronted with the prospect of this loss, Crummell elected to renounce his chosen ministry. Split in twain, "he turned and passed into the Valley of the Shadow of Death"—which here, too, has new meaning: His was "the world-wandering of a soul in search of itself, the striving of one who vainly sought his place in the world, ever haunted by the shadow of a death that is more than death,—the passing of a soul that has missed its duty" (ibid.). Du Bois, insulted by his classmate, quieted his rage and flew above the Veil. The retreat was at once tactical and self-affirming. It may have left him aloof and often alone, but it did not disarm him for the battle that lay ahead. The parallel situation of inflicted indignity and swallowed anger resulted in a more dangerous and difficult flight for Crummell. He fled across the Atlantic to England and Cambridge, and then to Liberia, but his soul found no rest: "In the fine old air of the English University he heard the millions wailing over the sea. In the wild fever-cursed swamps of West Africa he stood helpless and alone" (p. 141). There but for fortune, we might think on Du Bois's behalf—meaning, there but for a nearly unbreakable will and self-confidence, and for the twist of fate that brought him to Fisk and led to the discovery that his people were no "lost group" before he went on to Harvard and Berlin.

Still, this difference between the two men should not blind us to the common core of their experience—that is, exposure to a racially determined situation of insult and injury; anger contained and risen above; and when the anger is suppressed, a melancholy retreat from the site of the injury. The precision and poignancy of Du Bois's imaginative reconstruction of the meeting between Onderdonk and Crummell speaks to his recognition of this bond. Hence the simple sincerity in his depiction of the priest's return from exile: "The Valley of the Shadow of Death gives few of its pilgrims back to the world. But Alexander Crummell it gave back" (ibid.). More than gave back: As J. R. Oldfield puts it, "Crummell emerged from [his exilic] experiences strengthened and revitalized and more confident than ever of the 'destined superiority of the Negro race.' Crummell's suffering, Du Bois believed, had made him a seer" (1995, p. 1). Now he had the strength to bear the burdens of his vocation. "He bent to all the gibes and prejudices, to all the hatred and discrimination, with that rare courtesy which is the armor of pure souls." And when the time came to lay that burden down, he expressed no regrets. He smiled and said, "The gate is rusty on the hinges" (*Souls*, p. 142). Du Bois mourns his passing, but not with the agonized pain that accompanied the loss of his young son. Ripeness is all. At "star-rise" the gate swings open and death liberates Crummell: "then the soul I loved fled like a flame across the Seas." Where to? Perhaps to "the dim world beyond," if it exists. Imagining it to be so, Du Bois pictures the King, the "dark and pierced Jew, who knows the writhings of the earthly damned," greeting this king among men as he returns from his spiritual wars, and granting him at last the recognition so long denied: "Well done!" (ibid.).

"Of the Coming of John"

African-American identity originates in the Middle Passage, and it seems likely that Du Bois's recurrent use of water imagery is meant to evoke its grim conflation of birth and death. The twofold symbolic meaning of the oceanic, often figured as the great mother from whom we come and to whom we must return, is not limited to this experience, however, and so we might say that the crying waters of *Souls* are both memorial and immemorial. Appropriately, therefore, Crummell's departing soul races across them and John Jones, facing death, turns toward them. But the one is portrayed as being at peace; the other is seeking it. The poetic inscription in "Of the Coming of John," from Elizabeth Barrett Browning's *A Romance of the Ganges,* expresses the young man's longing:

> What bring they 'neath the midnight,
>   Beside the River-sea?
> They bring the human heart wherein
>   No nightly calm can be;
> That droppeth never with the wind,
>   Nor drieth with the dew;
> O calm it, God; thy calm is broad
>   To cover spirits too.
>   The river floweth on. (p. 142)

Jones is a man with a troubled heart; he experiences the contradiction of two-ness to the depth of his being. But unlike the hero-narrator of *Souls,* he cannot contain the contradiction. He is overcome by a murderous rage and, in its aftermath, yearns for the promised calm of the River-sea. Hence, too, the appropriateness of the musical inscription:

> You may bury me in the East,
> You may bury me in the West,
> But I'll hear the trumpet sound on that morning. (p. 157)

In the chapter on the Sorrow Songs, Du Bois pairs "You May Bury Me in the East" with a "heathen melody" passed down from his "grandfather's grandmother," who was stolen by a Dutch trader from her African home; and he characterizes it as a "song of exile" (p. 157). John proves to be an exile in more senses than one, and, when he hears the trumpet of freedom sound, it is in his time of dying.

Sorrow has been our more or less constant companion as we have traveled through the world within the Veil. Its habitual companion, the black anger generated by white supremacy, has been there as well. Viewed from one angle, the narrative as a whole is suffused by and gives sublimated expression to it; viewed from another, it is a layered defense against it; viewed from a third, it is marked by symptomatic moments in which the anger breaks through. Consequently we may say that the two-ness of Du Bois's authorial persona and racial identity is affectively overdetermined by his struggle against an underlying and unwelcome rage, an ambivalent battle in which it is maddeningly difficult to distinguish between the temptation of Hatred and the demand for retributive justice. Du Bois lives out one side of the dilemma; he rises above the desire for revenge. John Jones lives out the other side; he enacts it. We are left to interpret the meaning of this enactment.

But perhaps this prefatory statement is too condensed or even question-begging. What, we might ask, is the relationship between this chapter and the rest of the text, and between its protagonist and the author?

The first question admits of two quite different answers. On the one hand, "Of the Coming of John" is plainly synoptic. John Jones advances from the happy-go-lucky ways associated with the descendants of plantation slaves we encountered in Dougherty County to the gravity, dissatisfaction, and sensitivity to insult that accompany education and enlightenment. Born in the South, he ascends to the North before reimmersing himself in Southern life. His return is occasioned by a painful instance of mis-recognition; and, once he has returned home, he is prepared to trod the well-worn path of self-sacrifice. But he finds that his education has alienated him from his native community as surely as from his innocent good-humor. More fatefully and fatally, he is trapped between the situationally imposed requirement of accommodation to white supremacy and a hard-to-master inclination to revolt and revenge. He suffers from double, or more than double, consciousness. John finally breaks out of his doubled bondage when, in a rage, he kills a white man, a childhood friend, who is sexually assaulting his sister. His story comes to its sad end with a lynching party approaching and then surrounding him. Riding at its head is the slain man's "broad shouldered gray-haired" (*Souls*, p. 144) father, the local judge and patriarch, kith and kin to "gray-haired gentleman" who stood "with hate in his eyes" to witness the dawn of freedom. Thus the tale functions as an aesthetically and affectively enhanced expression of the major themes in *Souls* as a whole. For this reason, we can reverse interpretive perspective and, beginning with "Of the Coming of John," generate the world of *Souls* from it. In short, it is at once the capstone of the text's narrative arch and its phenomenological kernel.

On the other hand, "Of the Coming of John" decenters or at least problematizes the larger narrative. Restraint of anger and renunciation of violence are fundamental to the value-structure of *Souls*; yet in the end John Jones lacks this restraint and is unable to forgo the use of force. To be sure, he dies for his sins, if this is how we are to view them. But we can scarcely condemn him for his intemperate action, even if he holds himself accountable. He is, indeed, so sympathetically portrayed that we are far more likely to identify with him than to stand in judgment of him. His final, anguished rebellion against the indignities and brutalities of white supremacy sends a charge of righteous wrath through the length and breadth of the territory Du Bois has opened up to us. What appeared as embedded elements in the collective life of black folk when we first encountered them—the racialized oedipal drama just alluded to, what we characterized as a courtroom scene in "Of the Training of Black Men," the Black Belt farmer with his veiled anger at white brutality, the lineage of rebellious ancestors—now seem more like fissures produced by the building up of internal pressure. We might even be reminded of a transitional moment in *Invisible Man*. The nameless protagonist has been tricked, humiliated, and abused by ill-intended paternal authorities, black and white, with this result:

> Somewhere beneath the load of emotion-freezing ice which my life had conditioned my brain to produce, a spot of black anger glowed. . . . A remote explosion had occurred somewhere . . . and it had caused the ice cap to melt and shift the slightest bit. (Ellison [1952] 1989, p. 259)

In a similar fashion, the explosion of John Jones's pent-up anger causes the topography of *Souls* to shift. That is, we see it from yet another angle.

Perhaps the shift in perspective is lessened if we interpret "Of the Coming of John" as a cautionary tale, a warning to black people not to choose the path of revolt and revenge.[5] If so—and this brings us to the question of the relationship between author and protagonist—it might be read as an internal admonition. Although John Jones is not Du Bois, Du Bois is recognizable in him. Jones's father is never mentioned in the tale told of him, mirroring the absence of a father in Du Bois's own life. Just as it was Mary Silvina who supported her son's educational ambitions, so it was Jones's "mother who wanted to send him off to school" (*Souls*, p. 143). The words used to describe the falling of the Veil in Jones's life—"he first noticed now the oppression that had not seemed oppression before, differences that erstwhile seemed natural, restraints and slights that in his boyhood days had gone unnoticed or greeted with a laugh" (p. 146)—echo the painful moment in Du Bois's when he recognized that "he was different from the others; or like, mayhap, in heart and life and longing, but shut out from their world by a vast veil" (p. 10). When Jones turns homeward, resigned to pursue his "manifest destiny"—that is, to do his duty and try to help "solve the Negro problems" in his place of birth—he says to himself (prophetically, as it turns out), "I will go in to the King, which is not according to the law; and if I perish, I perish" (p. 148).[6] Du Bois had written these same words, taken from the Book of Esther, to himself at the end of that late night reverie in Berlin in which he articulated and confronted his own destiny.[7] Short of such a regal audience, however, each man must humble himself before a local white "superior." In Alexandria, Du Bois is offered a meal by the commissioner, from whom he is asking permission to open a school. But he must wait until the family has eaten, and then he eats alone (p. 48). Jones, likewise seeking permission to open a school in his hometown of Altamaha, Georgia, arrives at the front door of the local judge and is told, "Go 'round to the kitchen door, John, and wait" (p. 150).[8]

Yet both men are highly cultured, more sophisticated and discerning than the white fathers to whom they must bend their knees. They also have tastes in common, specifically Richard Wagner's opera *Lohengrin*, of which Du Bois wrote: "[Wagner] uses myth, he uses poetry, he uses sound and sight, music and color. And he uses human actors on a stage. The result is beautiful, as in the bride-song, but it is more than that: it rises to a great and glorious drama, which at times reaches the sublime" (1936, p. 130). Finally, each of them, in treading the path of renunciation, walked quite alone, separated by education and a certain inward reserve from the easy familiarity and emotional expressiveness of ordinary black folk.

There are differences between author and protagonist as well: Jones's southern versus Du Bois's northern origins; Jones's youthful plantation-hand attitudes and affects versus Du Bois's New England propriety; Jones's difficulty in disciplining his mind and cultivating his intelligence versus Du Bois's precocious intellectuality. Most of all, there is Jones's tragic flaw, his inability to master his anger, compared to Du Bois's almost unwavering self-discipline. But the opposition between mastering anger and being mastered by it is not so easily split apart into separate selves. It is better seen as an internal struggle, in this instance played out between the author and his invention.[9] For the impulse of revolt and revenge was not foreign to Du Bois. Although partially sublimated into forceful advocacy of his people's cause, it could not be extirpated. Hence we may fairly say that here we are witness to a return of the repressed, with the result that the "unreconciled strivings" (*Souls*, p. 11), the "double life" and "double thoughts" (p. 127) in African-American identity are writ large. And thus written, these dualities signify the fusion of anger and melancholy we first glimpsed in the visiting-card incident. When Du Bois characterizes "Of the Coming of John" as "a tale twice told but seldom written" (p. 5), he may well have had Nathaniel Hawthorne's well-known *Twice-Told Tales* in mind; but the original articulation, in Shakespeare's *The Life and Death of King John*, is more to the point:

> There's nothing in this world can make me joy.
> Life is as tedious as a twice-told tale
> Vexing the dull ear of a drowsy man;
> And bitter shame hath spoiled the sweet world's taste,
> That it yields naught but shame and bitterness. (act 3, scene 4, lines 108–111)

The words are spoken by Lewis, the French Dauphin, after he has been defeated in battle. For Jones, life's tediousness is the eternal and depressing return of the insults and contumely of white supremacy. Unable to escape them, he comes to know the defeats and bitter shame that spoil the sweet world's taste. He falls victim to the temptation of Despair that both Crummell and Du Bois were able to rise above.

Jones's life began innocently enough. Filled with "bubbling good-nature and genuine satisfaction with the world," he was judged a "good boy" by the white folk of Altamaha (*Souls,* p. 143). No hint of two souls in one breast in this young man! Yet in a sense, his identity had already been doubled. His childhood companion was also named John, a "fair-haired" boy, the son of the local dignitary, Judge Henderson. Black John is white John's namesake. He was named after him. But the nominal identity is deceptive. The childhood companions are destined to play different and unequal social roles. The judge sends his son off to Princeton—"It'll make a man of him," so he hopes—with the expectation his son would return home, become the town's mayor and maybe, someday, even the governor of Georgia. By contrast, after Jones has gone north to school, the judge says to Jones's younger sister Jennie, "Too bad, too bad your mother sent him off,—it will spoil him" (p. 144). The name assigned to Jones was intended to signify his dependence and inferiority. He is to remain a "good boy" while his erstwhile playmate is to become a man. Or, to state it in Hegelian terms, two individuals, each equally a self in the abstract (I = I, John = John), are to take up roles in a relationship of lordship and bondage determined by race (White I > Black I, John Henderson > John Jones). The middle term (>) in this relationship of inequality is precisely the Veil. John Jones's fate is sealed from the moment that he recognizes its presence. This is what "spoils" him for the performance of his preassigned social duties.

Even after he went north to Johnstown and the Wells Institute, Jones was not eager to taste the fruit of the tree of racial knowledge.[10] One might say of him, "when ignorance is bliss, 'tis folly to be wise." Why not hold fast to the "time when meadow, grove and stream / The earth, and every common sight . . . did seem / Aparell'd in celestial light," even if this was only the "glory and the freshness of a dream"? In this instance, the dream is racially specific: Du Bois explicitly identifies young John Jones with the mythic happy darky of the Old South.[11] He is heir to the "joyous abandon and playfulness which we are wont to associate with the plantation Negro" (p. 85). In the white racial imaginary, this figure is overlaid on the equally mythic blissfully ignorant child, especially the pre-oedipal male child for whom his mother's body is meadow, grove, and stream, and who does not yet fear the Father or know that he is destined to live within the Law. The latter myth helps to sustain the former. This is not to deny—as is true of most myths, as is true of dreams—that there is a fragment of reality captured in them. But infantile ignorance is blissful only intermittently. Even the beloved young Burghardt's moods changed like the sky "from sparkling laughter to darkening frowns" (p. 132); and the stereotypical good-nature of the slaves and their heirs is a second nature, not human nature. What in the racial myth is taken to be the primordial identity of black people is rather the product of conditioning within a historically specific master-slave relationship. Sometimes this second nature is merely a mask, a disguise or protective veil formed in conformity to the Veil, allowing for a possibly advantageous invisibility. In *Invisible Man*, for example, the protagonist's grandfather, who had seemed to be the very model of racial deference, says on his deathbed: "I never told you, but our life is a war and I have been a traitor all my born days, a spy in the enemy's country ever since I gave up my gun in the Reconstruction. . . . I want you to overcome 'em with yeses, undermine 'em with grins, agree 'em to death and destruction, let 'em swoller you till they vomit or burst wide open" (Ellison [1952] 1989, p. 16). But sometimes the mask, once assumed, adheres, and becomes nearly organic. The role is internalized, the slave identifies with the master, the distinction between dream life and waking life is weakened. This, too, albeit in quite a different way, has its advantages. For the dreamer, John Jones in this instance, oppression does not seem like oppression, restraints and slights can go unnoticed or be laughed off (*Souls*, p. 146). Life goes by, all innocence and untroubled sleep. But once Jones awakened and the dream dissolved, his bubbling good-nature was replaced by a predisposition to anger and a "vague bitterness" (ibid.). He recognized when he was not being recognized; peace of mind became a thing of the past; and, if he listened carefully, he, too, would have heard the voice of Time intoning, "Entbehren sollst du, sollst entbehren."

Jones's awakening was the result of a benevolent paternal intervention. The faculty at the Institute finally had enough of his tardiness, carelessness, poor lessons and neglected work, and noise and disorder and decided to suspend him (pp. 144–145). The young man was surprised and confused when the "gray-haired" dean told him the news. Childlike innocence had come up against the Law of the Father. It took him only a moment to understand that he had been truly seen, not mis-recognized, and to grasp the seriousness of the encounter: "But you won't tell mammy and sister,—you won't write mammy, now will you? For if you don't I'll go out into the city and work, and come back next term and show you something" (p. 145). Whatever Judge Henderson may have thought, Jones had been sent north to become a man among men, to bring honor to himself and his family, and in time to return to his community as exemplar and educator. If he failed, he would not only disgrace himself but also bring dishonor and disappointment to his mother and sister. The failure to gain recognition at the Institute would be wounding to those he loved the most; shame would be compounded by guilt. Knowing this, he struck a bargain: He would undertake the hard work of self-transformation in exchange for a second chance to make his mother proud. So doing, he paid the inevitable price: "the serious look that crept over his boyish face that afternoon never left it again" (ibid.).

He succeeded in this great undertaking. He advanced from preparatory school to college, entered into a "world of thought" and made that world his own, and in due time won the prize of graduation. But now he hesitated. He was destined to return to Altamaha, but he "found himself shrinking from the choked and narrow life of his native town" with a "nameless dread" (p. 146). We readers recognize the foreshadowing this feeling expresses, the calamity that awaits an educated, proud, and independent black man who dares to carry the Gospel of Sacrifice into the nether regions of the white supremacist South. Jones knows only that he is reluctant to turn homeward and—as fate would have it—seizes the opportunity to go north with the Institute quartet for the summer vacation.[12] He finds himself in New York, amid shifting crowds that remind him of the sea (Altamaha was on the Georgia coast). Without really thinking about it, he follows the flow, including more particularly a "tall, light-haired young man and a little talkative lady" (ibid.). Again, we see the pieces of the puzzle coming together. Jones, however, simply finds himself entering a theater and buying what turns out to be a reserved seat ticket. Behind him, a young white woman says to her male escort, "you must not lynch the colored gentleman simply because he is in your way." The man responds with a defense of white and black relations in the South, including his recollection of the "little Negro" who was his "closest play-fellow," and who was named after him (ibid.). Jones, in a "half-maze minding the scene," is apparently unaware of this interaction, and of the white man's anger and distress when he sees a Negro sitting next to the orchestra seats he had reserved.

A true tragic hero, Jones is being carried along on a tide of fortune toward his eventual doom. Henderson, his white alter ego, embodies and articulates the childhood innocence and adult hypocrisy of Southern race relations. He remembers his little Negro playmate nostalgically but cannot abide having a black man sitting next to him. He instructs an usher to arrange for the interloper's removal. Meanwhile the performance—of Wagner's *Lohengrin*—begins. Jones is rapt. He doesn't notice that his arm touched the lady's and that she recoiled. He feels the power of the music within him and his mind drifts:

> If he but had some master-work, some life-service, hard,—aye, bitter hard, but without the cringing and sickening servility, without the cruel hurt that hardened his heart and soul. When at last a soft sorrow crept across the violins, there came to him the vision of far-off home,—the great eyes of his sister, and the dark drawn face of his mother. And his heart sank below the waters, even as the sea-sand sinks by the shores of Altamaha, only to be lifted aloft again with the last ethereal wail of the swan that quivered and faded away into the sky. (p. 147)

Here Du Bois and Jones are almost perfectly fused. Mother-love and the love of Wagner's music unite them aesthetically; the acceptance of the imperative of renunciation, hard work, and self-sacrifice unites them spiritually; and neither of them can tolerate the servility the white masters require of their black bondsmen. The crying waters—at once the voice of Du Bois's heart and the voice of the sea—with which *Souls* began are now the waters of *Lohengrin* and the remembered waters of Altamaha, into which Jones's heart sinks.

Then comes the decisive moment of mis-recognition, the childhood visiting-card incident transformed into the confrontation of two men. The usher has returned and asks Jones to follow him. Rising, he

> looked full into the face of the fair-haired young man. For the first time the young man recognized his dark boyhood playmate, and John knew that it was the Judge's son. The white John started, lifted his hand, and then froze in his chair; the black John smiled lightly, then grimly, and followed the usher down the aisle. (Ibid.)

There is a rough, painful and infuriating, equality in this confrontation. Although the Law of the Father dictates the removal of John Jones from his seat, the two men, like the unbound selves that initially encounter each other in the Hegelian tale, see each other eye (I) to eye (I). Henderson is now the one caught in confusion; his lifted hand and frozen body reveal him as suspended between childhood intimacy and adult antipathy. Jones's light smile mirrors the hand gesture, his grim smile a quick putting away of childish things that have no relevance to adult realities. Angry he must be, but like the young Du Bois, like Crummell with Bishop Onderdonk, he restrains his anger and walks away—out of the Valley of Humiliation and, all unknowing, into the Valley of the Shadow of Death. Freed of the illusion that he can ignore the color-line in the North, he accepts his "manifest destiny" and writes to his mother and sister that he is coming home.

The black folk of Altamaha were prepared to greet John in the manner of a conquering hero, but they barely recognized the "silent, cold" man who stepped off the train (p. 148). Partially John was gloomily preoccupied with the indignity of riding in the "Jim Crow" car; partially he was oppressed by a sense of the "sordidness and narrowness" of his hometown. He was impaled on the hyphen of his African-American identity.[13] Not recognized as fully human in the white world, he was alienated from the black world as well; and he experiences his duality as a kind of soul-sickness. He is perhaps a kindred spirit to Alexander Crummell or to Du Bois without his high self-confidence and his elective affinities with the sorrow songs. Or, to revert to a Hegelian trope, he is all Enlightenment and no Superstition (Hegel [1807] 1977, p. 329). He is committed to racial progress and uplift, but he has lost his connection to the spiritual—religious—wellsprings of his culture. Consequently his first speech to the community, gathered in the Baptist Church, was a disaster. Speaking "slowly and methodically" of the broad ideals of "human brotherhood and destiny," of industrial schools and philanthropic work, he left his audience as cold as they found him to be. Worse still, he concluded by denouncing religious bickering and deprecating the value of religion altogether. "What difference does it make whether a man be baptized in river or wash-bowl, or not at all? Let's leave all that little-ness, and look higher" (*Souls*, p. 149). The result was predictable, if not to Jones himself: "A painful hush seized the crowded mass. Little had they understood of what he said, for he spoke an unknown tongue, save the last word about baptism; that they knew, and they sat very still while the clock ticked" (ibid.).[14] He had denigrated the faith of the fathers, the Law of the Father as black folk had legislated it for themselves. Fittingly, "an old bent man arose . . . and climbed straight up into the pulpit":

> He seized the Bible with his rough, huge hands; twice he raised it inarticu-late, and then fairly burst into words, with rude and awful eloquence. He quivered, swayed, and bent; then arose aloft in perfect majesty, till the peo-ple moaned and wept, wailed and shouted, and a wild shrieking arose from the corners where all the pent-up feeling of the hour gathered itself and rushed into the air. (pp. 149–150)

We are carried back to Alexandria, Tennessee, and the time when Du Bois first experienced "the frenzy of a Negro revival in the untouched back-woods of the South" (p. 120). But where he had simply been a newcomer who was fairly overwhelmed by the "pythian madness," Jones was being "held up to scorn and scathing denunciation for trampling on the true Reli-gion." He recognized himself in the old man's contempt: "he realized with amazement that all unknowingly he had put rough, rude hands on some-thing this little world held sacred" (ibid.). His "rough, rude hands" parallel the old man's "rough, huge hands"; and in this hand-to-hand contest he was necessarily the loser. Silently he walked out of the room and to the bluff overlooking the sea (see also Fontenot 2003, pp. 142–143).

The members of his community did not understand the Gospel of Sacri-fice Jones was teaching, but only the Gospels preached by the old man. For his part, Jones never "knew clearly what the old man said" (*Souls*, p. 150). Each spoke a language the other did not understand; the mutual alienation is, at this moment, complete. Du Bois does not disavow either side of this cultural antithesis. Rather, his authorial persona contains them both, in the sense and hope of merging "his double self into a better and truer self" (p. 11). Yet the story is told of John Jones. He is the one who experi-ences the pain of renunciation and is, in that regard, akin to his creator. And despite his defeat and even humiliation at the hands of the church father, his spiritual vocation is affirmed. His sister Jennie follows him when he leaves the church, offering consolation and seeking it. He looks at her "sor-rowfully, remembering with sudden pain how little thought he had given her" (p. 150). Here, Du Bois implies, is another hazard of enlightenment. In carrying forward one's missionary work, one may lose not only an integral connection to the folk community but also to the internal wellsprings of human sympathy and love. The mission can displace the people for whom it is undertaken.[15] But in this instance, Jones is called back to himself and to the familial ties that bind. He holds Jennie, who cries out her sorrow at her brother's pain, and her tears quiet his heart.

In this scene of reconciliation, we might feel the presence of Du Bois and his mother, whose sadness he shared and who supported his educational ambitions. The substitution of sister for mother would fall within this affective configuration. We might even see the role of sister as joining the positions of mother and daughter, for as elder brother in a family without a father John commands something like paternal respect. Jennie asks him, "Does it make every one—unhappy when they study and learn lots of things?" (p. 150). It does, he acknowledges. "And, John, are you glad you studied?", she continues. He is, he replies, "slowly but positively." Unhappiness is the cross willingly borne by those who walk the path of renunciation. "I wish I was unhappy . . . I think I am, a little," Jennie says, simultaneously affirming his choice of vocation and suggesting that she will walk in his footsteps. In this way, Du Bois gives Jones an emotional grounding for his educational work.[16]

Like Du Bois in Alexandria, Jones in Altamaha wishes to open a school; and like Du Bois, he needs the permission of the local embodiment of the Law of the White Father, in this case Judge Henderson. And once again he breaks the Law, by going to the judge's front door instead of the back. Put in his place for his impropriety, he muses to himself: "What on earth had come over him? Every step he made offended some one. He had come to save his people, and before he left the depot he had hurt them. He sought to teach them at the church, and had outraged their deepest feelings. He had schooled himself to be respectful to the Judge, and then blundered into his front door" (p. 150). We might say he had developed a mind of his own and, in the process, had lost the instinct for deference, whether to the mores of his own community or to the authority of white folk. Yet his missteps are not all of equal gravity. His relations with black folk were marred by his loss of innocence and of affective connection to community values. His faux pas with the judge is more in the nature of a Freudian slip; that is, an unconsciously determined forgetting of a conscious intention. Jones has schooled himself to accept the role of humble petitioner for the judge's favor, but his suppressed rebellion against the ritual of humiliation guides his feet to the front instead of the kitchen door.

The ensuing mise-en-scène is set in apposition to the one between Crummell and Bishop Onderdonk. The bishop would prefer to have no truck with black folk, while the judge is the archetypal benevolent white father. "You know I'm a friend of your people," he reminds John: "I like colored people, and sympathize with all of their reasonable aspirations; but you and I both know, John, that in this country the Negro must remain subordinate, and can never expect to be the equal of white men" (pp. 150–151).

Responsibility, not equality, is the law of the land. And so the question is posed: "I knew your father, John, he belonged to my brother, and he was a good Nigger. Well—well, are you going to be like him, or are you going to try to put fool ideas of rising and equality into these folks' heads, and make them discontented and unhappy?" (p. 151). The answer, one might think, is obvious. Jones is a free man, with a mind of his own. His father figures, if any, are his teachers at the Wells Institute. Returned to Altamaha, he is no longer his father's son, but rather father to himself. And he is precisely about the business of making his people discontented and unhappy. One might imagine him echoing Crummell's reply to Onderdonk, when the bishop demanded the acceptance of racial inferiority as a condition for occupying a pulpit in Philadelphia: "I will never enter your diocese on such terms" . . . "I will never open a school on such terms," we hear him saying. But Jones swallows his pride, and his anger along with it: "I am going to accept the situation, Judge Henderson," he replies. But again, the response was given "with a brevity that did not escape the keen old man" (ibid.). A hint of "social equality" slipped through the veil of "social responsibility." Despite this warning signal, however, the judge is as good as his word and, a friend of John's people (!), gives him conditional approval to open a school.

Meanwhile John Henderson has returned home as well. The judge wants him to stay and become a leader of the community, but he is restless and does not wish to abide by his father's commands. Like John Jones, he, too, has been corrupted by his exposure to the great world beyond Altamaha; and he is even more reluctant to defer to patriarchal authority. For his part, Judge Henderson has been irritated by his son, who had been so insensitive as to characterize *his* little kingdom, Altamaha, as a "God-forgotten town with nothing but mud and Negroes" (p. 151); and on the fateful day, the judge was on the edge of confronting the young man. But their conversation is cut short by company, which includes the postmaster. This local worthy was keen to report that "John is livenin' things up at the darky school," that he heard "somethin' about his givin' talks on the French Revolution, equality, and such like. He's what I call a dangerous Nigger" (p. 151). His accusation appears to be a malicious rumor rather than fact. When questioned by the judge, the postmaster admits that he's not personally heard the young man say "anything out of the way," although his wife had heard "a lot of rot" from their girl, Sally (p. 151). Still, the details are beside the point: "I don't need to heah a Nigger that won't say 'sir' to a white man" (p. 152). In short, John Jones is an uppity nigger whose behavior, if not the content of his teaching, points toward a rebellious upsetting of the racial order. And then the offense is doubled, or more than doubled. Learning the identity of the offending party, John Henderson angrily reports the theater incident: "it's the darky that tried to force himself into a seat next to the lady I was escorting" (p. 152). This misrepresentation, paralleling the original scene of mis-recognition, sexualizes the situation. John Jones is now doubly an outlaw. He is presumed to be encouraging rebellion against the white supremacist order of things, and he stands accused of symbolically violating the racialized incest taboo—of forcing himself upon a white woman. This is, of course, the fantasy of the white man, who projects his sexual desire into his racial Other.

From this point forward the story is one of the loss of self-control and the intervention of chance; that is, apparent chance as the outward form of inward necessity and fate. It has, in other words, the archetypal features of classical tragedy. The judge had been skeptical of the postmaster's report, but he was already "nettled" with his own son. His anger is easily displaced onto the other John and, with a "half-smothered oath," he goes off to shut down the school (p. 152). His son, whom Du Bois claims is "not a bad fellow, just a little spoiled and self-indulgent, and as headstrong as his proud father," is at loose ends (ibid.). His restlessness is accentuated by the lack of "a girl worth getting up a respectable flirtation with" in Altamaha (ibid.).Wandering aimlessly toward the pines, he spots John's sister Jennie on her way home and notices her "trim little body" (p. 153). Sexually stimulated, he asks her for a kiss and—when she, frightened, passes him by—abandons restraint and chases after her.

For his part, John Jones had been struggling with his educational mission. Like the young Du Bois in Alexandria, he found the black community to be dubious about his efforts: "the parents were careless, the children irregular and dirty, and books, pencils, and slates largely missing" (p. 152). But he could detect signs of progress and was in a cheerful, patient mood when the judge, red-faced and angry, burst into the classroom: "John, this school is closed. . . . Clear out! I'll lock the door myself!" (ibid.). In front of the children he had been teaching, Jones is treated like a disobedient child. Once again, he has been humiliated. He has been stripped of his manhood, symbolically castrated. He is powerless in the situation; there is nothing he can do but walk away—and yet he is ashamed. He can't face his mother and so veers off toward the pines, hoping to break the news first to his sister. He is broken as well. Self-restraint shattered, "the fierce, buried anger surged up into his throat. He waved his arms and hurried wildly up the path" (p. 153)— no longer the path of renunciation for, to use the relevant juridical term, he was no longer responsible for his actions. Hurrying forward in a daze, he is started "as from a dream" by a frightened cry. He sees "his dark sister struggling in the arms of a tall and fair-haired man." The climactic moment has arrived: "He said not a word, but seizing a fallen limb, struck him with all the pent-up hatred of his great black arm; and the body lay white and still beneath the pines, all bathed in sunshine and in blood" (ibid.).

The judge's unjustified wrath and his son's rapacious lust lead, with tragic necessity, to John Jones's ultimate act of revolt and revenge. The white man who we know falsely accused him of racial-sexual impropriety is assaulting his sister. John strikes him down in what might seem to be a justifiable rage. But Du Bois has already painted him as irrationally enraged and emotionally out of control. His rebellious action is not intellectually and morally mediated; and, despite the provocation, it might be judged excessive. Enacting this judgment, Jones cannot affirm his action. He is, rather, in a kind of fugue state. His anger is left behind with the corpse, which he had looked at "dreamily." This mirrors the distracted state of mind he was in earlier, when he was started "as from a dream" by his sister's frightened cries. He returns home and tells his mother that he is going away, that he is "going to be free" (p. 153). She asks him if he is going North again and he, looking out "where the North Star glistened pale upon the water," answered yes. But it is the oceanic mirroring of the North Star he will follow, and not the star itself. Still in a dissociative daze, he returns to the scene of his—what? crime? rebellion? There he awaits the death that will set him free. He hears the "faint sweet melody" of the sea and, as if in counterpoint, the earth trembling "with the tramp of horses and murmur of angry men" (ibid). Joining his voice to this threnody, he hums the "Song of the Bride" from *Lohengrin,* the opera he had happened upon in New York.[17] Music, ocean, and death are fused into the idealized pre-oedipal mother, the matrix of death's other kingdom, the great consolation for the trials and tribulations of life within the Veil. At last he sees the lynch mob approaching, "sweeping like a storm" and led by "that haggard white-haired man, whose eyes flashed red with fury" (p. 154). "Then, as the storm burst around him, he rose slowly to his feet and turned his closed eyes to the Sea. And the world whistled in his ears" (p. 154). The rebellious black man must pay the price for violating the Law. Yet, with Sam Hose in mind, we might see the lynching as a crucifixion.

Du Bois leaves his tragic hero suspended in that moment. There is a trace of ambiguity in the manner of his dying. One might picture him plunging into the seas, returning in this way to the Great Mother and evading the final enactment of the Law of the White Father.[18] But the lynch mob is depicted as sweeping toward him "like a storm" and, in the end, the "storm burst around him." He is surrounded. Nor had he offered any resistance, but only watched the Judge approaching and wondered if he had "the coiling twisted rope" (p. 154). We are led to imagine the noose tightening around his neck and the final moment when the "world whistled in his ears." Which is to say, Du Bois sets up the scene as a hanging; and we know that lynching was very much on his mind. Yet the distinction between being murdered and suicide is not hard and fast; and we might even find a certain nobility in the manner in which Jones accepted his fate. Standing there beside the River-sea, he is, at last, calm. His rage is spent; he will greet death as a groom meets his bride. With the bride-song merged with the music of the sea, the moment might even be thought sublime. At the least, he has already risen above the Veil; and from this height, when he looks down at the enraged white man riding toward him, he feels only pity (ibid.). He,

Jones, has renounced hatred; the judge is driven by it. Jones will honor the Law: an eye (I) for an eye (I), a life for a life. The judge will continue to live in violation of it, until his time of judgment comes.

As we stand witness to John Jones in his time of dying, we are necessarily reminded of the death of Jesus Christ, whose crucifixion was both a self-sacrifice and a judicial murder, and perhaps of Sam Hose, who was also crucified by a lynch mob. But we might wonder if Du Bois had another coming of John in mind, with another fatal and fateful conclusion—John Brown's raid on Harper's Ferry. In his biography of Brown, written some six years after *Souls*, Du Bois characterizes the public response to the raid this way: "A great surging throb of sympathy arose and swept the world. That John Brown was legally a law-breaker and a murderer all men knew. But wider and wider circles were beginning dimly and more clearly to recognize that his lawlessness was in obedience to the highest call of self-sacrifice for the welfare of his fellow men" ([1909] 1962, p. 356). John Brown did with forethought and willingly what John Jones did without thought and at least half against his will. Each paid the price for his violent action with his life. But Jones merely escaped from the vale of tears, while Brown rose to glory. He is reported to have said: "I can trust God with both the time and the manner of my death, believing, as I now do, that for me at this time to seal my testimony for God and humanity with my blood will do vastly more toward advancing the cause I have earnestly endeavored to promote, than all I have done in my life before" (ibid., p. 357).

In August 1906, the men and women of the Niagara movement met at Harper's Ferry. In the early morning light, they "marched barefoot on dewy grass with candles cupped against the morning breeze in silent procession down the steep road from their hilltop residence halls to pay homage to Brown's memory in the old arsenal" (Lewis 1993, p. 329). And at the meeting's conclusion they heard these words:

> We do not believe in violence, neither in the despised violence of the raid nor the lauded violence of the soldier, nor the barbarous violence of the mob, but we do believe in John Brown, in that incarnate spirit of justice, that hatred of a lie, that willingness to sacrifice money, reputation, and life itself on the altar of right. And here on the scene of John Brown's martyrdom we reconsecrate ourselves, our honor, our property to the final emancipation of the race which John Brown died to make free. (Lewis 1995, p. 369)

In this way, Du Bois drew the moral of the twice-told, or more than twice-told, tale of John.

The Wayfarer

Before completing our journey through the lifeworld of *Souls*, let us pause to consider one last time the relationship between author and text and to take up the question, unavoidable but thus far avoided, of the relationship between Du Bois and the God of his fathers.

Selfhood, Mis-recognition, and Renunciation (Reprise)

Although Du Bois suffered the wounds of John Jones and was animated by the will to self-sacrifice and defiant spirit of John Brown, his passions did not lead him to travel the road of revolt and revenge. His conscience—a self-restraint grounded in deeply rooted moral principle—precluded that choice. We might even see him in the image of the Stoic empjeror Marcus Aurelius, one of the souls with whom he communed above the Veil (*Souls*, p. 74), or in that of Epictetus, the Roman ex-slave and Stoic philosopher with whom Marcus Aurelius is historically paired. Of Stoicism, Hegel says, "in thinking, I *am free*, because I am not in an *other*, but remain simply and solely in communion with myself, and the object, which is for me the *essential* being, is in undivided unity my being-for-myself" (Hegel [1807] 1977, p. 120). Stoicism is the form of consciousness that emerges from and "has a negative attitude towards the lord and bondsman relationship": "whether on the throne or in chains, in the utter dependence of individual existence, its aim is to be free" (ibid., p. 121).[19] Du Bois was perhaps too passionate to be a Stoic in the full sense; but then again, don't we see in Stoicism itself an internal battle for peace of mind? When Epictetus guides his auditors toward the path of mental tranquility, isn't it because that path is not so easily found and followed? In other words, when Du Bois brings himself before us as a father mourning the death of his son; in the image of Crummell, a man worthy of being his father; or in the opposite image of John Jones, the man he was determined not to become, we are witness both to a stoic capacity to rise above the temptations of a rebellious spirit and the temptations themselves.

Du Bois characterized Crummell as facing the three temptations of Hate, Despair, and Doubt. These are inherent in the problem of the color-line. The paradigmatic interaction of white and black along that line is recognition denied. That denial is something more and other than a simple nay-saying. In itself, it is an interpellation and a demand for compliance—"niggerization," in Ossie Davis's unflinchingly direct characterization. To repeat: "The process of niggerization is always a two-sided one, shared by two consenting individuals, one black, one white. The price of consent exacted from the black person, however, can be his life, livelihood, and all that he holds dear" (Davis and Dee 1998, p. 44). Sometimes the ritual can be interrupted. One turns away, as Du Bois did in the visiting-card incident. But even then there is a wound, and the wounding generates anger, even rage. The anger is unavoidable and, initially, self-preservative. It is the affective force that must be employed if the negation of selfhood is to be negated, whether by engaging the would-be master or even in refusing the engagement. But the danger here—illustrated by the parable of John Jones—is that anger itself can negate the self, overwhelm or undermine it, so that action becomes blind and mindless. Alternatively, anger can grow into a settled attitude of hatred; and hatred, Du Bois believed, is a disease of the soul, an inner cancer or corruption. The imperative is therefore the sublimation of rage and anger into such traits of character as determination, perseverance, tenacity, steadfastness. This is Stoicism on the ground level, a hard-to-achieve union of self-restraint and disciplined self-assertion; and Du Bois could rightly pride himself in being, in just this sense, a free man. Still, he paid a price for this great accomplishment: "I did not seek white acquaintances, I let them make the advances and they therefore thought me arrogant. In a sense I was, but after all I was in fact rather desperately hanging on to my self-respect" (*Autobiography*, p. 283).

Du Bois's aloofness and reserve are as distant from Despair as restraint and disciplined self-assertion are from Hate. But in the one case as in the other, there is a relationship. Although aloofness can be quite without affect, a kind of numbed self-enclosure, Du Bois's self-protective and self-restorative retreat from the hurts and humiliations inflicted on black folk was unmistakably tinged with melancholy. We think of him "sadly musing" as he rode to Nashville in the Jim Crow car (*Souls*, p. 54), or caught in the spell of death and decay at the Waters-Loring plantation in Dougherty County (p. 81), or lamenting the loss of his infant son. His sorrow did not cross that other line, the one marking the boundary between life and death; but his portrayal of John Jones as the young man stands ready to make the passage reveals that he knew about death as a remedy for despair. We can imagine the ease with which he could identify with Faust, who was tempted in just this way: "The flood tide of my spirit ebbs away / To open seas I am shown forth by signs, / Before my feet the mirror-water shines, / And I am lured to new shores by new day" (Goethe 1965, p. 30). But unlike Faust, Du Bois was not tormented by questions about the meaning of life or the purpose of his own existence. Even when heartsick from the loss of his son, grief does not slip over into despair: "I shirk not. I long for work. I pant for a life full of striving" (*Souls*, p. 132).

The temptation of Doubt is also intrinsic to the experience of the Veil. Black people striving for "Liberty, Freedom, Opportunity" are shadowed by the afterthought, "Suppose, after all, the World is right and we are less than men? Suppose this mad impulse within is all wrong, some mock mirage of the untrue?" (p. 63). One of the components of double-consciousness is just such self-doubt. Individually, Du Bois was not much subject to it. He was blessed with an extraordinary self-confidence. He did not, in any fundamental way, doubt his own abilities nor the rightness of his call to racial leadership. Did he, however, worry about the cultural capacities of black folk? Did he, standing before the monuments and citadels of European civilization, share the haunting afterthought? Perhaps so; but if so, *Souls* itself, with its painstaking sociohistorical exploration of the African-American experience, helps lay that ghost to rest.

We might approach these affective or spiritual dimensions of the problem of the color-line from another, more basic direction. Stated with stark
simplicity, the denial of recognition is the infliction of psychical pain. We as
a species (and not only our species) have two primary, instinctually based
responses to pain, psychical pain included: flight and fight. Flight is the
simpler of these two drives. It is the true opposite of the drive toward pleasure, while fighting is a more complex response to the problem of pain.
Practically speaking, however, the two come joined together, united both
by the situation of pain and the affects of anxiety and anger. As a rough
approximation, when anxiety predominates in the mix, flight is the likely
outcome; when anger predominates, the propensity is to fight. Mental development, that is, coming to have a mind of one's own—freedom in something like the Stoic sense—requires tolerating this bedeviling mixture of
feelings and impulses long enough to size up the problem that has been
thrust upon one.

The visiting-card incident with which Du Bois introduces himself in
Souls is at once just such a situation of psychical pain and the moment in
which he began the process of developing a *racial mind of his own*, a mind
strong enough to withstand the temptations of Hate, Despair, and Doubt.
Henceforward, he would fight, but only with the weapons of intellect and
imagination. He would take flight, but only into the self-restorative refuge
of his inner world. This twofold renunciation was at the same time a profound self-determination. Where there might be Hatred, there was instead a
Will to Freedom; and where there might be Despair, there was a willingness
to spread, tirelessly and with his own hands, the Gospel of Sacrifice. And
therefore, as a result of this self-mastery, where there might be Doubt, there
was a life full of striving. Even so, the achievement of this truly admirable
Stoic resolve is precisely that, an achievement. It is not easy nor can it be
complete. For Du Bois, there would always be the shadow figure of John
Jones, a deeply wounded core self he would neither affirm nor disavow. He
brings this wounded self before us, this man for whom "bitter shame hath
spoiled the sweet world's taste," who is in so many ways the photographic
negative of the New England youth who was undaunted by the falling of
the Veil. But this duality of light and shadow is precisely the aesthetic/af-
fective dimension of double-consciousness, the complement and complica-
tion of a soul split between Africa and America. Once again, we might be
tempted to say, *Ecce Homo!* Behold the Man!

For Du Bois, renunciation functioned as the negation of the negation.
For John Jones, it became the experience of negation itself, carried in the
end to the extreme of self-annihilation. The common determinant of both
is the Veil, with its multiple negations of the possibilities of recognition
and self-development. If this primary loss, this unwilled, involuntary sacrifice of black bodies and souls on the altar of white supremacy, is to be
contested, then renunciation in the Stoic sense is required.[20] Self-sacrifice

of this type is self-creative, an expression of will to power (overcoming resistance) in an affirmative mode. Up to a point, one gains strength in waging this battle, especially when one doesn't wage it alone. But that point can be reached. The color-line is a continuum of pain, from everyday abrasions, annoyances, and irritations through deeper hurt and humiliation to actual trauma. The white girl's peremptory refusal of Du Bois's visiting-card would have been of the everyday sort, were it not for its critical role in the formation of his character. Onderdonk's humiliating devaluation of Crummell, because there is a premeditated cruelty in it, falls closer to the middle of the continuum. The niggering of the Du Boises as they numbly walked in Burghardt's funeral cortege was not a matter of settled design, but its very casualness bespeaks a lack of fundamental human sympathy that was salt—no, acid—in the wound.[21] For John Jones, the cumulative impact of the confrontation with his childhood friend in the theater, the judge's humiliating closing of his school, and the rapacious assault on his sister was traumatic. The pain was overwhelming, self-shattering in its impact. The annihilation of these fragments of selfhood was as close to freedom and peace as he could come. Renunciation of innocence, of vocation, of faith in the future, of faith in oneself: As the pain increases and the anger (expressed or contained) mounts, the hold on life weakens. At the end of the line, it seems a better thing to forgo life than to suffer its agonies. This is the point at which death is merciful.

From my fifteenth year I remember Harry Belafonte singing:

> I think I heard him cry, when they was nailing in the nails,
> I think I heard him cry, take my mother home.
> Then I'll die easy, take my mother home.
> I'll die so easy, take my mother home.[22]

We might sing the song in remembrance of John Jones, who spared his mother the pain of witnessing his crucifixion and died because the sins of the fathers were so terribly visited upon the sons.

Man and God

The vertical dimension of *Souls* plunges down into the spiritual and historical depths of the African-American experience and reaches up to spiritual heights "aparell'd in celestial light." In the chapter on the sorrow songs, these polarities, like the beginning and end of a circle, are joined. But what, we may ask, is the nature of that celestial light? Enlightenment, to be sure; but is it also divine, the "true Light, which lighteth every man that cometh into the world" (John 1:9)?

Du Bois was born into a world where the Old and New Testaments provided a virtual second language, and he was both proficient and at home in the use of it. He was not, however, conventionally religious. For example:

> I landed [at Wilburforce] with the cane and gloves of my German student days; with my rather inflated ideas about what a 'university' ought to be and with a terrible bluntness of speech that was continually getting me into difficulty; as when, for instance, the student leader of a prayer meeting into which I had wandered casually to look local religion over, suddenly and without warning announced that "Professor Du Bois will lead us in prayer." I answered simply, "No, he won't," and as a result nearly lost my new job. (*Autobiography,* p. 186)

John Jones's disastrous speech in the Altamaha Baptist Church seems drawn from the same secular well. Yet we might distinguish between the institutional and spiritual aspects of religious life. Du Bois was decidedly anticlerical: "From my 30th year on I have increasingly regarded the church as an institution which defended such evils as slavery, color caste, exploitation of labor and war" (ibid., p. 285). And at the personal level, he would not heed any call to orthodoxy nor tolerate any interference with his freedom of thought and belief. Neither was he, however, entirely alienated from the faith of the fathers. He was susceptible to the Music and the Frenzy, even if he was skeptical of the Preacher. He may not have literally believed in the immortality of the soul ("If still he be, and he be There, and there be a There, let him be happy, O Fate!"), but he held to the thought and the comfort of it: "Perhaps now he knows the All-love, and needs not to be wise. Sleep, then, child,—sleep till I sleep and waken to a baby voice and the ceaseless patter of little feet—above the Veil" (*Souls,* p. 134).

Correspondingly, Du Bois did not have an orthodox belief in God. Late in life, he wrote to a Cuban priest: "[If] you mean by 'God' a vague Force which, in some incomprehensible way, dominates all life and change, then I answer, Yes; I recognize such Force, and if you wish to call it God, I do not object" (quoted in Lewis 1993, p. 66). Yet Du Bois does have a relationship to God. His "Credo" opens with four great affirmations: (1) "I believe in God who made of one blood all races that dwell on earth"; (2) "Especially do I believe in the Negro Race"; (3) "I believe in pride of race and lineage and self"; and (4) "I believe in Service" [we would say, in the Gospel of Sacrifice] (Du Bois 1905, p. 214). A scant year later, following the terrible race riots in Atlanta, he wrestles with God more fiercely than Jacob with the angel. "A Litany of Atlanta" begins "O Silent God, Thou whose voice afar in mist and mystery hath left our ears a-hungered in these frightful days—*Hear us, good Lord!*" Then, with increasing pain and anger, he asks: "Is this Thy justice, O Father, that guilt be easier than innocence, and the innocent crucified for the guilt of the untouched guilty?" He questions, "Is not the God of the fathers dead?" And answers, "Thou are not dead, but flown afar . . . " (Du Bois 1906, pp. 215–216). And he invokes and prays to

Him in *Souls*. One might object that he takes the name of the Lord in vain; that is, that he uses it for rhetorical effect, not with religious intent. Lewis attributes to him a "serene agnosticism" (1993, p. 65) that would fit with such a judgment. But as we have just seen, Du Bois's agnosticism was hardly serene. There was too much spiritual passion in him, and too strong a visceral connection to the religious life of black folk, for the Almighty to be an indifferent place-holder or signifier in a completely secularized worldview. It would be closer to the truth, although still not the truth entire, to align his attitude with the characteristically double meaning of the hymns and spirituals he names the sorrow songs. When singing, "deep river, I'm going over Jordan," the crossing is at once to heaven above and freedom up north. This intended ambiguity is captured in John Jones's final words with his mother. She asks him if he's going North. He looks at the North Star and answers, yes. The North is at once the (to be sure, problematical) land of freedom and enlightenment, and death's other kingdom.

I am not claiming that Du Bois purely and simply believed in a divine presence or providence, or in a life after death. But these notions are integral to the vertical dimension of *Souls*. They anchor it from above, paralleling the way in which the universities are the roots of the common schools, and the Talented Tenth pulls the mass of black folk upward with it. They fill a space that is organic to the lifeworld of the text. Moreover, they are focal points of affective intensity. They are not mere stage props, but rather an animating force—for ordinary black folk and, *through them*, for Du Bois as well.[23]

This transcendental tendency is reinforced by the Romanticism in Du Bois's perspective, German Romanticism most obviously (Goethe, Schiller) but also the more explicitly Neoplatonic version of Wordsworth's "Intimations" ("trailing clouds of glory do we come from God, who is our home: Heaven lies about us in our infancy"). There is little difficulty, therefore, in using *The Republic* as a vehicle for elucidating the political and cultural aspects of *Souls*, or the *Phaedo* to give philosophical meaning to the idea of death-as-liberation. It would be a far greater stretch to align this spiritual dimension of the text with Hegelian notions of the Absolute Spirit. Here is the version of the concept Du Bois would have read in Martineau's *A Study of Religion*, in that course he took with William James at Harvard:

> Absolute Knowledge . . . is not a Nature foreign to the subject and in negative relation to it, but a phase of universal Reason of which the individual is a self-discriminating function; and the latter is not a flash of intuitive vision, directed upon a fixed object, but a process moving through traceable stages from simple consciousness through self-consciousness, reason, the moral law, religion, to absolute Thought, in which all antitheses return to unity. In each of these stages, the movement takes the form of a triple pulsation, of affirmation, denial, and reconciling emergence into something higher. The

universe, being but the life of one thinking principle, repeats this law of movement in all its fields—in outward Nature, in human history, and in the individual experience. This is *Idealism;* because it never quits the realm of its ideas; all that I know is the process of universal Mind; and my knowing is the process of my own function in it. And it is *absolute*, because it unifies objective and subjective sides of the relation, and makes one immanent law co-extensive with the All. (Martineau 1888, 1:82)

Whatever affinities we may find between Du Bois and Hegel, they do not extend to the identification of the Real and the Rational. Hence in a later work we find Du Bois commenting that Marx's notion of the inevitability of communism "is undoubtedly not true and simply a result of his academic training in Hegelianism" (1935, p. 175). But along with the dialectical turn in his style of thinking and the fit between the problematics of recognition and the problem of the color-line, there is a correspondence between his articulation of the relationship between Man and God and Hegel's notion of the Unhappy Consciousness. In *The Phenomenology of Spirit,* Consciousness emerges from the relationship of Lordship and Bondage with a mind of its own. This subjective freedom is Stoicism, as we find it in Marcus Aurelius, Epictetus, and (at least approximately) Du Bois. It is followed by Scepticism, the outward expression of that freedom, the power of thought directed critically or negatively toward objects outside of the self. When this power is turned back upon Consciousness, an internal relationship of alienation is created. Consciousness as subject longs for unification with its object, experienced as Unchangeable Being. This is the paradigmatic form of religious life, captured dramatically in Christianity by Christ's final agony: "My God, my God, why hast Thou forsaken me?"(Matt. 27:32, 46). We hear angry as well as anguished echoes of these words in "A Litany of Atlanta"; and for the transported Africans who slaved in the Americas, it is the paradigmatic religious moment. Around Christ's suffering cluster the images of the divine that shine through in the sorrow songs and that Du Bois brings before us in *Souls:* the "great Avenger" who looks down upon the "Dawn of Freedom"; the "All-love" that awaits young Burghardt and the "dark and Pierced Jew" who awaits Alexander Crummell; the "God of Right" (p. 162) whose altar stands amid the nation's strife and striving, its "fire and blood, prayer and sacrifice"; "Eternal Good, pitiful yet masterful," in whose good time, it is hoped, "America shall rend the Veil and the prisoned shall go free" (p. 163); and finally "God the Reader," to whom Du Bois addresses his prayer that his "book fall not still-born into the world-wilderness" (p. 164).

Most of all, there are the sorrow songs themselves, through which Du Bois most securely joined himself to black folk in their suffering, and through which black folk in their suffering had joined themselves to the hope of liberation and redemption.

Consolation

The Sorrow Songs
In the Forethought to *Souls,* Du Bois concludes his summary of the book's contents by saying, "All this I have ended with a tale twice told but seldom written," referring (as discussed above) to "Of the Coming of John." From one perspective, this claim is plainly inaccurate. The chapter on the sorrow songs follows it. But "The Sorrow Songs," the last to be written, is of a different character from the ones preceding it. Although in it Du Bois brings forward new and important dimensions of African-American life, the chapter is itself a twice-told tale; that is, a retelling of *Souls* in musical terms. Hence Du Bois can fairly maintain that the narrative line ends with the death of his tormented protagonist.[24] And when we look back from that climactic moment, it is easy to see why Susan Mizruchi argues that *Souls* "can be read as a book of the dead" (1996, p. 286). She points to its opening words, "Herein lie buried many things . . . " and the ubiquity of references to death as the narrative unfolds. True enough, and notably so when we plunge nearly out of history and into the inner recesses of the Veil in Chapters XI through XIII.

Yet *Souls* is also, and more largely, a book of and for the living. This duality is captured in the dedication: "To Burghardt and Yolande, The Lost and the Found" (*Souls,* p. 4). Yolande—Nina Yolande, more formally—was born October 21, 1900. She was a "large, lively baby girl, cafe-au-lait in color. Her parents were delighted; the new baby brought them closer together than they had been since Burghardt's death" (Lewis 1993, p. 251). Her birth did not fully heal the wound of her brother's death, in her parents singly or in their relationship to each other. But her nominal presence in *Souls* signifies its delicate balance between the living and the dead, between morning and mourning—as in the instance of the sorrow song that echoes the ambiguity of freedom born and freedom stillborn in "Of the Dawn of Freedom." The imperative of renunciation likewise bears this double marking. As the self-sacrifice required by the spiritual strivings of black folk, it is life-affirming, a sublimation of the life-drives of individuals and peoples. As the sacrifice of the self when the pain of engagement has become unbearable, it is a vehicle of the death-drive, with its aim of the cessation of suffering and sometimes the consoling hope that, in death's other kingdom, "my mother will be there." Now, as we turn to the sorrow songs themselves, the same duality is inscribed in both words and melody—not just, or even primarily, because the interpenetration of life and death is the womb of the human condition but because it could not be otherwise for a people born of the "death-ships" of the Middle Passage.

Du Bois presents the sorrow songs in two quite different ways. In each chapter except the last, they are wordless.[25] For those who can both read music and know the songs themselves, the words come to mind directly.

For those who are lacking in both regards, they convey only a musical intention. But taken as they are presented, they are melody pure and simple; and, as we look at the first page of each chapter, it seems as if their words are printed above them, so that African and African-American melody is to be united with European and European-American poetry. Then, in Chapter XIV, their lyrical content is brought forward, although not in full, and we are asked to contemplate the historical experience they reflect. Sundquist takes them up in this way and uses them as an optic through which to read the text as a whole. We will follow his lead in a moment. Yet the initial impression of melody and poetry is suggestive in its own right. I am thinking here of Nietzsche's distinction between the Apollonian and the Dionysian in *The Birth of Tragedy,* which was evoked (in Chapter V) when we followed Du Bois into his first Negro revival meeting. The idea behind the paired concepts, although not the concepts themselves, Nietzsche took from Schopenhauer, who believed that the Will, reality itself, could be directly experienced through our bodies and in music. Individuality and intellection were problematically and, in part, defensively related to this matrix of Being. Nietzsche viewed Greek tragedy as an especially wonderful union of the two. Primordial reality was expressed in Dionysian music and dance, individuality in narratives drawn from the epic tradition. The combination of African-based melody and European-based poetry in *Souls* has something of the same effect. One might even imagine—although I am far from claiming this as Du Bois's intent—the one being read against the background of the other. Thus, in "Of Our Spiritual Strivings," we might hear "The Crying of Waters," itself so akin to the sorrow songs, spoken over the melody of "Nobody Knows the Trouble I've Seen." That might indeed suggest that "mind and soul according well / May make one music as before, / But vaster" (*Souls,* p. 119).[26]

I hasten to add that any such Nietzschean trope must be used with restraint. The ecstatic loss of self in a revival meeting and in a Dionysian festival do have something in common. Indeed, the early Dionysian rituals turned on the sufferings of the god and so have a kinship with Christian rituals that center on the crucifixion. But the Frenzy is only a part of the story of African-American religious life and, conceptually, Du Bois differentiates it from the Music, which (as we remember) he treats as "the one true expression of a people's sorrow, despair, and hope" (p. 120). Or, as he says in the opening line of Chapter XIV, "They that walked in darkness sang songs in the olden days—Sorrow Songs—for they were weary at heart" (p. 154). Where the Dionysian ritual and, for example, an Easter mass sweep forward to the moment of resurrection and redemption, the sorrow songs center on the weariness of the long and lonely passage through the Valley of the Shadow of Death. They contain the promise of freedom, in this life or the next; they undoubtedly shine a spiritual light into the dark night of the imprisoned soul. But as Du Bois offers them to us, "they are the music of an unhappy people, of the children of disappointment; they tell of death and suffering and unvoiced longing toward a truer world, of misty wanderings and hidden ways" (p. 157).

If we envision the topography of *Souls* from this perspective, we would see it as encircled by a mighty but melancholy stream of melody, resembling in part the River Ocean that the archaic Greeks believed to be the outermost boundary of their world.[27] The stanzas of poetry heading each chapter are then, each in its own way, the "voice of the sea" (p. 9)—Du Bois's voice as he gives articulate form to the currents of suffering, sorrow, and hope that roil these historical waters. One after the other they appear, until in the final chapter they give way to the words of the sorrow song, "To Lay This Body Down":

> I walk through the churchyard
>   To lay this body down;
> I know moon-rise, I know star-rise;
> I walk in the moonlight, I walk in the starlight;
> I'll lie in the grave and stretch out my arms,
> I'll go to judgment in the evening of the day,
> And my soul and thy soul shall meet that day,
>   When I lay this body down. (p. 154)

Here we have the profound yearning for the death that liberates, with its promise of the reunion of separated souls. We think, naturally, of mother and child, but also of the "two souls, two thoughts, two unreconciled strivings" that result from the alienation of Africa and America. Perhaps, in other words, the promise is one of spiritual reconciliation, of a soul at one with itself. But this intimation of the sublime quiet of the grave is reached only through the great chain of poetic utterances, beginning with "The Crying of Waters," that tells of sufferings here below and the struggle to bring them to a this-worldly end. Moreover, the musical notation is from "Wrestlin' Jacob," in which the meeting of souls is precisely a matter of spiritual striving. In Genesis 32, Jacob famously wrestles with the angel of the Lord, refusing to give up the struggle until he has been blessed. The angel accedes to this most forceful of prayers, and says, "Thy name shall be called no more Jacob, but Israel: for as a prince hast thou power with God and with men, and hast prevailed" (Gen. 32:28). This is a battle for recognition quite different from the one thematized by Hegel, with quite the opposite outcome. "Wrestlin' Jacob" preserves the drama of this encounter and, appropriately, Du Bois characterizes it as a "paean of hopeful strife" (p. 158). In the end, black folk will be blessed by God and will prevail. But in the long meanwhile, it is not the angel of the Lord that they confront but

rather the ungodly power of white supremacy. Just as appropriately, therefore, we have the first line of the chapter, cited above: "They that walked
in darkness sang songs in the olden days—Sorrow Songs—for they were
weary at heart." The will to carry on the struggle and the weariness it en-
tails are thus juxtaposed against the image of death the liberator in "To
Lay This Body Down"; and once again we have the doubled meaning of
renunciation.

When we look at "The Sorrow Songs" this way, it is of a piece—affectively,
aesthetically, spiritually—with the chapters immediately preceding it. And
like them, it is strongly marked by Du Bois's personal experiences. We remember that he began *Souls* with an affirmation of racial identity: "need
I add that I who speak here am bone of the bone and flesh of the flesh of them
that live within the Veil?" (p. 6). He confirms this identification by defining
his relationship to the songs:

> Ever since I was a child these songs have stirred me strangely. They came
> out of the South unknown to me, one by one, and yet at once I knew them
> as of me and mine. Then in after years when I came to Nashville, I saw the
> great temple builded of these songs towering over the pale city. To me Jubi-
> lee Hall [built with the proceeds of the international tour of the Fisk Jubilee
> Singers] seemed ever made of the songs themselves, and its red bricks were
> red with the blood and dust of toil. Out of them rose for me morning, noon,
> and night, bursts of wonderful melody, full of the voices of my brothers and
> sisters, full of the voices of the past. (p. 155).

As Sundquist observes, "the opening rhetorical question of Du Bois's
preface has now become a stirring declaration that the songs are 'of me
and mine.' The souls with which Du Bois has ritually joined himself over
the course of *The Souls of Black Folk* are in great part the souls of the black
South, the souls of slavery, those who have gone before and yet speak still
in the bequeathed voices of the sorrow songs" (Sundquist 1993, pp. 526–527).
His two-ness is alluded to ("they came out of the South unknown to me")
but is simultaneously overcome ("yet at once I knew them as of me and
mine"). The unifying link is secured by his own descent into the South,
with Fisk itself as the geographical nexus of the joining. This link was not
created, however, by these rituals of cultural immersion. Not only does Du
Bois claim a natural affinity for African-American folk culture ("ever since
I was a child these songs have stirred me strangely"), he also brings forward an authenticating familial connection to this spiritual heritage: "My
grandfather's grandmother was seized by an evil Dutch trader two centuries ago; and coming to the valleys of the Hudson and Housastonic, black,
little, and lithe, she shivered and shrank in the harsh north winds, looked
longingly to the hills, and often crooned a heathen melody to the child
between her knees" (*Souls*, p. 157).[28] Both the melody and an approximation

of the words were passed down, generation to generation. Thus among the languages of *Souls*—English, German, French, Latin—we have:

> Do ba–na co–ba, ge–ne me, ge–ne me!
> Do ba–na co–ba, ge–ne me, ge–ne me!
> Ben d' nu–li, nu–li, nu–li, ben d' le. (Ibid.)

The language of Africa, transmitted through his matrilineage, was Du Bois's own proper inheritance—transmitted, and untranslatable, lost and found. We "sing it to our children," he tells us, "knowing as little as our fathers what its words may mean, but knowing well the meaning of its music" (ibid.).[29] Just so, it is tempting to hear the African words as remnants of a mother tongue, untranslatable because it is a language before language, sensuously encoded like a cradle-song sung by a mother to a nursing baby, but lost with the mother's death. One is then left longing for a moment, like the one in the "Overture" to Proust's *Swann's Way*, when Marcel tastes the "petite madeleine" soaked in tea and the floodgates of memory open, making accessible the sublimity of the mother-world. But in the present instance, the magical moment is forever foreclosed.

Although "The Sorrow Songs" is autobiographically grounded, it is sociohistorically extended. In this regard, it mirrors "Of the Faith of the Fathers," which initiated the descent into the deeper recesses of the Veil. That chapter began with Du Bois's experience in the revival meeting and included his powerful affirmation of the African origins of African-American religion. It was primarily given over, however, to the kind of social and institutional analysis that is generally characteristic of the first part of the text. The present chapter includes an analysis of the transmission and development of the songs, as well as of their institutionalization. But the emphasis is on the way in which they express the spiritual strivings of black folk, especially during the long years of bondage. Hence, compared to the earlier chapter, the affective and aesthetic accent is reversed. Or, to carry the point a bit further, in "Of the Faith of the Fathers" Du Bois builds his analysis around the intertwined elements of the Preacher, the Frenzy, and the Music. In "The Sorrow Songs," the Music is separated out from its religious integument, and we are swept back by it, not only to Africa but also to the passage through slavery to freedom that shaped African-American identity. Simultaneously, this formative experience is brought forward, and this in a twofold sense. On the one hand, the sorrow of the songs confronts the (especially white) reader with the pain and suffering that slavery imposed on black folk. On the other, Du Bois views the Music as one of the great gifts of black folk to this nation, and as a singular cultural achievement. Already in "Of Our Spiritual Strivings," he put forward the claim that "there is no true American music but the wild sweet melodies of the Negro slave" (p. 16). Here he maintains that "the Negro folk-song—the rhythmic cry of the slave—stands today not simply as the sole American music, but as the most beautiful expression of human experience born this side the seas" (p. 155). If the "Gentle Reader" would but listen to the songs, taking in the suffering and the sublimity palpable in them, they might pierce the Veil and make possible a moment of recognition and spiritual communion.[30]

We have, then, three interrelated concerns: slavery, the gifts of black folk, and the prospects for mutual recognition. As we know, Du Bois was willing to grant that American slavery was not "the worst . . . in the world," that one could find in it "something of kindliness, fidelity, and happiness" (p. 26). But it was a "guilty nation" that had instituted it and black folk were a "wronged race" (p. 32). American slavery had "classed the black man and the ox" together (p. 27), and the centuries of dehumanization had taken their toll. The emancipated slave entered the world "handicapped" by the "weight of his ignorance,—not simply of letters, but of life, business, of the humanities; the accumulated sloth and shirking and awkwardness of decades and centuries shackled his hands and feet" (p. 14). Nowhere do we find Du Bois echoing Washington, who in *Up From Slavery* claims that "we must acknowledge that, notwithstanding the cruelty and moral wrong of slavery, the ten million Negroes inhabiting this country, who themselves or whose ancestors went through the school of American slavery, are in a stronger and more hopeful position . . . than is true of an equal number of black people in any other portion of the globe" (Washington 1901, p. 37). Yet, as Gooding-Williams emphasizes, neither does he adopt the position advanced by Crummell in "The Need for New Ideas and New Aims for a New Era"—that African-Americans must not "dwell morbidly and absorbingly on the servile past," but must rather "escape the 'limit and restraint' of both the *word* and the *thought* of slavery" (1994, p. 256; see also Sundquist 1993, pp. 516–517). Instead, Du Bois aims at the preservation and transmission of the history of enslaved black folk, a history that he would neither idealize nor devalue. Indeed, the tale he wishes to tell cannot be completed without this portion of the narrative. There is, first, a matter of justice: Slavery was a wrong that has yet to be righted. The case cannot be brought before the historical bar without the evidence of the crime. And second, the realities of slavery constitute a vital, in a way *the* vital, basis for the sociological explanation of the current condition of black folk, including the veiled relationship of black and white.

Beyond such matters of justice and judgment, Du Bois finds, through the medium of the sorrow songs, a living cultural link—or rather a succession of links—to Africa. He traces out four developmental steps, of which the first two are predominantly African: "African music," like the song inherited from his great-great grandmother or "You May Bury Me in the East" [the "song of exile" which "heralds 'The Coming of John'"); and

"Afro-American" music, like "March On" ("Of the Training of Black Men") and "Steal Away Home" ("Of the Faith of the Fathers") (*Souls*, p. 158). The third step is a "blending of Negro music with the music heard in the foster land. The result is still distinctively Negro and the method of blending original, but the elements are both Negro and Caucasian" (ibid.). Instances are "Bright Sparkles in the Churchyard" ("Of the Black Belt") and "I Hope My Mother Will Be There" ("Of the Passing of the First-Born"). This might be seen as a further instance of two-ness, or of two-ness overcome. The fourth step is a two-sided white appropriation of Negro music: songs like those of Stephen Foster, which Du Bois mentions without criticism, and the debased and imitative forms—"the Negro 'minstrel' songs, many of the 'gospel' hymns, and some of the contemporary 'coon' songs,—a mass of music in which the novice may easily lose himself and never find the real Negro melodies" (p. 158). These last-mentioned amount to a musical version of the Veil. But the first three form a musical umbilical cord, joining African-Americans to their native land, while they strive to build a life for themselves in their "foster land."[31]

Du Bois establishes his own place in this lineage not only by his transmission of his familial song of Africa but also by his revoicing of the sorrow songs themselves. It is as if the blood of the African griot runs in his veins. He teaches and preaches and sings the songs, in a narrative rhythm at once highly individual and deeply racial.[32] And through the re-presentation of the songs, he conveys the "articulate message of the slave to the world" (p. 156). In speaking for them, or rather in allowing them to speak through him, he is refusing to accept the judgment that they have nothing meaningful to say.[33] At the same time, he is refusing to internalize one of the most debilitating pathologies of double-consciousness; namely, an acceptance of mis-recognition and humiliation that takes the form of being ashamed of one's ancestors, one's family of origin. Such a dis-identification is not necessarily a full-blown identification with the oppressor, but it does necessarily leave one adrift between the devil and the deep blue sea. Du Bois, by contrast, affirms himself through his identification with his enslaved ancestors and affirms his ancestors through their identification with him. This is the double-bond, rather than double-consciousness, he affirmed in his "Credo:" "I believe in Pride of race and lineage and self."

If Du Bois is the messenger of his ancestors, what, then, is the message? It is, most basically and as already indicated, a story of "death and suffering and unvoiced longing toward a truer world." Or, again: "Of nearly all the songs . . . the music is distinctly sorrowful." They—speaking here especially of a selection of the spirituals and hymns he characterizes as master songs—"tell in word and music of trouble and exile, of strife and hiding; they grope toward some unseen power and sigh for rest in the End" (*Souls*, p. 159). They reveal the slaves' feeling for Nature, and their use of natural images to convey their spiritual concerns—as when, for example, the "wild thunder-storms of the South" become "My Lord calls me, / He calls me by the thunder, / the trumpet sounds it in my soul" (ibid.). They speak of "monotonous toil and exposure" to the elements and of the desire to escape to "something that's new" (p. 160). Reflecting the fragmented kinship relations of the plantation South, "mother and child are sung, but seldom father [here we think of Du Bois's natal family]; fugitive and weary wanderers call for pity and affection, but there is little of wooing and wedding; the rocks and the mountains are well known, but home is unknown" (ibid.). Correspondingly "love-songs are scarce," while of "death the Negro showed little fear, but talked of it familiarly and even fondly as a simple crossing of the waters, perhaps—who knows?—back to his ancient forests again" (p. 161).

This suggests another way of organizing the songs. Paralleling the melodies that are distinctly African, there are African survivals in the lyrics, like the "'Mighty Myo', which figures as a river of death" (p. 159), and less specifically the longing for and mourning of a lost home. Next there are the manifold ways in which the songs reflect the long exile from the African homeland and the lifeworld of the slaves. This condition of alienation extends, as Du Bois repeatedly emphasizes, long past the dawn of freedom so-called and down into the present. Consequently when we hear in the sorrow songs a "faith in the ultimate justice of things" identified with this world and not only the next, a third stage is implied—"that sometime, somewhere, men will judge men by their souls and not by their skins" (p. 162). Sometime, somewhere: well might we ask along with Du Bois, "Is such hope justified? Do the Sorrow Songs sing true?" (ibid.).

Du Bois's answer to this question is framed, as it necessarily must be, by the problem of the color-line. For plainly the hope is not justified so long as the prejudice against and denigration of black folk remains in force, so long as they are imprisoned behind a Veil of mis-recognition that reduces them to stereotypical fragments of human beings. "Your people are unfortunately incapable of contributing to the great work of civilization," says the voice of the Veil. "They are simply inferior to the members of the white race, and must accept their lot in life." This is the truth as the white supremacist knows it, even those like Judge Henderson who fancy themselves a friend of colored people. Du Bois does not repeat it in so many words, but the two lines of argument he now introduces presuppose it.

From one direction, Du Bois challenges the claim of the inherent superiority of the white race: "Such an assumption is the arrogance of peoples irreverent toward Time and ignorant of the deeds of men. A thousand years ago such an assumption, easily possible, would have made it difficult for the Teuton to prove his right to life" (ibid.). Germanic culture—near and dear to Du Bois's heart—developed over time. It was not biologically given nor a gift of God. But a species of historical ignorance hides this obvious fact: "So woefully unorganized is sociological knowledge that the meaning of progress, the meaning of the 'swift' and 'slow' in human doing, and the limits of human perfectibility, are veiled, unanswered sphinxes on the shores of science" (ibid.). Sociological knowledge, Du Bois continues to hope, can play a part in clearing the racial air. But *we* might note the double-bind in this formulation. The Veil itself precludes questioning the sphinx on the meaning of human progress, makes it seem that there is no question to be asked—that the answer has already been given and the Josies of the world are sacrificing themselves for nothing. It is precisely *this* conundrum that pushed Du Bois beyond the program of the Verein political economists. Beyond it, but not to its abandonment: The appeal across the color-line must engage the passions of white folk along with their intelligence. In this regard, the aim of *Souls* is to generate a common pathos, a shared experience of suffering and human sympathy, that would provide an affective foundation for mutual recognition.

From the other direction, Du Bois again asserts the claims of African-Americans to recognition, not simply on the basis of common humanity but more particularly because they, too, have been builders of the American nation. How came it to be "your country," he asks the white reader?

> Before the Pilgrims landed, we were here. Here we have brought our three gifts and mingled them with yours: a gift of story and song—soft, stirring melody in an ill-harmonized and unmelodious land; the gift of sweat and brawn to beat back the wilderness, conquer the soil, and lay the foundations of this vast economic empire two hundred years earlier than your weak hands could have done it; the third, a gift of the Spirit. (p. 162)

The first two of the three gifts are self-explanatory, at least at this late point in the narrative. The Spirit, too, is familiar to us, although we have not attempted to pin it down. Nor is it easily confined within definitional boundaries. There is the obvious Christian instance, the Spirit of the Lord that passes through the worshippers in the Frenzy or Shouting. Just as obviously, given Du Bois's roots in German cultural life, there is the notion of *Geist,* with its overdetermined meanings: spirit, soul, mind, intelligence, or essence; historical extensions of the notion, like *weltgeist* or *zeitgeist;* and the *Geisteswissenschaften,* the cultural or social sciences. We are mindful, too, that the title of the introductory chapter, "Of Our Spiritual Strivings," might be used to characterize *Souls* as a whole, as when in the Forethought Du Bois tells us that his aim is to open up "the spiritual world in which ten thousand thousand Americans live and strive" (p. 5). But there is also spiritual as opposed to material or, more pointedly, spiritual values as opposed to materialistic ones—as when, in "Of the Wings of Atalanta," Du Bois would not have the cultivation of the soul lost in attending to the needs of the body.

All of these meanings, I believe, play their part in the narrative and argument of the text. But in the present context, "Spirit" has the specific meaning of the soul of the nation, the source of its character or identity, and this in a twofold sense. On the one hand, Du Bois asserts that American national character was formed around the Negro problem: "out of the nation's heart we have called all that was best to throttle and subdue all that was worst; fire and blood, prayer and sacrifice, have billowed over this people, and they have found peace only in the altars of the God of Right" (ibid.). Slavery, Abolition, and the Civil War; negation, and the negation of the negation. On the other, he tells us, "our gift of the Spirit [has not] been merely passive. Actively we have woven ourselves with the very warp and woof of this nation, . . . [In] generation after generation [we] have pleaded with a headstrong, careless people to despise not Justice, Mercy, and Truth, lest the nation be smitten with a curse" (ibid.). Black folk have been at the center of the struggle over national identity; and they have been the nation's conscience, its prophetic voice, its incarnate call to righteousness and rectification. Accordingly the question—"Is such a hope justified? Do the Sorrow Songs sing true?"—may be rephrased: Will the prophetic voice be heard, the call acknowledged, the warning heeded? Will the time come when it can truly be said, "they *recognize* themselves as *mutually recognizing* one another" (Hegel [1807] 1977, p. 112).

The answer is not given in the asking nor is there one that Du Bois can give. Recognition is a two-party affair, and there is no guarantee that white folk will play their part. Necessarily, therefore, *Souls* ends with an aporia: "If somewhere in this whirl and chaos of things there dwells Eternal Good, pitiful yet masterful, then anon in His good time America shall rend the Veil and the prisoned shall go free" (p. 163). Time will tell; meanwhile, we are carried back to Du Bois's first reference to Wordsworth's "Intimations" when the "shades of the prison-house" closed round him after his visiting-card was peremptorily refused. Yet even then the spiritual realm was open to him, when on wings of imagination he would proudly soar into "a region of blue sky" above the Veil; and he never lost the keys to this kingdom. We remember him at a later date, stationed at Atlanta University, where he could "dwell above the Veil" and sit with Shakespeare, who "winces not." And there, in the groves of the academy, we leave him, with the "sunshine trickling down the morning" into the "high windows" of his study, while simultaneously "fresh young voices" well up to him from below, "swelling with song, instinct with life, tremulous treble and darkening bass." "My children," he names them, "singing to the sunshine" and to him. Yet the song they sing is not one of jubilation but rather akin to the sorrow songs: "Let us cheer the weary traveller . . . Along the heavenly way" (*Souls,* p. 163). The Call to self-sacrifice cannot be ignored; the high road of spiritual striving beckons: "And the traveller girds himself, and sets his face toward the Morning, and goes his way" (p. 164).

In this, the last scene in the tale Du Bois has told, we again have a doubled, or more than doubled, meaning. Set in the morning, with the sunshine trickling down to him and "his children," we cannot help but recall the eventide that carried his young son away. ("I knew life and death. The passing of my first-born son was an experience from which I never quite recovered.") The Lost is signified by the Found. The voices of these, his spiritual children, reach him from below; his very elevation separates him from them. ("I did not know my students as human beings; they were apt to be intellects and not souls. To the world in general I was nearly always the isolated outsider looking in and seldom part of that inner life" [*Autobiography*, p. 283].) It is as if, like a true Platonic philosopher, he is bathed by the light of the Good but is not at home in the cave where ordinary people dwell. His fate, his mission and destiny, is to bear the burden of Enlightenment and, when he descends into the cave, to spread the Gospel of Sacrifice with his own hands. He must travel on, a weary and wayfaring stranger, until he comes at last to the morning of the Great Jubilee, the one so soulfully heralded by the Fisk Jubilee Singers: "My Lord, My Lord, what a morning, / When the stars begin to fall." Yet we cannot forget that there is mourning even on this morning or that, when celebrating "no more auction block for me," the counterpoint is "many thousands gone." These are, after all, the sorrow songs, sung by those who walked in darkness and were weary at heart. Du Bois, the weary traveler, is bone of the bone and flesh of the flesh with them. His sadness, likewise his mother's sadness . . . his own Song of Songs ("Do ba–na co–ba, ge–ne me, ge–ne me!") came to him through her . . . mingles with theirs.

So, too, their struggle is his, his struggle is theirs. The chiaroscuro of renunciation shades *The Souls of Black Folk*, gives it an autumnal hue. Only in autumn, however, is it possible to "reap the harvest wonderful"; and a stoic renunciation is required if one is to wage, unceasingly, the battle for recognition. Thus the hero-narrator of this epic tale returns again and again to the place where the Veil falls, speaking through it, piercing it with his voice, so that "the ears of a guilty people tingle with truth, and seventy millions sigh for the righteousness which exalteth nations, in this drear day when human brotherhood is mockery and snare" (p. 164).

Even now, in our own drear days, we might wonder, who has ears to hear and eyes to see?

Involuntary Sacrifice

Because we end with the sorrow songs, hence with the Middle Passage and the long years of slavery that fixed, through traumatic impact, the two-ness of African-American identity, we might add a few words about the many thousands gone—not those who chose to spread the Gospel of Sacrifice, but those who *were* sacrificed on the altar of the white man's cupidity and cruelty. In mating the sorrow songs with the poetry of European-American high culture, Du Bois offers them a recognition that white supremacy precludes. And yet: Recognition is not redemption. Those who suffered, suffered; those who died, died. Their suffering, their deaths, cannot be undone. Perhaps Nietzsche's Zarathustra would see it differently: "To redeem those who lived in the past and to recreate all 'it was' into a 'thus I willed it'—that alone should I call redemption" (Nietzsche 1883–1885, p. 251). His exemplary individual, the overman, wills the eternal return of the same and so redeems the past. But the overman, the phantasmal shadow of Plato's philosopher-king, lacks the signal attributes of those who are capable of voluntary sacrifice: love and compassion. He has no soul. The hero-narrator of *Souls*, by contrast, stands his ground amid the human, all-too-human; and for him the problem of redemption cannot be so heartlessly solved.

For those who have been involuntarily sacrificed, no redemption is possible. But for those who are their heirs, it may be. In *Jazz*, Toni Morrison brings before us Golden Gray, the beautiful man-child of a white mother who raises him and a black father he has never met. Torn apart by the duality of his racial identity, he seeks out his missing father in order to kill him and kill off his blackness, seeks out his missing father because he is missing the father in himself. Overwhelmed and split apart, he stands benumbed by a well in the Virginia backwoods. His mind is "soaked and sodden with sorrow, or dry and brittle with the hopelessness that comes from knowing too little and feeling too much" (Morrison 1992, p. 161). Then, from deep in the well, "where the light does not reach, a collection of leftover smiles stirs, some brief benevolent love rises from the darkness." He feels it, a "serene power that flicks like a razor and then hides." And then hides. "But once the razor blade has flicked—he will remember it, and if he remembers it he can recall it. That is to say, he has it at his disposal" (ibid.). The well draws its waters from the Black Atlantic. If Golden Gray can tolerate its sorrow, he can feel at the same time the laughter and love of his ancestors. They cannot be redeemed, but he can be redeemed through them. This is the gift of the Spirit, and one may be grateful for it. Grateful as well to the author of *Souls*, who so richly conveys it, who speaks to us in "a personal and intimate tone of self-revelation" in each of its chapters and asks only for the recognition that he himself willingly gives.

Notes

Chapter 1. Setting the Stage

1. The scholarly community owes a special debt to Du Bois's friend and literary executor Herbert Aptheker, who did so much to ensure the publication and enduring recognition of his work. Yet despite his dedicated efforts, Arnold Rampersad—writing in 1989, thirteen years after the original publication of his *The Art and Imagination of W. E. B. Du Bois*—could still comment "I hardly know how to characterize the stillness that has surrounded his name since my book appeared" ([1976] 1990, p. vi). That silence has been definitively broken, and the students of Du Bois's life and work now have a rich and diverse critical literature at their disposal. There is also the W. E. B. Du Bois Institute for African and African American Research at Harvard University, which publishes the *Du Bois Review*, dedicated to social science research on race. And the Center for Contemporary Black History at Columbia University publishes *SOULS: A Critical Journal of Black Politics, Culture, and Society*. These publications are a fitting tribute to the man who, more than any other, initiated these research programs.

As to *Souls* itself, in his "The Survey on Issues in African Studies: A First Report," Fabio Rojas reports that "only one book has achieved a nearly unanimous status as a canonical text, W. E. B. DuBois' *The Souls of Black Folk*" (2005, p. 2).

2. It quickly will become evident to the reader how much I rely on the work of the community of Du Bois scholars. This community is large, and it seems almost inevitable that I have overlooked some of its members. For any such oversight, I offer sincere apologies.

3. Robert Stepto ([1979] 1991, pp. 53–55) discusses some of the specific textual changes Du Bois made in these articles.

4. "[In *Souls*], the soul of W. E. B. Du Bois, his sufferings, his virtues, his gifts, [is] offered as exemplary of the best achievement of the Afro-American people" (Rampersad [1976] 1990, p. 88).

5. Du Bois cites *Faust* in *Souls*, and the case for its affinities with the Platonic and Hegelian texts will be made as we proceed. As to Wagner's *Gesamtkunstwerk*, Anne E.

Carroll contends Du Bois did have it in mind, or at least in the back of his mind. But even if we were to conclude that he wasn't consciously modeling himself on Wagner, we still might follow Carroll in viewing *Souls* as "a new kind of total work of art, a new form of creative and expository text hashed out to meet the demands of the unique situation of African Americans in America" (2005, p. 252).

6. "Of Our Spiritual Strivings" is a revised version of "Strivings of the Negro People," published in *Atlantic Monthly* (August, 1897). The titular change is strongly indicative of the unifying tendencies that run through the text. The object "the Negro People" is replaced by the first person plural, and the strivings of the people are characterized as spiritual. We'll consider the way Du Bois interpenetrates individual and collective identity and the multiple meanings of spiritual life and strivings as we proceed.

7. Du Bois himself places Chapter X, "Of the Faith of the Fathers," in the second part of *Souls*. We'll return to this issue of interpretation in Chapter 5.

8. The last of the sorrow songs is "let us cheer the weary traveller," followed by: "and the traveller girds himself, and sets his face toward the Morning, and goes on his way" (*Souls*, pp. 163–164).

9. "The chapters on the death of his son, on Alexander Crummell, and on the sacrificial death of the fictive but semi-autobiographical John are bound together by their representation of death as the moment of final salvation—what had always been represented in the spirituals as the movement into freedom but which, in the realm of Du Bois's secular prophecy, remains inevitably provisional, as much a dark trope of potential cultural declension and loss as of ultimate spiritual triumph" (Sundquist 1993, pp. 524–525).

10. "The 'souls' of the title is a play on words. It alludes to the 'twoness' of the black American that Du Bois initially suggests in his first chapter" (Rampersad 1989, p. 117).

11. "Both seventh sons and those born with a caul [a part of the amniotic membrane that only rarely envelops the head of a newborn child] have the abilities to communicate with spirits, to perform magic, and to heal the sick. Both are considered to be blessed with good fortune and those with a preserved veil are protected against drowning" (Byerman 1978, p. 81).

12. To my mind, Gooding-Williams (2003) provides the most incisive analysis of the relationship of second-sight, double-consciousness, and two-ness. Bruce (1992, pp. 236–244) is especially good on the notion of double-consciousness; Reed (1997, chap. 7) reviews many of the received opinions. See also Lewis (1993, p. 281); and Zamir (1995, chap. 4).

We'll give further consideration to the triad of second-sight, double-consciousness, and two-ness in Chapter 2.

13. For a reading of *Souls* that questions the interpretive adequacy of the concept of recognition, see Siemerling 2001.

14. The second part of chapter 4 of *The Phenomenology of Spirit* concerns "Stoicism, Skepticism, and the Unhappy Consciousness." The last of these configures a proto-religious relationship in which a subject is alienated from the Unchangeable. This is at once an internal division and—to state it bluntly—a representation of the gulf between the human and the divine. The subject's yearning for union with the Unchangeable adds a vertical dimension to the problem of constituting selfhood, complementing the phenomenology of recognition that unfolds on a horizontal plane. Hence these notions, too, can be used in framing interpretations of *Souls*, and especially of its more personal part.

15. I offer a version of Nietzsche's perspectivism suitable for psychoanalytic employment in Wolfenstein 2000a, chap. 3. This approach to psychoanalytic inquiry does

not preclude the possibility of unifying or even foundational interpretations, but it does involve a certain suspicion of such truth-claims and a predisposition to listen with a third and even a fourth ear.

16. Probably the most notable and, in aesthetic terms, successful literary use of this masculinist understanding of the psychology of race relations is in Ralph W. Ellison's *Invisible Man* ([1952] 1989). I attempt to bring it, and some of its limitations, into focus in "Race, Rage, and Oedipus in Ralph W. Ellison's *Invisible Man*" (Wolfenstein 2003). For a reading of *Invisible Man* that calls this psychological framing into question, see Claudia Tate 1987, "Notes on the Invisible Women in Ralph Ellison's *Invisible Man.*"

17. For my own use of the concept of recognition to frame matters of human identity, see Wolfenstein 1993, chap. 6, and Wolfenstein 2000a, chap. 1. Within the expansive field of psychoanalytic feminism, my own primary influences include (most prominently) Dorothy Dinnerstein ([1976] 1999), and then Jessica Benjamin (1980, 1988, 1995), Nancy Chodorow (1978, 1989, 1994), and Jane Flax (1990, 1993). The journal *Studies in Gender and Sexuality* is a rich source of contemporary discussion and criticism.

Chapter 2. Through a Glass Darkly

1. The lyrics of the sorrow songs, along with their opening musical bars, are available in the *Musical Hypertext Edition of THE SOULS OF BLACK FOLK* (http://way.net/SoulsOfBlackFolk/SoulsOfBlackFolk.html).

2. We will consider the meaning of Du Bois's juxtaposition of poetic words and wordless melodies in Chapter VI. Meanwhile, we'll follow Sundquist's lead in linking the lyrics of the songs to the context in which the melody is displayed.

3. Susan Mizruchi claims that Symons is referencing the slave trade in this poem (1998, p. 348). That seems unlikely. It is a plausible surmise that, in beginning the spiritual journey of *Souls* with "The Crying of Waters," Du Bois had this intent. But Symons had a different orientation. He is best known for his advocacy of and participation in the Symbolist movement. "The Crying of Waters" is in the collection of poems, *The Loom of Dreams*, which he privately published in 1901. The volume also included "The Ecstasy," reflecting his sense of spiritual kinship with John Donne, whom he viewed as a Symbolist. It's a rather large step from these airy preoccupations to the experiences of black folk in another time and place. Du Bois, by contrast, bridged this gap. As we shall see, his terrestrial involvements did not prevent him from being drawn to transcendental poetic themes.

For *The Loom of Dreams*, see Symons, *Collected Works*, vol. 2. For interpretations of Symons as aesthetician and poet, see Munro 1969 and Markert 1988.

4. For an analysis of Du Bois's struggles with the genre of autobiography, see Mostern 1999, chap. 3.

5. On the dating of this incident, see Lewis 1993, pp. 33–34, and 590.

6. Harris adopts an Adlerian approach to the interpretation of *Souls* in general and this incident in particular. The choice is sensible because Adler focuses so clearly on issues of superiority and inferiority, issues that white supremacy brings to the fore. See also the continuation of her analysis, pp. 228–229.

7. Reactions to insult and intended humiliation are complex and variable. Sometimes the demeaning words slip like water off the proverbial duck's back. Sometimes the recipient is stunned or (so it would appear) simply hurt. But the most characteristic response, as the history of race relations and political life ubiquitously shows, is anger, either expressed or (if the situation precludes its expression) suppressed. When it is manifestly absent, one wonders if it is latently present; that is, repressed or sublimated

rather than simply suppressed. In the present instance, there are strong indications of both of these trends. Du Bois's determined opposition to white supremacy was surely fueled by appropriately sublimated aggressivity; and, as we shall see, *Souls* is marked by symptomatic expressions of an anger that he strove to rise above (see also Wolfenstein 2000b).

8. Zamir offers a thoughtful and quite extended analysis of the visiting-card incident (1995, pp. 134–143). He emphasizes the way in which it functions rhetorically as an appeal to sympathy across the color-line, while at the same time advancing a critique of the semblance of sympathy that was so often passed off as the real thing. Substantively, he uses the trope of the Unhappy Consciousness in *The Phenomenology of Spirit* to good effect in characterizing the self-division and the struggle that the incident initiates. Thus: the "white girl who rejects the black boy is . . . internalized in the abstract as the cultural ideals of the world to which she belongs and is . . . placed in opposition to a black self newly aware of its status as 'a Negro' distinct from being 'an American,' and with a unique 'message to the world'" (p. 146).

9. Gooding-Williams (2003, pp. 2–5) calls attention to Du Bois's use of the verse that opens this chapter in the introduction to his Fisk University commencement address of 1898, "Careers Open to College-Bred Negroes." There, he argues, the usage couples the sublime and the liberal arts. Du Bois's address ends with part of the verse from James Russell Lowell's *The Present Crisis* that heads Chapter II of *Souls* (Du Bois 1898, p. 17): "Truth forever on the scaffold,/Wrong forever on the throne. / Yet that scaffold sways the future,/And behind the dim unknown/Standeth God within the shadow, /Keeping watch above his own." In thus balancing the sublime and high culture with the righteous and wrathful God who stands guard over his children, Du Bois doubly anticipates the vertical dimension of *Souls*.

10. "According to Du Bois, the interpersonal veil that divides black from white in America is internalized with the result that the black American develops not merely the two consciousnesses appropriate to being a (white) American on the one hand and a black (non-American) but also the veil between them. And because white and black are veiled from one another, the American Negro is veiled from himself, able to see himself either as an American or as a Negro but not as both at the same time" (Bull 1998, p. 121).

Chapter 3. "Be Your Own Father"

1. In my view, psychobiographical interpretations are intrinsically more speculative than textual ones. Although it would take us too far afield to do more than touch on this subject, it can be argued that—allowing for appropriate contextualization and assuming a well-authenticated text—textual analysis involves a relatively stable object of representation and therefore a relatively unambiguous standard for assessing the degree of interpretive recognition. This is not to deny that, in the manner of all aesthetic objects, it is properly finished by the reader in the creative moment of mutual interpellation. But the object itself, or the object in-itself as a Hegelian might say, is quite unambiguous. A life history, by contrast, is intrinsically indefinite. Even if such a history is lived artistically, it is not an aesthetic object nor a stable object of representation. The autobiographical and biographical records inevitably contain gaps and fissures, and the ambiguity of the interpretive enterprise is intensified if the individual is presumed to be motivated by unconscious conflicts and tendencies as well as conscious intentions. Hence it seems prudent to treat biographical portraits of the present kind as akin

to "just-so" stories and to judge them by heuristic and communicative standards of narrative coherence and plausibility rather than by strict criteria of veridicality.

2. In *Dusk of Dawn* Du Bois contextualizes his birth a bit differently. After noting the enfranchisement of freemen in the South, he observes: "Thaddeus Stevens, the clearest-headed leader of this attempt at industrial democracy, made his last speech impeaching Andrew Johnson on February sixteenth and on February twenty-third I was born" (*Dusk*, p. 8). Here the identification is with a white spiritual ancestor who, like his dark-skinned inheritor, challenged the authority of the Great White Father.

3. "The family-romance pattern is completed with the necessary self-fathering of the son. If the father cannot be a model, then the son must generate an identity of his own" (Byerman 1994, p. 4).

4. Du Bois was inclined toward chivalric values, and not only in *Souls*. He dedicated *Dusk of Dawn* to his friend and coworker in the NAACP Joel Spingarn: "To keep the memory of Joel Spingarn, Scholar and Knight."

5. The notion of a transitional psychological space originates with D. W. Winnicott, who characterizes it this way:

> Transitional objects and transitional phenomena belong to the realm of illusion which is at the basis of initiation of experience. This early stage in development is made possible by the mother's special capacity for making adaptation to the needs of her infant, thus allowing the infant the illusion that what the infant creates really exists.
>
> This intermediate area of experience, unchallenged in respect of its belonging to inner or external (shared) reality, constitutes the greater part of the infant's experience, and throughout life is retained in the intense experiencing that belongs to the arts and religion and to imaginative living, and to creative scientific work. (1971, p. 14)

6. In positing that his lifeworld become interpenetrated with racial meaning over time, rather than viewing it as raced *ab initio*, I am following Du Bois's lead. His self-presentation is consistently one of racialization. He becomes aware of the Veil with a "certain suddenness" when he is on the edge of adolescence, and it was not until he goes to Fisk that he becomes, in an affirmative sense, a Negro. This does not mean he was born with an ocular defect of color-blindness, but only that the definition or boundary of selfhood was not initially the color-line.

7. Du Bois's characterization of himself as a teacher is supported by data collected by Dorothy Yancy (1978).

8. Claudia Tate explores the theme of the search for the lost mother in her subtle reading of Du Bois's second novel, *Dark Princess* ([1928] 1995). In her view, the search begins in ambivalence and resultant guilt:

> When [Mary Silvina's] death made it possible for Du Bois to accomplish what her continued existence could not, all of his prior guilty wishes to be rid of her assailed him and probably complicated his already ambivalent feelings for her. I suspect that Du Bois transformed his guilty grief into a lifelong process of mourning and reparation in the only emotional economy that had given him sustained pleasure—the satisfaction of work. Du Bois's labor for the race would be like an act of reparation to his internalized mother and to his heroic image of himself. His writings would unconsciously inscribe his devotion to the memory of his mother and repair his assaulted ego. For these reasons his energy for accomplishment was virtually inexhaustible. (Tate 1998, p. 58)

This is a plausible interpretation and overlaps with the one developed here. It differs in emphasis. I see guilt and ambivalence as the minor theme in Du Bois's relationship with his mother, love and devotion as the major theme. As I read her, Tate reverses the relationship.

I might add that Tate draws on the analysis of Allison Davis in his *Leadership, Love, and Aggression* (1983). Davis emphasizes doubly determined defenses against shame. On the one hand, such defenses were needed to ward off the blows to self-esteem and self-respect that are suffered by black children in a white racist society (p. 114). On the other, they were required to ward off the shame involved in the questionable probity of Mary Silvina and the poverty her son experienced along with her (pp. 111–114). Beyond these plausible inferences, he contends that Du Bois "felt sorry for his mother, he nursed her, and he expressed concern and solicitude for her. But these are not love. In fact, they might have been defensive expressions of guilt from resenting her for having disgraced him" (p. 116). As is often the case when one gives oneself over to the interpretive exercise of suspicion, here Davis steps too far. Du Bois's account of his childhood and of his relationship to Mary Silvina may require interpretive amplification, but I do not see that we have license to overturn it.

Chapter 4. *Humani Nihil A Me Alienum Puto*

1. Act 1, scene 1 from P. Terentius Afer, *Heautontimoroumenos: The Self-Tormenter*, ed. Henry Thomas Riley, Perseus Digital Library, http://perseus.uchicago.edu/hopper/text.jsp?doc = Perseus:text:1999.02.0115.

2. What follows is not an attempt to capture the complexity of Du Bois's intellectual development. It includes just enough to make the generative tensions of *Souls* perspicuous. For more detailed treatments see Broderick 1971; Rampersad [1976] 1990, chaps. 2 and 3; Lewis 1993, chaps. 4–6.

3. In "Of the Coming of John," the Wells Institute, where the young man advances from innocence to enlightenment, is on Carlisle Street.

For a sense of Carlyle's impact on Du Bois's style, compare the After-Thought of *Souls* with the closing words of *The French Revolution:* "And so here, O Reader, has come the time for us two to part. Toilsome was our journeying together; not without offense, but it is done. To me thou wert a beloved shade, the disembodied or not yet embodied spirit of a brother. To thee I was but a voice." (Carlyle 2002, p. 775).

4. Along related lines, Houston Baker points to the affinities between Du Bois and Matthew Arnold. Both honor "a knowledge of the classics, a grounding in broad human sympathies, and a struggle for self-realization through the arts of the Western world. [Further,] the cultured man is elevated above the scenes of clerical and secular life; he is at some remove from the people, a man of astute sensibility who can wisely and justly criticize the state of society" (Baker [1972] 1990, p. 97).

5. Zamir "overstates his case . . . when he implausibly attempts to map 'quite precisely' (114) the parallels between Du Bois's brief recounting of a childhood experience in the second paragraph of 'Of Our Spiritual Strivings' and Hegel's complex account of the transition to self-consciousness . . . in the *Phenomenology*" (Gooding-Williams 1997, p. 855).

For an exceptionally thorough analysis of Du Bois's Harvard years, see Richard Cullen Rath 1997.

6. Du Bois's library included a copy of James's *Principles of Psychology* and both volumes of Martineau's *A Study of Religion* (Du Bois 1980, reel 89).

7. Gooding-Williams offers a more extended discussion of Hegelianism at Harvard and its possible influence on Du Bois in "Evading Narrative Myth, Evading Prophetic Pragmatism" ([1991–1992] 2006, pp. 75—78). See also Adell 1994, chap. 1; Lewis 1993, pp. 139–140.

8. Lenin once remarked that Marx's *Capital*, vol. 1, could not be understood without a prior familiarity with Hegel's *Science of Logic*. The same can be said of *Souls* and Du Bois's rootedness in the *Geisteswissenschaften*, the cultural or social sciences. This extends to the concept of "spirit" (spiritual life, spiritual striving) itself, which plays such an important role in *Souls* and the many meanings of which are contained in the concept of *Geist* (see chapter 6, pp. 143).

We might also note that Du Bois was enrolled in a course with Wilhelm Dilthey in 1893. We can't be sure what he took from this experience or even if he regularly attended the lectures, but, as Gooding-Williams (2005) demonstrates, there are affinities between Dilthey's *Introduction to the Human Sciences* of 1893 and Du Bois's "Conservation of Races," delivered at the founding meeting of the American Negro Academy in 1897.

Dilthey aside, the more general thrust of Gooding-Williams argument is to place Du Bois's approach to race matters squarely within the purview of the *Geisteswissenschaften*. From this perspective, we might use Hegel along with Goethe to signify Du Bois's susceptibility to German Romanticism, and his affiliation with Schmoller and Wagner to signify his more empirical/historical bent.

9. Mizruchi (1998, chap. 4) details the extreme racial bias of the social sciences and the pseudo–social sciences in the fin de siècle United States. The Veil Du Bois sought to pierce with the hard truth of science was woven in part from racialized science itself.

10. Aptheker (1985, p. 28) has Du Bois saying that his own best development is "now" one and the same with the best development of the world. In his autobiography, Du Bois quotes himself as saying his own best development is "not" one with the world's best development (*Autobiography*, p. 171). The latter seems correct, not only because it comes from Du Bois's own hand but also because it fits with his conception of voluntary self-sacrifice.

11. This is a slight modification of Esther's statement as she is about to intercede for her people: "and so will I go in unto the king, which *is* not according to the law; and if I perish, I perish" (Esther 4:16). As we will see, Du Bois uses it as well in "Of the Coming of John."

12. "Recognizing imagination as a source of black strength, and confirming the power of the imagination in Africa, slavery, and thereafter, also freed Du Bois as a thinker and a writer. . . . [He based *Souls*] on his scholarly knowledge of history and sociology, but the eye and mind of the artist are given almost free play" (Rampersad 1989, p. 116).

13. The use of the past tense reflects changes in the concept of race between 1900 and 1940 (ibid.).

14. The lynching, "followed in May by the death of his son Burghardt from diphtheria, shocked and depressed Du Bois" (Blight and Gooding-Williams 1997, p. 208). Lewis comments that, after the Hose lynching and the death of Burghardt, "Atlanta was like a poisoned well" for the Du Boises (1993, p. 228). Mizruchi (1996) joins the two events in her brilliant reading of Chapter XI of *Souls*.

15. As the reference to the landlord's wife indicates, Du Bois did not have access to all of the facts.

16. Alexander Crummell had died the previous September. The proximity of his death to Burghardt's may account in part for Du Bois's desire to eulogize him.

Chapter 5. Go Down, Moses

1. Eric Sundquist, who also sees interpenetrated horizontal and vertical dimensions in *Souls*, characterizes their relationship as one of ancestors and descendents: "The spirits of the ancestors, in the homeland as well as in the diaspora, need to be

fused with those present generations who continue to lead an oppressed 'underground' existence. Those who have gone before thus sustain and raise up those who live still on the soil of American slavery, the vertical (spiritual) figure of death and resurrection coinciding with the horizontal (secular) figure of memory and progress" (1993, p. 499). This formulation concisely captures the unifying effect of the sorrow songs on the topography of the text. It also glosses over the opposition between the horizontal and vertical dimensions, the way in which this duality reflects the soulsplitting effects of experiences of mis-recognition.

2. Du Bois deepens the analysis of the life and death of the Freedmen's Bureau in *Black Reconstruction in America*, but he holds to the same conclusion: "The Freedmen's Bureau did an extraordinary piece of work but it was a small and imperfect part of what it might have done if it had been made a permanent institution, given ample funds for operating schools and purchasing land, and if it had been gradually manned by trained civilian administrators" (p. 230).

3. "Though not overtly religious, [*Souls*] more than any other establishes its author as a prophetic voice . . . " (Byerman 1978, p. 75). See also Gates and Oliver 1999, p. xxxii; Zamir 1995, p. 195.

4. Except in this last regard, she is not a subject in her own right, but rather the object of masculine strivings and the stimulus in the ambivalent battle for recognition waged by white men and black men, fathers and sons. She is, in short, figured within the racialized version of the masculine imaginary.

5. We will feel the presence of these racialized oedipal relations in the background of the later chapters of *Souls*, intruding here and there, until they reemerge fully formed in "Of the Coming of John."

6. "The role which the great Negro Toussaint, called L'Ouverture, played in the history of the United States has seldom been fully appreciated. Representing the age of revolution in America, he rose to leadership through a bloody terror, which contrived a Negro 'problem' for the Western Hemisphere, intensified and defined the anti-slavery movement, became one of the causes . . . which led Napoleon to sell Louisiana for a song, and finally, through the interworking of these effects, rendered more certain the final prohibition of the slave-trade by the United States in 1807" (Du Bois [1896] 1970, *The Suppression of the African Slave-Trade*, p. 70).

7. On the same page in *Up From Slavery* where Washington mocks the young man who is learning French, he makes fun of young men with middle initials in their names: "When I asked what the 'J' stood for, in the name of John J. Jones, it was explained to me that this was part of his 'entitles'" (p. 94). Hence we might read "Of the Coming of John" as, in part, a counter to Washington's conception of racial enlightenment.

8. These parodic themes are concisely captured in this bit of song, collected by John Lomax in 1917:

Niggers gettin' mo 'like white folks,
Mo'like white fo'ks eve-y day.
Niggers learnin' Greek an' Latin,
Niggers wearin' silk an' satin,
Niggers gettin' mo'like white fo'ks eve'y day. (quoted in Levine 1978, p. 245)

Lomax viewed the lyrics as presenting "the cheerful side of improving social conditions." Levine observes that "they could as easily, and perhaps more meaningfully, be seen as an example of lower-class black satire and anger directed at those Negroes who were trying to become culturally 'white'" (ibid.).

9. This experience probably lies behind the parallel moment in "Of the Coming of John," in which John Jones requires Judge Henderson's permission to open a school (*Souls*, pp. 150–151). See Chapter 6 for further discussion of this parallel.

10. "In Josie, [Du Bois] honors the black woman, not for her success, but for her selflessness, for her love of family, for her belief in a better future for black people, and for her strength, willingness, and determination to work for a better life. . . . [His] sensitivity to the pain and anguish as well as the hopes and dreams of those women whose lives and work appeared to fill only small circles is noteworthy" (McKay 1986, p. 270).

11. Carrie Cowherd (2003) delineates and analyzes the classical references and representations in this chapter and *Souls* more generally. She also makes the case for Du Bois's Platonic influences and leanings (pp. 292–295).

12. In *The Autobiography* Du Bois acknowledges that, early on, he "conceived that the foundations of world culture were laid, the way was charted, the progress toward certain great goals was undoubted and inevitable" (1968, p. 155). He continues: "What the white world was doing, its goals and ideals, I had not doubted were quite right. What was wrong was that I and people like me and thousands of others who might have my ability and aspirations, were refused permission to be part of this world" (ibid., p. 156). In his later, more Marxist years, he became more critical of world culture. Still, Marx, too, held a view of history in which "the progress toward certain great goals was undoubted and inevitable"; and an important aspect of his critique was precisely the exclusion of a group of people—the proletariat—from social and cultural participation. Which is to say, certain commonalities result from viewing a shared historical situation from the perspective of oppressed peoples. That there are also meaningful or even fundamental differences—in this instance, opposed views of social class—is, of course, also true.

13. I would align myself with Arnold Rampersad in this regard, who sees a kind of Platonism in Du Bois without treating Du Bois as a Platonist: "he held strongly to what might be called a Platonic view of the ultimate significance of life. The true aim of work was not simply the accumulation of wealth. The pursuit of the ideals of truth, beauty, and love, of which work was prophetic, dominated his imagination" ([1976] 1990, p. 85).

14. The complex history of Du Bois's later views of racial leadership is not part of our story. See, e.g., Marable 1986; Reed 1997; Lewis 2000.

15. Any such feminization of blackness drops a veil over the spiritual strivings of individual black women. As Barbara McCaskill argues in her balanced assessment of this issue, "a scrutiny of *The Souls of Black Folk* confirms a presentation of African American womanhood that reinforces Victorian assumptions of respectable femininity that African American men like Du Bois—and numbers of their African American sisters—were accustomed to inserting in their projects of racial advancement" (2003, p. 74). See also Hazel Carby's analysis of the gender codes at work in *Souls* in her *Race Men* (1998, chap. 1) and Jane Flax's comments on the metaphysics of the feminine in her *Thinking Fragments: Psychoanalysis, Feminism, and Postmodernism in the Contemporary West* (1990, pp. 212—216).

16. This is the view taken by Stepto: "The 'white world' of *The Souls*—in Du Bois's estimation the first nine chapters" depict the "travels and travails of blacks in a white world, as well as the dialectics of race ritual between a black and white world." With Chapter X, by contrast, we enter a "black world" ([1979] 1991, p. 56).

17. "Du Bois's New England eyes prevent him from conceiving this scene from any other perspective than that of a witness; a stranger to physical slavery, he cannot be a

participant in the way that Douglass, Stamp Paid, or Baby Suggs Holy [the latter two characters in *Beloved*] were 'witnesses and participants,' or as Equiano was a witness and a participant in Essaka's communal dance" (Samuels 2001, p. 60).

18. Is Du Bois thinking here of Aristotle's famous characterization of man as a political animal?

19. Korang contends that the church Du Bois "came to observe was . . . , in his view, an example of the American accommodationism that did not sit well with him. We might say that his critical reconstruction of its history . . . was to test the possibility of recovering for his brand of black nationalism the inner Africanity this church had, but lost" (2001, p. 176).

Chapter 6. My Home Is Over Jordan

1. Dorothy Dinnerstein's analysis of the ways in which the infant's experience of the infant/mother dyad results in burdening women with expectations they cannot possibly fulfill remains unsurpassed. As she so ably argues, "woman, who introduced us to the human situation and who at the beginning seemed to us responsible for every drawback of that situation, carries for all of us a pre-rational onus of ultimately culpable responsibility forever after" ([1976] 1999, p. 234). From the infant's perspective, the mother is all-powerful. She is therefore responsible for all hurts and injuries, all suffering, and responsible, too, for their amelioration. From the mother's perspective, the situation is one of infinite responsibility and extremely finite power. Paradigmatically, she is therefore always on trial before a judge who will find her guilty; and she, herself, may well be one of the judges.

2. Crummell had a more literal connection to Du Bois's patrilineage: He was the first rector of the Episcopal Parish of St. Luke in New Haven, which Du Bois's grandfather Alexander helped to establish (*Dusk*, p. 108).

3. Gooding-Williams goes further and contends that "Du Bois's essay on Crummell is a masterpiece of indirection, and that Du Bois sets forth in it a substantive critique of Crummell's social philosophy" (1994, p. 245). Leaving aside any questions there might be concerning the plausibility of such a view in textual terms, it is hard for me to imagine Du Bois engaging in a covert strategy of this kind. He was a man who prided himself on his honesty (*Autobiography*, p. 277) and who "always tried to give the other fellow his due. . . . It became a point of honor never to refuse appreciation to one who had earned it, no matter who he was" (p. 284). To criticize Crummell while appearing to honor him would have cut very much against the grain. It also would have been to speak ill of the dead, even if by indirection, and of a man whose death was temporally linked to Burghardt's. This is not to deny the larger point, that there were significant differences between the two men, most notably on the importance of keeping alive the memory of slavery (see also Zamir 1995, pp. 169–170). But if these differences were in the back of Du Bois's mind, there (I would say) they stayed.

For Crummell's appreciation of Du Bois, see his "The Attitude of the American Mind toward the Negro Intellect" (1898; in Moses 1992, p. 299).

4. In Sundquist's view, Du Bois's "idealization of Crummell's prophetic calling was a means of giving new scope to the imaginative, spiritual tendencies in his own thought which had been held in check by the methods of historical and sociological writing in which he had been trained" (1993, p. 518). As indicated earlier, I would not limit this claim to the present chapter.

5. In common with earlier references to the tendency toward revolt and revenge in black political culture, it can also be read as a warning to white people. Stated in the

language of biblical justification, "an eye for an eye, a tooth for a tooth." Stated in the language of the streets, "what goes around comes around."

6. The notion of "manifest destiny" is drawn from the annals of Anglo-American expansion: White people would move westward, bringing democracy to all who were capable of practicing it. American Indians and Negroes, needless to say, lacked this capability. When Jones returns to the South he, too, is on a civilizing mission, but his people are precisely the ones the white supremacist doctrine excludes.

7. This connection is also drawn by Blight and Gooding-Williams (1997, p. 217) and Charles Nero (2005, pp. 267–269).

8. There is a town of Altamaha in Georgia, but unlike Altamaha in *Souls*, it is inland rather than coastal. Why Du Bois chose the name is not clear. *Alt* is "old" in German and *maha* contains *ma*; but I'd not place any weight on this bit of amateur philology.

9. "'Of the Coming of John' may well be the author's sublimated revenge on those whites who called him and his dead son 'niggers'. . . . John may not be one of the Talented Tenth, but the very anger with which he acts is the same anger with which his creator frequently wrote. His murder in a just cause is simultaneously repulsive and attractive to the writer" (Byerman 1978, p. 106).

10. As noted earlier, the "Carlisle" in Carlisle Street is a reference to Thomas Carlyle, and so evokes the heroic strivings that Du Bois made his own. "Johnstown" provides another double for John Jones.

11. Chester Fontenot (2003, pp. 134–148) provides a subtle and sustained reading of "Of the Coming of John." On this issue he observes: "Du Bois's language [in describing Jones when he is newly come up from the South] suggests that John embodies the representation of nineteenth-century black males—undependable, innocent, happy, and lacking responsibility and purpose" (p. 135).

For an interpretation of the story from a psychoanalytic perspective quite different from the one employed here, see Zwarg (2002).

12. Here again we have a piece of Du Bois's biography. The summer after graduating from Fisk, he and some friends went north to work in a resort hotel in Minnesota. The work included waiting tables, for which Du Bois was ill-suited, and promoting (as well as singing in) a glee club, for which he was well-suited (*Autobiography*, pp. 127–129).

13. The disjunction that Du Bois depicts has a painful, ongoing currency. We still hear of young people of color who overcome all manner of obstacles to attend elite (white) colleges and universities, only to find that the further they progress along the road to educational attainment, the more they are viewed with suspicion by their peers who stayed behind—and who then find in themselves an uncomfortable or even lacerating sense of distance and difference from their communities of origin. (There are, to be sure, other stories to be told, of community pride in educational achievement and a reciprocal sense of gratitude for and connection with home and community.)

14. Readers of *Souls* often see John in the image of John the Baptist. Concerning this scene, Blight and Gooding-Williams wittily remark that "here, ironically, Du Bois's John the Baptist appears as John the 'anti-Baptist'" (1997, p. 217).

15. After Nina died, Du Bois wrote a simple eulogy for her, in which he movingly describes her enduring sense of bereavement from the loss of her first-born. Of himself he remarks: "I was not, on the whole, what one would describe as a good husband. The family and its interests were never the main center of my life. I was always striving to guide the world and certainly the Negro group, so that I was always ranging away in body and in soul and leaving the home to my wife" (quoted in Lewis 1995, p. 142). The well-being of his family was, if not sacrificed to, at least compromised by his service to the race.

16. Following the consonants (*J*), one might also see in Jennie a trace of Josie and, through Josie, link John to Joan—Joan of Arc, as in Du Bois's use of Schiller's *The Maid of Orleans*. The common thread—common, too, in the allusion to John the Baptist and (in the end) to the crucified Jesus Christ—is self-sacrifice for a spiritual cause.

17. In Wagner's opera, Lohengrin appears magically to rescue Elsa, when she is falsely accused of her brother's murder. He successfully defends her honor, as John Jones does the honor of his sister. Lohengrin then asks for Elsa's hand in marriage and she willingly consents. He tells her he has a secret she must never ask him to reveal. On their wedding day, she cannot resist asking the question. He must then reveal that he is a knight of the Holy Grail and that he must now return to the castle of the Grail. So he, too, like the hero-narrator of *Souls*, follows the path of renunciation.

Charles Nero offers a quite different interpretation of this moment and of "Of the Coming of John" more generally. He reads the story as a bitter commentary on the impossibility of establishing "biracial male homosocial" bonds (2005, p. 260) in turn-of-the-century America. This is not an implausible interpretation of the meaning of sympathy between men of different races; framing it this way, Nero sees the relationship between John Jones and John Henderson as the central issue. His conclusion, however, does seem implausible: "Du Bois's melodramatic ending of this short story is a recording of homosexual panic or an apprehension of his inability to participate in socially accepted public heterosexuality. Black John Jones must kill his beloved, white John Henderson, if he is to restore his own gender integrity" (ibid., p. 276). I don't see that Du Bois gives us license to see an intense but tragically failed or flawed homoerotic bond between the two men. A more restrained interpretation—that their deaths testify to the failure of interracial sympathy and the situational impossibility of black and white rising together—would seem to be a better fit with the textual evidence.

In the course of making his general argument, Nero brings forward gender matters that are commonly overlooked. As we have noted, Du Bois himself in his midnight musings in Berlin and his protagonist as he turns toward home cite lines spoken by Queen Esther as they envision the mission they are about to undertake. Nero calls attention to the use made of Esther by African-American women at the turn of the century and asks why Du Bois would "align his male protagonist with a socially feminized text" (p. 267). Even bracketing this contextualization, Esther is, after all, a woman, and hence one might see in Du Bois's authorial choice an "appropriation of the feminine for John" (p. 269). This fits with Nero's further argument that, as John awaits lynching and death, he identifies himself with Elsa, as he hums the "Song of the Bride": "John approaches the act of submission [to death, in this instance] as a bride approaches her husband on the wedding day" (p. 264).

This interpretation of the bride-song moment fits with John's passivity, which was gendered feminine at that time. But his acceptance of death is also explained by a combination of guilt (acceptance of responsibility for his actions) and despair; and I think the stronger reading of this moment positions John as the groom, not the bride. On the other hand, the identification with Esther does suggest a "feminine" (although definitely not passive or submissive) component in the personality of both Du Bois and his protagonist. The question then becomes, how do we construe this purported femininity? In my opinion, by reference to Du Bois's identificatory relationship with his mother: We might suppose that, in taking up his mission and in bearing the sacrifices it entailed, he was not only acting *for her* but also acting *in her stead*. Or, as argued in Chapter 3, the internalization of his relationship with Mary Silvina formed the matrix of his character. Although such identifications are characteristically disavowed in the formation of normative male heterosexuality, they are nonetheless constitutive of it.

Femininity in this sense is therefore distinct from both the feminine in women and from homoerotic components of personality in men.

ɩ 18. In *Two Warring Ideals*, Byerman asserts that Jones "commits suicide by jumping into the sea" (1978, p. 103). Later, in *Seizing the Word*, he characterizes the last moment as Jones's "calm, almost suicidal wait for the lynch mob" (1994, p. 33). The latter seems just right. The earlier interpretation is in tune with Jones's suicidal intent but ignores the textual markers of the event. The later one nicely combines them.

19. I hope I will not be held too strictly to philosophical account in my bending of the notion of Stoicism to fit the present circumstance.

20. "Du Bois's 'Gospel of Sacrifice' redefines the rite as possession rather than dispossession. As such, it becomes the basis of a social mission. Sacrifice is monumentalized, writ large, to remember collective sufferings" (Mizruchi 1998, p. 365). To remember them, and to end them.

21. "When Whites look at these mourners and mutter "Niggers," they are defining Blacks through their exclusion from sympathy as outside the borders of community" (Mizruchi 1996, p. 278).

22. Negro spiritual. Recorded by Harry Belafonte, August 10, 1955.

23. Martineau remarks of agnosticism: "to make it good, you must be careful not to look beyond phenomena, as empirical facts: you must abjure the enquiry into *causes*, and the attempt to trace invisible *issues*: never lift the veil that bounds experience, and you will need nothing and know nothing of the transcendental world" (1888, 1:vii). Du Bois's settled position was precisely agnostic: "My thought on personal immortality is easily explained. I do not know. I do not see how any one could know. Our whole basis of knowledge is so relative and contingent that when we get to argue concerning ultimate reality and the real essence of life and the past and the future, we seem to be talking without real data and getting nowhere" (quoted in Lewis 1995, p. 134). Nonetheless, I am suggesting that Du Bois could not resist lifting the veil that separates life and death, at least to the extent of filling his transcendental metaphors with a passion and a yearning his restrained agnosticism would not seem to allow.

24. The publication history is also relevant. Gates and Oliver observe: "without the publisher's insistence, this last, unifying chapter would not have been included in *Souls*" (1999, p. xxxi). Du Bois had submitted a manuscript ending with "Of the Coming of John," and it was his editor who asked, "Is it too late to carry out your original intention of having a chapter on 'Sorrow Songs of the Negroes'?" (ibid.).

25. "In [*Souls*], Du Bois boldly honors slave music as a way of rehabilitating African American folk culture. The lyrics remain hidden until the final chapter . . . , a device that modeled the slaves' clandestine creation and expression of this music" (Blight and Gooding-Williams 1997, p. 217).

26. Alexander Weheliye takes a further step along this line: "Poems by Schiller, Byron, Lowell, and Whittier thus form a symbiosis with the spirituals. Du Bois slyly forces these Western texts to testify to slavery and the absent presence of black subjects, both as empirical entities and as apparitions integral *to* and unequivocally *of* Western modernity. Read or listened to in tandem with the musical bars, then, the poems *are* the lyrics of the 'Sorrow Songs,' creating a new form of spiritual in their admixture" (2005, pp. 331–332).

27. In the *Phaedo*, Plato places the River Ocean at the outermost rim of the world, with the River of Pain just inside it and flowing in the opposite direction. Running through and beneath the world there are two other great rivers: the River of Burning Fire and the River of Wailing (in Rouse 1956, pp. 516–517). Plato's aim in this mythic presentation is to set the context for the judgment of souls after they have left the

company of the body. With better historical license, African-Americans might see the Atlantic as an unholy combination of all four rivers, a gloomy prospect relieved only by the thought and memory of the distant African homeland.

28. In the last chapter of *Souls*, there is "an authorial self-fashioning and an autobiographical narrative of Du Bois's development from infancy (when the African song is first heard) to youthful immersion (in Tennessee) and to mature self-consciousness (at Atlanta University)" (Zamir 1995, p. 183).

29. "The music . . . signifies slavery and the inheritance of ancestral strength as well as ancestral hardship; the words lack of meaning [is, among other things,] the utmost sign of the loss of ancestral language (or, in a more accurate sense, of its fragmentary survival in the words and phrases that have entered American English)" (Sundquist 1993, p. 528. See also Samuels 2001, pp. 60–61).

30. "Du Bois locates the sublime in black religion in general and the sorrow songs in particular. Du Bois does this to reverse the idea that black people were aesthetically impoverished and incapable of using symbolic language. Through their religious expression, New World Africans challenge an Anglo-European conception of the sublime. They transmute their experience in America into black oral expressive culture, the sublime in a 'blue note' of black cultural productions, and they produce a sublimity and a beauty that is congruent with their reality, thereby deconstructing the social text called America" (Hubbard 2003b, p. 313).

31. Rath frames his analysis of the sorrow songs this way: "Du Bois laid claim to both Europe and Africa, each from the frontier of the other. He wrote from what ninety years later is called the liminal, the hybridized, the in-between, the middle ground, the creolized—that which must create a legitimacy the world without has tried to deny it" (1997, pp. 490–491). The permutations of the sorrow songs reflect this cultural location.

32. Sundquist approaches this point differently. He sees Du Bois as identifying himself with the figure of the Preacher in "Of the Faith of the Fathers," and, through this mediation, with the functions of bard and cultural priest (1993, pp. 482–483). I'd say that Du Bois's opinion of the Preacher is at best ambivalent and so an unlikely object of such identification. But there is no doubt that the sorrow songs moved him deeply, and that he "sang" them from his soul. Because by his own account they are of African origin, it is then at least permissible to assign him the role of griot.

33. Zamir goes a step further, arguing that "by replacing high art's claims for representing the health of national cultural with the counterclaims for the higher authenticity of black *folk* art, Du Bois is able to relativize the criteria by which racist evolutionary theories provided alibis for Anglo-Saxon superiority and for the assimilation or exclusion of minority groups" (1995, p. 175). And this challenge to the distinction between high and folk culture has a reflexive implication: "against the grain of his own dichotomization of primitive and civilized, he is at least able to grope his way to the idea that once the criterion for judging the 'progress' or 'backwardness' of a people is shifted from technological or imperial achievement to poetry, the hierarchy between 'civilized and 'primitive' becomes unstable" (ibid., p. 176).

References

Adell, Sandra. 1994. *Double Consciousness/Double Bind: Theoretical Issues in Twentieth-Century Black Literature.* Chicago: University of Illinois Press.

Aptheker, Herbert, ed. 1970. *A Documentary History of the Negro People in the United States, Volume II.* New York: The Citadel Press.

——, ed. 1973. *The Correspondence of W. E. B. Du Bois, 1877–1934.* Amherst: University of Massachusetts Press.

——, ed. 1985. *Against Racism: Unpublished Essays, Papers, Addresses, 1887–1961, By W. E. B. Du Bois.* Amherst: University of Massachusetts Press.

——, ed. 1986. *Newspaper Columns of W. E. B. Du Bois, Volume 1.* White Plains, NY: Kraus-Thompson Organization Limited.

Aristotle. 1998. *Politics.* Trans. Ernest Barker. New York: Oxford University Press.

Baker, Houston A. [1972] 1990. *Long Black Song: Essays in Black American Literature and Culture.* Charlottesville: University of Virginia Press.

Barkin, Kenneth D. 2000. "'Berlin Days,' 1892–1894: W. E. B. Du Bois and German Political Economy." *boundary 2* 27 (3):79–101.

Benjamin, Jessica. 1980. "The Bonds of Love: Rational Violence and Erotic Domination." *Feminist Studies* 6:144–174.

——. 1988. *The Bonds of Love: Psychoanalysis, Feminism, and the Problem of Domination.* New York: Pantheon Books.

——. 1995. *Like Subjects, Love Objects.* New Haven: Yale University Press.

Benston, Kimberly, ed. 1987. *Speaking for You: The Vision of Ralph Ellison.* Washington, DC: Howard University Press.

Blight, D. W., and R. Gooding-Williams, eds. 1997. *THE SOULS OF BLACK FOLK by W. E. B. Du Bois.* Boston: Bedford Books.

Broderick, Francis L. 1971. "The Search for a Career." In Logan 1971, pp. 1–37.

Bruce, Dickson D., Jr. 1992. "W. E. B. Du Bois and the Idea of Double Consciousness." In Gates and Oliver 1999, pp. 236–244.

Bull, Malcolm. 1998. "Slavery and the Multiple Self." *New Left Review* 231:94–126.

Burnet, John. 1930. *Early Greek Philosophy.* London: A. & C. Black.

Byerman, Keith. 1978. *Two Warring Ideals: The Dialectical Thought of W. E. B. Du Bois.* Ph.D. diss., Purdue University.

——. 1994. *Seizing the Word: History, Art, and Self in the Work of W. E. B. Du Bois.* Athens: University of Georgia Press.

Carby, Hazel. 1998. *Race Men.* Cambridge: Harvard University Press.

Carlyle, Thomas. 1965. *Past and Present.* New York: New York University Press.

——. 1966. *On Heroes, Hero-Worship and the Heroic in History.* Lincoln: University of Nebraska Press.

——. 2002. *The French Revolution: A History.* New York: Modern Library.

Carroll, Anne E. 2005. "Du Bois and Art Theory: *The Souls of Black Folk* as a 'Total Work of Art'." In Gooding-Williams and McBride 2005, pp. 235–254.

Chodorow, Nancy. 1978. *The Reproduction of Mothering.* Berkeley: University of California Press.

——. 1989. *Feminism and Psychoanalytic Theory.* New Haven: Yale University Press.

——. 1994. *Femininities, Masculinities, Sexualities.* Lexington: University of Kentucky Press.

Collins, Patricia Hill. 1990. *Black Feminist Thought.* New York: Routledge.

Cowherd, Carrie. 2003. "The Wings of Atalanta: Classical Influences in *The Souls of Black Folk.*" In Hubbard 2003a, pp. 284–297.

Crummell, Alexander. 1898. "The Attitude of the American Mind toward the Negro Intellect." In Moses 1992, pp. 289–300.

Cummings, E. E. 1972. *Complete Poems (1913–1962).* New York: Harcourt Bruce Jovanovich.

Davis, Allison. 1983. *Leadership, Love, and Aggression.* New York: Harcourt Brace Jovanovich.

Davis, Ossie, and Ruby Dee. 1998. *With Ossie and Ruby: In This Life Together.* New York: Harper-Collins.

Dinnerstein, Dorothy. [1976] 1999. *The Mermaid and the Minotaur.* New York: Other Press.

Douglass, Frederick. [1845] 1997. *Narrative of the Life of Frederick Douglass, An American Slave, Written By Himself.* New York: W. W. Norton.

Du Bois, W. E. B. [1896] 1970. *The Suppression of the African Slave-Trade to the United States of America, 1638–1870.* Mineola, NY: Dover.

——. 1897. "Strivings of the Negro People." *Atlantic Monthly* 80:194–198.

——. 1898. "Careers Open to College-Bred Negroes." In Foner 1970, pp. 86–101.

——. [1899] 1996. *The Philadelphia Negro.* Philadelphia: University of Pennsylvania Press.

——. 1903a. *The Souls of Black Folk.* In Gates and Oliver 1999.

——. 1903b. "The Talented Tenth." In Paschal 1971, pp. 31–51.

——. 1904. "The Souls of Black Folk." In Blight and Gooding-Williams 1997, pp. 254–255.

——. 1905. "Credo." In Gates and Oliver 1999, pp. 214–215.

——. 1906. "A Litany of Atlanta." In Gates and Oliver 1999, pp. 215–218.

——. 1907. "St. Francis of Assisi." In Paschal 1971, pp. 290–302.

——. [1909] 1962. *John Brown.* New York: International Publishers.

——. [1911] 2004. *The Quest of the Silver Fleece.* Philadelphia: Pine Street Books.

——. [1920] 1969. *Darkwater: Voices from within the Veil.* New York: Schocken Books.

——. [1928] 1995. *Dark Princess.* Jackson: University Press of Mississippi.

——. 1935. "The Present Economic Problem of the American Negro." *National Baptist Voice.* In Paschal 1971, pp. 163–179.

——. [1935] 1992. *Black Reconstruction in America.* New York: The Free Press.

——. 1936. "Opera and the Negro Problem." In Aptheker 1986, pp. 129–131.

——. 1937. "Race as Class." *Philadelphia Courier,* June 5, 1937. In Aptheker 1986, p. 207.

——. [1940] 1975. *Dusk of Dawn.* Millwood, NY: Kraus-Thomson Org. Ltd.

——. [1946] 1965. *The World and Africa.* New York: International Publishers.

——. 1961. *W. E. B. Du Bois: A Recorded Autobiography.* Folkways Record FH 5511 [Recorded by Moses Asch].

——. 1968. *The Autobiography of W. E. B. Du Bois.* New York: International Publishers.

——. 1980. *The Papers of W. E. B. Du Bois, 1868–1963.* Sanford, NC: Microfiling Corp. of America.

———. 1999. *Musical Hypertext Edition of THE SOULS OF BLACK FOLK*. University of Virginia: Electronic Text Center, http://way.net/SoulsOfBlackFolk/SoulsOfBlackFolk.html.

Ellison, Ralph W. [1952] 1989. *Invisible Man*. New York: Vintage Books.

Emerson, Ralph Waldo. 1843. "The Transcendentalist." In Emerson 1950, pp. 87–103.

———. 1950. *The Selected Writings of Ralph Waldo Emerson*. Ed. Brooks Atkinson. New York: Modern Library.

Fanon, Frantz. [1952] 1967. *Black Skin, White Masks*. New York: Grove Press.

Flax, Jane. 1990. *Thinking Fragments: Psychoanalysis, Feminism, and Postmodernism in the Contemporary West*. Berkeley: University of California Press.

———. 1993. *Disputed Subjects*. New York: Routledge.

Foner, Philip S. 1970. *W. E. B. Du Bois Speaks: Speeches and Addresses, 1890–1919*. New York: Pathfinder.

Fontenot, C. J., M. A. Morgon, and S. Gardner, eds. 2001. *W. E. B. Du Bois and Race*. Macon, GA: Mercer University Press.

Fontenot, Chester J. 2003. "Du Bois's 'Of the Coming of John,' Toomer's 'Kabnis,' and the Dilemma of Self-Representation." In Hubbard 2003a, pp. 130–160.

Franklin, John H., ed. 1965. *Three Negro Classics*. New York: Avon Books.

Freud, Sigmund. 1900. *The Interpretation of Dreams*. In vols. 4–5 of the *Standard Edition of the Complete Psychological Works of Sigmund Freud* [hereafter *SE*]. Edited and translated by James Strachey. 24 vols. Londgon: Hogarth, 1953–74.

———. 1917. "Mourning and Melancholia." In Freud, *SE*, vol. 14.

———. 1937. "Constructions in Analysis." In Freud, *SE*, vol. 23.

Gates, Henry Louis, Jr., ed. 1990. *Reading Black, Reading Feminist: A Critical Anthology*. New York: Meridian.

Gates, Henry, and Terri Oliver, eds. 1999. *W. E. B. Du Bois, THE SOULS OF BLACK FOLK: A Norton Critical Edition*. New York: W. W. Norton.

George, Andrew J., ed. 1904. *The Complete Poetical Works of Wordsworth*. Boston: Houghton Mifflin.

Goethe, J. W. 1965. *Faust*. Trans. C. E. Passage. New York: Bobbs-Merrill.

Gooding-Williams, Robert. 1994. "Du Bois's Counter-Sublime." In Gates and Oliver 1999, pp. 245–262.

———. 1997. "*Dark Voices* . . . By Shamoon Zamir." Book Review. *American Literature* 69 (4): 855–856.

———. 2003. "Intimations of Immortality and Double Consciousness." Presented at the Du Bois Symposium, Eastern Division Meeting of the American Philosophical Association, Washington, DC, December.

———. 2005. "Politics, Race, and the Human Sciences." Presented at a conference on "Du Bois and the Scientific Study of Race," Yale University, New Haven, CT.

———. 2006. *Look, a Negro!* New York: Routledge.

———. [1991–1992] 2006. "Evading Narrative Myth, Evading Prophetic Pragmatism." In Gooding-Williams 2006, pp. 69–86.

Gooding-Williams, Robert, and Dwight McBride, eds. 1997. *W. E. B. Du Bois: THE SOULS OF BLACK FOLK*. Boston: Bedford Books.

———. 2005. *100 Years of THE SOULS OF BLACK FOLK: A Celebration of W. E. B. Du Bois*. A Special Issue of *Public Culture* 17 (2).

Hanchard, Michael. 2006. *Party/Politic: Horizons in Black Political Thought*. New York: Oxford University Press.

Hancock, Ange-Marie. 2005a. "W. E. B. Du Bois and the 'Outsider Within'." Presented at a conference on "Du Bois and the Scientific Study of Race," Yale University, New Haven, CT.

———. 2005b. "W. E. B. Du Bois: Intellectual Forefather of Intersectionality?" *Souls: A Critical Journal of Black Politics, Culture, and Society* 7 (3–4): 74–84.

Harris, Shanette M. 2003. "Constructing a Psychological Perspective: The Observer and the Observed in *The Souls of Black Folks*." In Hubbard 2003a, pp. 218–250.

Hart, Albert Bushnell. 1891. "Why the South Was Defeated in the Civil War," *The New England Magazine* 11 (3): 363–376.

Hegel, G. W. F. 1956. *The Philosophy of History.* New York: Dover.

———. [1807] 1977. *The Phenomenology of Spirit.* Trans. A. V. Miller. New York: Oxford University Press.

Hubbard, Dolan, ed. 2003a. *The Souls of Black Folk: One Hundred Years Later.* Columbia: University of Missouri Press.

———. 2003b. "W. E. B. Du Bois and the Invention of the Sublime in *The Souls of Black Folk.*" In Hubbard 2003a, pp. 298–321.

James, William. 1890. *The Principles of Psychology.* Vol. 1. New York: Henry Holt.

Kaufmann, Walter, ed. 1959. *The Portable Nietzsche.* New York: Penguin Books.

Korang, Kwaku Larbi. 2001. "As I Face America: Race and Africanity in Du Bois's *The Souls of Black Folk.*" In Fontenot, Morgan, and Gardner 2001, pp. 166–186.

Lattimore, Richmond, trans. 1965. *The Odyssey of Homer.* New York: Harper & Row.

Lemke, Sieglinde. 2000. "Berlin and Boundaries: *sollen* versus *gesehehen.*" *boundary 2* 27 (3):45–78.

Levine, Lawrence. 1978. *Black Culture, Black Consciousness.* New York: Oxford University Press.

Lewis, David Levering. 1993. *W. E. B. Du Bois: Biography of a Race.* New York: Henry Holt.

———, ed. 1995. *W. E. B. Du Bois: A Reader.* New York: Henry Holt and Company.

———. 2000. *W. E. B. Du Bois: The Fight for Equality and the American Century.* New York: Henry Holt.

Litwack, Leon. 1998. *Trouble in Mind: Black Southerners in the Age of Jim Crow.* New York: Alfred A. Knopf.

Logan, Rayford, ed. 1971. *W. E. B. Du Bois: A Profile.* New York: Hill and Wang.

Lomax, Alan, ed. 1964. *The Penguin Book of American Folk Songs.* Baltimore: Penguin Books.

MacLeod, Fiona [William Sharp]. 1913. "Dim Face of Beauty." *From the Hills of Dream: Threnodies, Songs and Later Poems.* London: William Heineman.

Marable, Manning. 1986. *W. E. B. Du Bois: Black Radical Democrat.* Boston: Twayne.

Markert, Lawrence W. 1988. *Arthur Symons: Critic of the Seven Arts.* Ann Arbor: U.M.I. Research Press.

Martin, Theodore, Anna Swanwick, and A. Lodge, trans. 1902. *The Maid of Orleans, The Bride of Messina, Wilhelm Tell, Demetrius. By Friedrich Schiller.* Boston: Francis A. Niccolls and Company.

Martineau, James. 1888. *A Study of Religion.* 2 vols. New York: MacMillan.

Marx, Karl. 1845. "Theses on Feuerbach." In Tucker 1978, pp. 143–145.

———. 1852. *The Eighteenth Brumaire of Louis Bonaparte.* In Tucker 1978, pp. 594–617.

Marx, Karl, and Friedrich Engels. 1848. *Communist Manifesto.* In Tucker 1978, pp. 469–500.

McCaskill, Barbara. 2003. "Anna Julia Cooper, Pauline Elizabeth Hopkins, and the African American Feminization of Du Bois's Discourse." In Hubbard 2003a, pp. 70–84.

McDowell, Deborah, and Arnold Rampersad, eds. 1989. *Slavery and the Literary Imagination.* Baltimore: The Johns Hopkins Press.

McKay, Nellie Y. 1986. "W. E. B. Du Bois: The Black Women in His Writings—Selected Fictional and Autobiographical Portraits." In Gates and Oliver 1999, pp. 263–272.

———. 1990. "The Souls of Black Women." In Gates 1990, pp. 227–243.

Mizruchi, Susan. 1996. "Neighbors, Strangers, Corpses: Death and Sympathy in the Early Writings of W. E. B. Du Bois." In Gates and Oliver 1999, pp. 273–295.

———. 1998. *The Science of Sacrifice: American Literature and Modern Social Theory.* Princeton, NJ: Princeton University Press.

Morrison, Toni. 1992. *Jazz.* New York: Penguin Books.

Moses, Wilson J., ed. 1992. *Destiny and Race: Selected Writings, 1840–1898 (Alexander Crummell).* Amherst: University of Massachusetts Press.

Moss, Donald, ed. 2003. *Hatred in the First Person Plural*. New York: Other Press.

Mostern, Kenneth. 1999. *Autobiography and Black Identity Politics: Racialization in Twentieth Century America*. New York: Cambridge University Press.

Munro, John M. 1969. *Arthur Symons*. New York: Twayne.

Nero, Charles I. 2005. "Queering *The Souls of Black Folk*." In Gooding-Williams and McBride 1997, pp. 255–276.

Nietzsche, Friedrich [1872] 1956. *The Birth of Tragedy*. Trans. Walter Kaufmann. New York: Doubleday.

——. 1883–1885. *Thus Spoke Zarathustra*. In Kaufmann 1959, pp. 100–439.

——. [1886] 1966. *Beyond Good and Evil*. Trans. Walter Kaufmann. New York: Vintage Books.

——. [1887] 1967. *On the Genealogy of Morals*. Trans. Walter Kaufmann. New York: Vintage Books.

Oldfield, J. R. 1995. *Civilization and Black Progress: Selected Writings of Alexander Crummell on the South*. Charlottesville: University Press of Virginia.

Paschal, Andrew G., ed. 1971. *A W. E. B. Du Bois Reader*. New York: Macmillan.

Plato. *Phaedo*. In Rouse 1956, pp. 460–521.

——. *Republic*. In Rouse 1956, pp. 118–422.

Rampersad, Arnold. [1976] 1990. *The Art and Imagination of W. E. B. Du Bois*. Cambridge: Harvard University Press.

——. 1989. "Slavery and the Literary Imagination: Du Bois's *The Souls of Black Folk*." In McDowell and Rampersad 1989, pp. 104–124.

Rath, Richard Cullen. 1997. "Echo and Narcissus: The Afrocentric Pragmatism of W. E. B. Du Bois." *The Journal of American History* 84 (2): 461–495.

Razaf, Andy, and Thomas Waller. 1929. "(What Did I Do to Be So) Black and Blue." Mills Music. Recorded by Louis Armstrong and His Orchestra, July 22, 1929.

Reed, Adolph L., Jr. 1997. *W. E. B. Du Bois and American Political Thought: Fabianism and the Color Line*. New York: Oxford University Press.

Ricoeur, Paul. 1970. *Freud and Philosophy*. New Haven: Yale University Press.

Ridolfi, Roberto. 1963. *The Life of Niccoló Machiavelli*. Trans. Cecil Grayson. Chicago: University of Chicago Press.

Rojas, Fabio. 2005. "The Survey on Issues in African Studies: A First Report." Department of Sociology, Indiana University, Bloomington.

Rouse, W. H. D., ed. 1956. *Great Dialogues of Plato*. New York: New American Library.

Samuels, Wilfred D. 2001. "Confluences, Confirmation, and Conservation at the Crossroads: Intersecting Junctures in *The Interesting Narrative of the Life* and *The Souls of Black Folk*." In Fontenot, Morgan, and Gardner 2001, pp. 45–69.

Sartre, Jean-Paul. [1963] 1968. *Search for a Method*. New York: Vintage Books.

Schiller, Friedrich von. 1801. *The Maid of Orleans*. In Martin, Swanwick, and Lodge 1902, pp. 1–133. Also in Project Gutenberg, http://onlinebooks.library.upenn.edu/webbin/gutbook/lookup?num=6792.

Schrager, Cynthia D. 1996. "Both Sides of the Veil: Race, Science, and Mysticism in W. E. B. Du Bois." *American Quarterly* 48 (4): 551–586.

Shakespeare, William. *Hamlet*. In Sisson 1953, pp. 997–1042.

——. *The Life and Death of King John*. In Sisson 1953, pp. 421–448.

Siemerling, Winfried. 2001. "W. E. B. Du Bois, Hegel, and the Staging of Alterity." *Callaloo* 24 (1): 325–333.

Sisson, C., ed. 1953. *William Shakespeare: The Complete Works*. New York: Harper.

Smart, C., ed. 1863. *The Works of Horace*. New York: Harper.

Sollors, Werner. 1986. *Beyond Ethnicity: Consent and Descent in American Culture*. New York: Oxford University Press.

Stepto, Robert B. [1979] 1991. *From Behind the Veil: A Study in Afro-American Narrative*. Chicago: University of Illinois Press.

Sundquist, Eric J. 1993. *To Wake the Nations: Race in the Making of American Literature*. Cambridge: Harvard University Press.

——, ed. 1996. *The Oxford W. E. B. Du Bois Reader*. New York: Oxford University Press.

Symons, Arthur. 1924. *The Collected Works of Arthur Symons*. Vol. 2, *Poems*. London: Martin Secker.

Tate, Claudia. 1987. "Notes on the Invisible Women in Ralph Ellison's *Invisible Man*." In Benston 1987, pp. 163–172.

——. 1998. *Psychoanalysis and Black Novels: Desire and the Protocols of Race*. New York: Oxford University Press.

Terentius Afer, P. *Heautontimoroumenos: The Self-Tormenter*. Ed. Henry Thomas Riley. Perseus Digital Library, http://perseus.uchicago.edu/hopper/text.jsp?doc=Perseus:text:1999.02.0115.

Tucker, Robert, ed. 1978. *The Marx-Engels Reader*. New York: W. W. Norton.

Washington, Booker T. 1895. "Atlanta Exposition Address." In Gates and Oliver 1999, pp. 167–170.

——. 1901. *Up From Slavery*. In Franklin 1965.

Weheliye, Alexander G. 2005. "The Grooves of Temporality." In Gooding-Williams and McBride 1997, pp. 319–338.

Winnicott, D. W. 1971. *Playing and Reality*. New York: Basic Books.

Wolfenstein, Eugene Victor. 1993. *Psychoanalytic-Marxism: Groundwork*. New York: Guilford Press.

——. 2000a. *Inside/Outside Nietzsche: Psychoanalytic Explorations*. Ithaca: Cornell University Press.

——. 2000b. "On the Road Not Taken: 'Revolt and Revenge' in W. E. B. Du Bois's *The Souls of Black Folk*." *Journal for the Psychoanalysis of Culture and Society* 5 (1): 121–132.

——. 2003. "Race, Rage, and Oedipus in Ralph W. Ellison's *Invisible Man*." In Moss 2003, pp. 69–113.

Wordsworth, William. 1807. "Ode: Intimations of Immortality From Recollections of Early Childhood." In George 1904, pp. 353–356.

X, Malcolm, and A. Haley. 1965. *The Autobiography of Malcolm X*. New York: Grove Press.

Yancy, Dorothy C. 1978. "William Edward Burghardt Du Bois' Atlanta Years: The Human Side—A Study Based Upon Oral Sources." *The Journal of Negro History* 63 (1): 59–67.

Zamir, Shamoon. 1995. *Dark Voices: W. E. B. Du Bois and American Thought, 1888–1903*. Chicago: University of Chicago Press.

Zwarg, Christina. 2002. "Du Bois on Trauma: Psychoanalysis and the Would-Be Black Savant." *Cultural Critique* 51:1–39.

Index